LANGUAGES OF POWER IN ISLAMIC SPAIN

edited by ROSS BRANN

CDL PRESS
Bethesda, Maryland

Library of Congress Cataloging-in-Publication Data

Languages of power in Islamic Spain / edited by Ross Brann.
p. cm. — (Occasional publications of the Department of Near Eastern Studies and the Program of Jewish Studies, Cornell University ; no. 3)
"Revised versions of presentations made at a conference ... held November 4-5, 1994 at Cornell University."
Includes bibliographical references and index.
ISBN 1-883053-28-5
1. Language and culture—Spain—Andalusia—Congresses. 2. Sociolinguistics—Spain—Andalusia—Congresses. 3. Andalusia (Spain) —Languages—Political aspects—Congresses. 4. Spain—Civilization —77–1516—Congresses. I. Brann, Ross, 1949– II. Series: Occasional publications of the Department of Near Eastern Studies and the Program of Jewish Studies, Cornell University ; v. 3.
P35.5.A47L36 1997
306.44′0946′80902—dc21 97-3720
CIP

CDL Press, P.O. Box 34454, Bethesda, MD 20827.
E-Mail: cdlpress@erols.com; Website: www.cdlpress.com

ISBN 1-883053-28-5

OCCASIONAL PUBLICATIONS OF THE

DEPARTMENT OF NEAR EASTERN STUDIES

AND THE

PROGRAM OF JEWISH STUDIES

CORNELL UNIVERSITY

NUMBER 3

Edited by

Ross Brann
and
David I. Owen

Vol. 1 – *A Witness Forever: Ancient Israel's Perception of Literature and the Resultant Hebrew Bible* by Isaac Rabinowitz

Vol. 2 – *Yours Always: A Holocaust Love Story* by Kitty Zilversmit

Vol. 3 – *Languages of Power in Islamic Spain* edited by Ross Brann

The publication of volume three of *Occasional Publications of the Department of Near Eastern Studies and the Program of Jewish Studies* was made possible by a gift from

Robert Malina '60
and
Fran Michaels Malina '60,

devoted Cornell University alumni and benefactors.

PREFACE

A WHOLLY SPURIOUS yet enduringly popular *ḥadīth* attributes to the Prophet Muḥammad a message to posterity concerning Islamic Spain: "al-Andalus, where the living are happy and the dead martyrs."

Whether one ascribes to the concept of a conflict-ridden Iberian society divided against itself along religious lines as imagined in the *ḥadīth*, to the notion of *convivencia* and the three cultures, to the idea of an Iberian culture variously expressed in Romance/Latin, Arabic, and Hebrew, or to some other interpretive paradigm, Spain was unique in the history of medieval Europe for its religious and ethnic diversity. From the Muslim conquest of al-Andalus in 711 until the Christian conquest of Granada in 1492, social, economic and intellectual interaction among Muslims, Christians, and Jews was a constant feature of social, economic, artistic, and intellectual life and the variety of cultural production within each of these religious communities was considerable.

The eight papers presented in this volume, the third in the series of Occasional Publications of the Department of Near Eastern Studies and Program of Jewish Studies, Cornell University, discuss among other things various aspects of that cultural interaction and investigate the significance of some of the contested cultural boundaries erected between and within the three monotheistic communities. The papers variously examine how the discursive languages of poetry of medieval Iberia, historiography, philosophy, linguistic research, polemic and other modes of cultural expression such as architecture and political institutions addressed problems of cultural domination and opposition, coexistence and contact between members of different groups. They further explore how various discourses mediated tensions between pietists and members of the courtly class, conflicts and rivalries among and within religious communities, and ethnic or socio-economic cleavages within Andalusi society and in Christian Spain. The papers represent revised versions of presentations made at a conference on the theme *Languages of Power in Islamic Spain* held November 4-5, 1994 at Cornell University.

I would like to acknowledge the generous support of the Department of Near Eastern Studies, the Program of Jewish Studies, the Society for the Humanities, the Institute for European Studies, the Medieval Studies Program, the Religious Studies Program, the Department of the History of Art, and the Departments of Romance Studies and Comparative Literature, without whose interest the conference could not have taken place. I would also like to thank Carmella Hall, Phyllis Emdee, and Bridget Garcia of the Department of Near Eastern Studies for their valuable assistance in organizing that venture, and Philip E. Lewis, the Harold Tanner Dean of the College of Arts and Sciences, for his longstanding interest in and support for Near Eastern Studies and Jewish Studies at Cornell University.

Ross Brann

CONTENTS

PREFACE

Ross Brann .... *vii*

THE *QAṢĪDAH* AND THE POETICS OF CEREMONY:
THREE ʻĪD PANEGYRICS TO THE CORDOBAN CALIPHATE

Suzanne Pinckney Stetkevych 1

PHILOLOGIANS AND POETS
IN SEARCH OF THE HEBREW LANGUAGE

Angel Sáenz-Badillos 49

REPRESENTATION AND IDENTITY IN MEDIEVAL SPAIN:
BEATUS MANUSCRIPTS
AND THE MUDEJAR CHURCHES OF TERUEL

D. Fairchild Ruggles 77

TEXTUALIZING AMBIVALENCE IN ISLAMIC SPAIN:
ARABIC REPRESENTATIONS OF ISMĀʻĪL IBN NAGHRĪLAH

Ross Brann 107

THE ARABICIZATION AND ISLAMIZATION OF THE CHRISTIANS OF AL-ANDALUS: EVIDENCE OF THEIR SCRIPTURES

Hanna Kassis 136

AMBIVALENCE IN MEDIEVAL RELIGIOUS POLEMIC: THE INFLUENCE OF MULTICULTURALISM ON THE *DIALOGUES* OF PETRUS ALPHONSI

Barbara Hurwitz Grant 156

LONGING, BELONGING, AND PILGRIMAGE IN IBN 'ARABĪ'S *INTERPRETER OF DESIRES* (*Tarjumān al-Ashwāq*)

Michael A. Sells 178

PRACTICAL INTELLIGENCE: DON JUAN MANUEL

Ciriaco Morón Arroyo 197

INDEX 211

CONTRIBUTORS 221

For Eileen

יַעֲלַת הַחֵן תִּשְׁאָלֵנִי: / ״אֶת מִי חָשַׁקְתָּ בִּצְבָאוֹת?״

וָאֹמַר לָהּ ״אִם לֹא תֵדְעִי – / הָסִירִי אֶת הַשֵּׁשׁ מֵאוֹת!״

(Judah Halevi)

THE *QAṢĪDAH* AND THE POETICS OF CEREMONY:

THREE ʻĪD PANEGYRICS TO THE CORDOBAN CALIPHATE

SUZANNE PINCKNEY STETKEVYCH *

> And what have kings, that privates have not too,
> Save ceremony, save general ceremony?
> And what art thou, thou idol ceremony?
> . . . .
> Art thou aught else but place, degree and form,
> Creating awe and fear in other men?
>
> *Henry V*, Act iv, Scene i

THE ROLE of the Classical Arabic language as a foremost attribute of religio and imperium in the classical Arabo-Islamic world, and in Muslim Spain in particular, has been widely recognized and studied. By contrast, the role of the *qaṣīdah* (panegyric ode), which for our purposes we may view as a meta-language, has been less well understood. The argument of the present study will be that the *qaṣīdah* performed a ritual ceremonial function as one of the insignia of power (and culture) and, further, that this function is in no way incidental to the poem as a literary work, but essential and formative. In this respect we will claim for the panegyric *qaṣīdah* what most recently David Quint has for the European epic, that the continuity of this literary form encodes and transmits an ideology of empire or, more precisely for the *qaṣīdah*, of Arabo-Islamic rule.[1] For the

---

* The research for this study was assisted by an award from the Joint Committee on the Near and Middle East of the Social Science Research Council and the American Council of Learned Societies, 1994.

[1] See David Quint, *Epic and Empire: Politics and Generic Form from Virgil to Milton* (Princeton: Princeton University Press, 1993), esp. p. 8, citing Thomas M. Greene, *The*

present purposes I have chosen three *qaṣīdahs* presented to Umayyad (Marwānid) caliphs in Cordoba on the occasion of two Islamic religious festivals, the first two on the ʿĪd al-Fiṭr (Festival of Breaking the Fast) of 363 H/974 CE and the third, under quite differing politico-military circumstances, on ʿĪd al-Aḍḥā (Festival of the Sacrifice) of 403/1013. It is my hope that by examining the quite explicit ritual, ceremonial, and political dimensions of these three *qaṣīdahs* we will better be able to perceive them in other poems where they may be only implied. In far broader terms I will propose that in the later flowering of more purely lyrical Andalusian verse the political force of the *qaṣīdah* was still present implicitly or in potentia. Finally, in light of the numerous modern studies of the relation of ceremonial to power, the ideological formulations of the panegyrics here treated will, it is hoped, serve to decode the sometimes inarticulate symbolic language of ceremony.

The first two of our *qaṣīdahs* are preserved in *Al-Muqtabis* of Ibn Ḥayyān where they occur as the first two of the poetry citations that conclude a detailed description of the ʿĪd al-Fiṭr ceremony in Cordoba for the year 363/974. The passage runs as follows:[2]

> The first day of the month of Shawwāl [= ʿĪd al-Fiṭr] fell on a Wednesday. On that day the Caliph al-Mustanṣir bi-Allāh held court to receive the ʿĪd greeting [*tahniʾah*], according to custom, on his throne in the east tribunal overlooking the gardens above the high extended terrace [text corrupt] in a session of the utmost magnificence, most renowned for its decorations and most elaborately arranged—this due to his consum-

---

Descent from Heaven: A Study in Epic Continuity (New Haven and London: Yale University Press, 1963).

[2] Abū Marwān Ibn Ḥayyān al-Qurṭubī, *Al-Muqtabis fī Akhbār Balad al-Andalus*, ed. ʿAbd al-Raḥmān ʿAlī al-Ḥajjī (Beirut: Dār al-Thaqāfah, 1965), 155-62. See also the Spanish translation, Emilio García Gómez, trans., *Anales palatinos del califa de Córdoba al-Hakam II, por ʿĪsā Ibn Ahmad al-Rāzī (360-364 H. = 971-975 J.C.) [El califato de Córdoba en el "Muqtabis" de Ibn Hayyān]* (Madrid: Sociedad de Estudios y Publicaciones, 1967), 196-202. Both the Arabic edition and the Spanish translation are based on a single extant nineteenth-century manuscript (see the introductions), and both are obscure in places. I have tried to produce a coherent English rendering.

mate joy over his triumph over Ḥasan ibn Qannūn al-Ḥasanī and his presence before him hastening in obedience, and over the harmonious extension of his dominion over hostile territory. On that day there attended him on his right the secretary-vizier, prefect of al-Zahrā' [and] Muḥammad ibn Aflaḥ, [the caliph's] client; and there joined the two rows after them the ranks of the major functionaries, consisting of the high and middle police commanders, then the commanders of the stores, and the treasurers and quartermasters, and others of the functionaries according to their ranks. Then the permission went out, and the first of the [Caliph's] brothers arrived. After the greeting [*taslīm*], his full brother Abū al-Aṣbagh 'Abd al-'Azīz sat on his right, and beneath him Abū al-Muṭarrif al-Mughīrah; and on the left sat Abū al-Qāsim al-Aṣbagh. After them, after the greeting, sat the viziers, after a gap between them, and beneath them sat Ja'far ibn 'Alī al-Andalusī, while his brother Yaḥyā ibn 'Alī stood in the row of the chamberlains, men of the retinue. Following them there arrived the high qāḍī, Muḥammad ibn Isḥāq ibn al-Salīm, and a group of his magistrates who sat, after the greeting, according to their rank. And there witnessed the ceremony the two Ḥasanīs, Ḥasan and Yaḥyā, the sons of [Ḥasan ibn Q]annūn who had been forced to surrender from al-Ḥajar. They alighted before permission [was granted] in the inner tribunals of the army quarters and arrived along with the Qurashīs of the blood. With them there arrived 'Alī, Manṣūr, and Ḥasan, the sons of Ḥasan ibn Qannūn, and the rest of the [defeated] Ḥasanid Idrīsids, repairing to the protection of the Commander of the Faithful. And at the head of their procession were Ḥasan and Yaḥyā. Right after the Qurashīs there followed to give their salutation the clients [*mawālī*], then the judges of the districts, the jurisprudents, counsellors of state, and after them the notaries [*'udūl*], the whites of the army, Andalusians and Ṭanjīs, and from the ranks of the black/slave regiments, the Khumsīs and Ṣaydīs, and the major Khumsīs and the knights of horsemanship, and others from the ranks of the retinue. So it was one of the most festive of customary spectacles and one of the most lavish of celebrations. During it the orators and the poets stood extemporizing and reciting many long and excellent [orations and poems], and among the best of what the poets recited that day was that of the foremost of them, Ṭāhir ibn Muḥammad al-Baghdādī, known as al-Muhannad, in a long poem of his, from which [we cite]:

[meter: *mutaqārib*]

1. An Imam chosen out of mercy for all creation
has spread wide mercy's veils.

2. The Throne's Master elected him from the elect
who trail their robes' trains above the sun.

3. He established Prophethood among their fathers
and upon their progeny conferred the Caliphate.

4. So he protected his flock, seeking victory
from the Throne's Master, guarding the untended.

5. He expended his wealth on them, unsparingly,
so that their wealth would multiply.

6. His beneficence dispelled their misery;
his grace turned their penury to plenty.

7. He assumed the caliphate in its epoch,
then by his piety perfected it.

8. His religion was its adornment;
his luminous days its very image.

9. Were any form of rule raised above it,
he would be the only ruler right for it.

10. No virtue of right guidance can be mentioned
that he has not already acquired.

11. So may God grant him joyous 'Īds
and bring him many more like them,

12. And multiply the sweetness of his fast
and of the burdens he imposes on his soul,

13. And reveal to him the thanks for his beneficence
and his attaining for the soul its hopes,

14. And for his subduing the might of his enemies
when he shackled them with his conquest.

15. He hastened their Resurrection [Day],
for [in him] they had witnessed it and its horrors.

16. Upon them his army launched an attack
and overtook their kings and princes,

17. And his Lord gave him dominion over their land,
[all] that it bore and [all] its goods.

18. His lions slew their lions;
his thick-necked lion-cubs their lion-cubs,

19. And when his army marched the night march toward them,
the very earth began to quake.

20. The enemy horizon seemed an infantry afoot,
but then [his] Lord severed their limbs.

21. [The caliph] swept their puddle into [his] sea;
He drowned their trickling stream in [his] fathomless depths.

22. He brought them in submission to his abode
to dwell therein and show their veneration.

23. When he took possession of them, they were in error;
then he forgave them and God guided their errant [steps] aright.

24. His beneficence erased their evil deeds;
his acts of virtue covered up their sins.

25. His noble nature revealed its graciousness;
his hands poured forth their favors.

26. Would it have become his magnanimity
had he requited the ignorant in kind?

27. How many a time did he forgive, though able [to punish],
until God clothed him in [forgiveness'] shirt.

28. May he ever triumph over his enemies
and obliterate the nights and their princes.

Then after him there arose his messenger Muḥammad ibn Shukhayṣ to recite a long poem of his in which he heaped [ignominy] upon the Banū Ḥasan who had been humbled by the caliph's victory, and did this to excess. The poem begins:

[meter: *basīṭ*]

1. Sha'bān completed what Rajab had begun
   even before hopes had expected it.

2. More than this the month of fasting met us with
   the best of two 'Īds: the full moon and the [new] moon rising.

3. In a year of lush abundance, its ascending stars
   surrounded us with victory and fertility,
   so perfidy and drought died out.

4. God's is the deed through which joy came to us
   before the dispatches and writs.

5. The very earth swaggered in wonder at him,
   but I think a swaggerer's wonder is no cause for wonder.

6. The horizon shone from the exuberance that engulfed it,
   and the earth blossomed from the delight that set it aquiver.

7. Then the rose mimicked the glow of bashful cheeks,
   and the chamomile the gleam of pearly teeth.

8. When the failed fool saw the unfolding events
   reveal to his eye harbingers of his destruction,

9. And that the assault of God's Commander reaches him
   whom neither steeds nor fine bred camels reach,

10. And that [the Caliph's] resolve was an irrevocable decree,
    his wrath destruction,
    and that this destruction and this wrath are on God's behalf,

11. And that even if he fled as far as China,
    it would not save him from [the Caliph's] sword

12. — For how can he whom God is bent upon pursuing
    ever hope for a refuge to save him? —

13. He hoped to flee, but then his hope informed him
    that ever-vigilant fate surrounded him.

14. Where is there a refuge from the shadow of heaven
    on a day when the tent ropes are loosed from the horizons?

15. [Ḥasan Ibn Qannūn's] surrendering authority to our lord
[the Caliph]
safeguarded his blood that I wanted to use to cure rabies.[3]

16. He barely escaped with the last breath of his life,
buffeted between life and death.

17. God hastened his misfortunes in this world,
[leaving him] neither life, nor kin, nor lineage.

And he digressed to mention Ḥasan and his defeated people, saying, in an excessive and unseemly manner,

18. A motley crowd claim Hāshim as their lineage,
but they have no true lineage to anyone.

19. Blind in perception, neither religion nor noble lineage
could bend their necks to pious deeds.

20. It increased their blindness that the first of them
threw down his staff [=settled]
where there was neither learning nor civility.

21. They grew up with wild beasts in a savage crowd
who have no thought nor aim but slurping soup.

22. Had they claimed to be the foremost of Quraysh,
events and suspicions would have forced denial of their claims.

23. All that burns can be extinguished,
but the evil after 'Uthmān['s murder] is extinguished only
to flare up again.

24. If Ḥasan goes forth as the head of the descendants of Ḥasan,
then who, I wonder, is the tail?

25. The dispatches and pens of a king [whom the Caliph] destroyed
proved untrue ever since the [Caliph's] spears and swords proved true.

26. Though folly may erode the resolve of the mighty,
[the Caliph's] might never lacks earnest resolve.

[3] It was believed that the blood of kings would cure rabies.

27. Nor has the mill of war been turned in his domain
unless his decision was its pivot.

28. A decision whose Endower guides him to success
when opinions differ and talk is diverse.

29. A decision that, when it reached generals,
gave them more support in war than all their clamorous army.

30. [The Caliph] threw [Ḥasan] into the abyss of the ravine
and then granted him a respite till he became the source
of his own afflictions.

31. God may be forbearing to a people to increase
their misery, and so He loosed their rope.

32. When [Ḥasan] came to the Peninsula there encircled his retinue
squadrons whose anger caused the very earth to tremble.

33. Every time he traversed the back of the earth
its highlands and lowlands countered him with cavalry and infantry.

34. Until when he drew near the precinct of our heartlands,
his heart throbbing and his intestines in commotion,

35. He found the armies whose march made him imagine
the haughty hills were locusts hopping round him.

36. They came altogether thanking God, extolling right guidance,
one after another and flowing [over the earth].

37. The followers of him who seeks victory from God [Mustanṣir bi-Allāh],
Their victory is the true perception—not feigning and lies.

38. Nothing prevented them from bringing [Ḥasan] every harm
that leads to death
except obedience and awe [of the Caliph].

39. [Ḥasan] kept crying, "There is no god but God!" out of anguish
like that of seafarers on the verge of shipwreck.

40. Hoping for life, fearing death, he was in two opposite states:
elation and dejection.

41. Until there appeared the star of good fortune [i.e., the
Caliph] that interceded for him;

and in battle each man gets what he rides.

42. Though I do not think that [Ḥasan] saw the Mahdī [Caliph],
since veils of his light veiled his eyes from his face.

43. If [the Caliph] had removed the veils [of his mercy] before
the Shi'ite [Ḥasan] [revealing his awful power],
[the Caliph's] sword would have been stained
with the blood of jugular veins,

44. [Mercy's veils] would have ended and passed away,
with religion crushed, the free man enslaved,
and property plundered.

45. [Ḥasan] withheld nobility, so it was withheld from him;
this brought him the rope by which sorrows are led.

46. And I said to the fool [Ḥasan] that kindled with his heedlessness
a fire for which the firewood of his soul was readied,

47. "Much discord have you sown in the Mahdī's state;
look at the state your strife has brought you to!"

And he says in it—may God be kind and gracious to him:

48. O invoker of God in the [gallant] deed
for the year of whose date poems and orations were composed.

49. Since the flames of war were kindled
your confidence has not flagged
in defending what divine decrees—not shooting stars—impose.

50. You took him captive after wresting his rule from his hand;
so in your grasp he became both plundered and plunder.

51. Your magnanimity has almost made one forget that you
gave him his soul [=life],
and that is something that cannot be given.

52. The liege-men have vowed [to you] their constant protection
and the Arabs have openly declared their obedience.

53. Unflagging was the resolve of the army who,
when a victor among them called out your name, were victorious.

54. The entire dominion of the west is now devoted to you;
its regions both far and near have given you obedience.

55. So why stop short of a direction [the east]
where Egypt is oppressed and Aleppo uprooted?

56. The reversal of the deserter's fortune informs us
that the good fortune of the renegades has been reversed.

57. You allowed access to your domain to followers of his call;
for unripe dates are eaten until ripe dates mature.

58. If the tent pole of Fusṭāṭ were felled by its stays,
neither the tent pegs nor the ropes would hold.

59. Nothing in the march [of prosperity] can match your numinous face
except our fruitful year.

60. So may God increase you in the might by which His blessing endures
for as long as the ages and epochs.

61. You are a gift to Islam from the 'Īd-Greeter
for what He gives and bestows.

62. May your army be flooded with bounty,
and the grades and ranks of all your generals exalted!

63. And may our summers be covered with the generous rain
of your limpid grace,
which, when a pouring stream is mentioned, pours forth.

64. A mighty victory and a prosperous fertile year for
[this 'Īd] al-Fiṭr
for which your newly polished days are named.

65. And surely the hair-parting of our lord and master Abū al-Walīd
should be turbaned with the crown of dominion.

66. The [crowning] of him whose grandfather is Marwān and whose father
is the Mahdī al-Wulāt
should not be postponed.

The third of the *qaṣīdah*s under consideration is by Ibn Darrāj al-Qasṭallī as preserved in *Al-Dhakhīrah* of Ibn Bassām and said to have been delivered to the caliph Sulaymān, probably on the occasion of ʿĪd al-Aḍḥā, 403/1013.[4]

> Abū Marwān ibn Ḥayyān related: When Sulaymān was able to establish himself in Cordoba, as we have described, those that remained of the ʿĀmirī poets that were still residing in Cordoba at that time began to compose panegyric for him in the hope of tapping the stores of his generosity. So they composed in his praise good poems in which they appealed to religion and manly virtue, and most of them recited them openly in his public audience. He listened with manifest delight, but then defrauded them in accepting the panegyric, for he neither rained down generous rewards upon them nor even sprinkled. Because of this the dispersal of the group [of poets] from Cordoba was completed and most of them abandoned his protection. Thus every trace of culture [*adab*] was erased there and was vanquished by barbarism, [Cordoba's] people reverted from their customary humanism to blatant vulgarity, and nobility was abandoned.
>
> Among those of this elevated class whose panegyric for the caliph Sulaymān was renowned in those days and whose words were preserved was the best of them, Abū ʿUmar Aḥmad ibn Muḥammad ibn Darrāj al-Qasṭallī. He was at that time residing in Cordoba and thought that Sulaymān would grant him refuge from fate, but his luck was not that good. He went before him at his first audience at the palace and recited to him the *qaṣīdah* that begins:
>
> [meter: *kāmil*]
>
> 1. The days bear witness to you that you are their ʿĪd:
> for you the desolate one yearned,
> to you the far-away returned;

---

[4] Abū al-Ḥasan ʿAlī Ibn Bassām al-Shantarīnī, *Al-Dhakhīrah fī maḥāsin Ahl al-Jazīrah* (Cairo: Lajnat al-Taʾlīf wa al-Tarjamah wa al-Nashr, 1939), 1:1:50-53. In the present discussion, I am using the poem as it appears in the *Dhakhīrah* in 34 verses, except where otherwise noted. Ibn Darrāj's *Dīwān* contains a much longer version of 89 verses, along with some variants in the common lines, which I hope to turn to *in toto* on another occasion. See Ibn Darrāj al-Qasṭallī, *Dīwān*, ed. Maḥmūd ʿAlī Makkī, 2d ed., (n.p.: Al-Maktab al-Islāmī, 1389/1969), poem no. 27, 51-57. The ellipses in the translation indicate breaks with regard to the *Dīwān* version.

2. The gloomy day was illumined,
the one of terror dispelled, the disobedient submitted,
the harsh relented.

3. By you the world was purified:
the aged regained their youth once more,
when before even the newborn had turned grey with age.

4. How solid froze the sea before your tempest,
but now its ice is broken by
your generous dew.

. . . .

5. Your house found repose in the broad valley of Mecca
until the return of days whose promised time
drew near,

6. For processions of cavalry whose steeds whinny for you,
and battalions whose banners flutter
over you,

7. Stirred to passion by your call,
by which their lowlands and their highlands
had long prospered.

. . . .

8. Until you rose to that station among ranks
that makes the noble and princely
mighty

9. In the domed tent of dominion whose ropes and pole
are the tribes of Ṣinhājah
and Zanātah.

. . . .

10. On battle-days their swords strike true to their promise;
when men contend for noble rank,
their pledge holds true.

11. O hour when blood kinship's bonds were cut,
and no veil stood between the witness
and the deed!

12. A day when the noble were humbled to the base
and free lords were assaulted
by their slaves,

13. Their heroes forsook them in a terror
that crippled the chieftains
and their braves.

14. Their guide, perplexed, did lead them on the road to escape,
nor did their shots
hit the target.

. . . .

15. Until you brought them a most auspicious new moon
whose good fortune rose above them
in the sky.

And from it [are the lines]:

16. On the two sides of the River Sharanbah[5]
they pitched a battle whose thunder made
the unshakable mountains shake.

17. They advanced to Shahbā' whose harvest-time had come;
the necks of iron-clad warriors
were the crop.

18. And to the ravines of Qantīsh where
the oppressor nations had gathered against them
in unstoppable numbers.

19. They left there a hill that just that morning
had been a hollow —
the hill was of enemy corpses.

20. And when the Frankish battalions ensnared you
with their followers, God turned them back
from you

[5] Following Ibn Darrāj, *Dīwān,* v. 56, p. 54.

21. With [steeds], swimmers in the depths of the sea,
trailing ample mail, spreading out to flood
the empty plain.

22. They made the eagle and the crow their guests that day,
and fed them their seducer
and leader.

23. A remnant of Ermengaud's army rallied round him
to advance, and then their masses
marched to hell.

24. They approached them at the Wadi Ār beneath cutting blades
in whose steel the Muslims' might
struck sparks.

25. After they had broken the spears and drawn
white blades as sharp
as they were Muslim.

26. Then it seemed as if their crucifixes had been raised
in the shadow of the battle-dust, and the time had come
for their prostrations.

27. On the left side so disheveled did their troops advance
that whoever saw them gave glad tidings
of victory.[6]

28. Their swords left such furrows in its defenders' skulls
that they had to use their cheeks for bridges.

29. In a battle that would back the excuse of the swords
if their steel had melted from
the battle heat.

30. And in which the brown Khaṭṭī spear had but a feeble excuse
for its shaft not sprouting leaves
while in your hand.

[6] I have filled in the lacuna in *Al-Dhakhīrah* 1:1:52, v. 27, from Ibn Darrāj, *Dīwān*, 55, v. 67.

31. In it you saw might wherever you liked,
and, wherever you liked,
ample robes of grace.

. . . .

32. Accept [this poem] for her dowry has been led to you
by matched praises,
their object not blameworthy,

33. [She is] a novelty of exquisite order,
her gems, both jewels and center stone,
precisely matched.

34. Let her enjoy days of glory, all of them 'Īds,
and you for those who obey you,
the 'Īd among those 'Īds!

. . .

Part I

'ĪD AL-FIṬR CEREMONY: CORDOBA: 363/974

Let me begin by noting that what I am analyzing here is not "the ceremony" as anthropologically witnessed, but Ibn Ḥayyān's text describing the ceremony, or as García Gómez points out, Ibn Ḥayyān's edition of al-Rāzī's text.[7] "Place, degree, and form" are evident characteristics in Ibn Ḥayyān's description of al-Ḥakam II al-Mustanṣir's holding court on 'Īd al-Fiṭr to receive the traditional felicitation, and, together with the magnificence of the spectacle, were certainly intended to create "awe and fear." But this alone explains neither the meaning of the ceremony nor why the historian has presented it to us in so much detail. It is our goal here to explore the meaning and function, and hence the importance, of this ceremony.

---

[7] García Gómez, *Anales palatinos,* 13. An important complement to the present study, which provides a detailed description and analysis of this volume of *Al-Muqtabis* (without, however, dealing with the poetry texts) is Gabriel Martinez-Gros, *L'idéologie omeyyade: La construction de la légitimité du Califat de Cordoue (X^e-XIe siècles)* (Madrid: Casa de Velázquez, 1992), ch. 5 "Le califat immobile: les *Annales* de 'Isā al-Rāzî," 129-55.

First, let us note the etymology of the Arabic word *ʿīd.* The classical lexicographers consider it to be from the root *ʿ-w-d* (to return) and thus to refer to holidays that recur annually. The two *ʿīds*, ʿĪd al-Fiṭr and ʿĪd al-Aḍḥā, must first of all be understood in light of the anciently attested "new year" and "seasonal" festivals of the Near East. For the present purposes Connerton's summary is the most concise:

> The celebration of recurrence is made possible, in the first instance, by *calendrically* observed repetition. Calendars make it possible to juxtapose with the structure of profane time a further structure, one qualitatively distinct from the former and irreducible to it, in which the most notable events of sacred time are assembled together and co-ordinated. Each day is thus locatable in two quite different orders of time: there is the day on which such and such events take place in the world, and there is the day on which one celebrates the memory of this or that moment of sacred or mythic history. While the co-existence of these two temporal orders runs through the course of the entire calendrical cycle, that cycle will normally contain special points at which the activity of recapitulation becomes the focus of communal attention. Throughout the semitic world, in particular, the ceremonials of the New Year are strikingly similar. In each of these systems, we encounter the same basic idea of annual return to chaos followed by a new creation. In each, there is expressed the conception of the end and the beginning of a temporal period, based on the observation of biocosmic rhythms, and celebrated in a sequence of periodic purification—purgings, fastings, confessions of sins—in preparation for the periodic regeneration of life. And in each, the ritual enactment of combats between two groups of actors, the presence of the dead, and saturnalia, gives expression to the sense that the end of the old year and the expectation of the new year is at once an annual repetition and the repetition of a primordial moment—the mythic moment of passage from chaos to cosmos.[8]

---

[8] Paul Connerton, *How Societies Remember* (Cambridge: Cambridge University Press, 1989), 65. He notes, too, that in Christianity "emphasis shifts in this schema from the prototype of creation to that of salvation" p. 65. See also A. J. Wensinck, "The Semitic New Year and the Origin of Eschatology," *Acta Orientalia* 1 (1923): 158-99; and the formulation of the "seasonal pattern" in Theodor H. Gaster, *Thespis: Ritual, Myth, and Drama in the Ancient Near East* (New York: Norton and Co., 1977). The latter is introduced into the interpretation of the Arabic *qaṣīdah* in Suzanne

A key element in the restoration of cosmos or order is the reaffirmation of the social order and the position of the ruler at the top of it. In this respect I believe we will find Kuhrt's remarks on the Babylonian New Year Festival quite translatable into the present context, for if, in her words, "what had been in origin merely a civic festival was transformed into an event of national significance in which not only Marduk's supreme power and world creation but also the king's position and the order for which he was responsible were confirmed and celebrated,"[9] we will observe here that the religious festival of the 'Īd al-Fiṭr has become an event of dynastic significance in which not only Allāh's supreme power, but also the Umayyad caliph's legitimate position and the social order of the Cordoban caliphal dominion are confirmed and celebrated.

However ancient and archetypal the origins of the Cordoban ceremony may be, it is nevertheless evident that Ibn Ḥayyān's description is concerned with contemporary religious and political matters, and it is the intersection of these two aspects—the cyclically repeated and the ephemeral contemporary, what we can otherwise term sacred and profane time—that most intrigues and concerns us here.

To begin with the cyclical repetition of the 'Īd, we note that in the first place, it serves to identify the polity as an Islamic one and to confirm the legitimacy of al-Mustanṣir's rule. Even a quick perusal of this volume of *Al-Muqtabis* reveals a certain periodization or punctuation by passages describing the two 'Īd celebrations of each year. I would argue that one effect of this is to create a rhythmic sense of the perpetuity or continuity of the Cordoban Umayyad dynasty. The association of the dynasty with Islamic custom has the effect of projecting it at once backward and for-

---

Pinckney Stetkevych, *The Mute Immortals Speak: Pre-Islamic Poetry and the Poetics of Ritual* (Ithaca, N.Y.: Cornell University Press, 1993), ch. 7 and eadem, "Pre-Islamic Panegyric and the Poetics of Redemption: *Mufaḍḍalīyah 119* of 'Alqamah and *Bānat Su'ād* of Ka'b ibn Zuhayr," in Suzanne Pinckney Stetkevych, ed., *Reorientations: Arabic and Persian Poetry* (Bloomington, Ind.: Indiana University Press, 1994), 1-57.

[9] Amélie Kuhrt, "Usurpation, conquest, and ceremonial: from Babylon to Persia," in David Cannadine and Simon Price, eds., *Rituals of Royalty: Power and Ceremonial in Traditional Societies* (Cambridge: Cambridge University Press, 1987), 31.

ward in time. The ceremony purports to reenact originary Islamic practice as established by the Prophet Muḥammad, thereby creating the illusion of the original and uninterrupted Islamic legitimacy of the Umayyad house. As Connerton puts it, "All rites are repetitive, and repetition automatically implies continuity with the past."[10] At the same time, the association of the dynasty with a perpetual calendrical cycle creates the illusion that it, too, can claim perpetuity. One could go as far as to suggest, as Kuhrt does, that the emphasis on such ceremony reveals anxieties both as to the origins and future of the dynasty.[11]

In the contemporary political and religious arena, however prosperous and peaceful al-Mustanṣir's reign, the Cordoban Umayyads' anxieties were not in the least unfounded. Within the Islamic polity, claims to political legitimacy were largely based on (alleged) descent from the family of the Prophet (the Banū Hāshim) or from his tribe, the Quraysh of Mecca (of whom the Banū Umayyah were a powerful clan), backed up by political and military success.[12] For all practical purposes, the latter confirmed the former.

During the time in question, the Umayyad house was competing ideologically, politically, militarily, and ceremonially with the Fāṭimid house which only a few years before (358 H/969 CE) had established its triumphant new capital, Cairo (al-Qāhirah = "the [city] triumphant"), as manifest proof of its caliphal claims. Although this shift of the Fāṭimid center of gravity to the west relieved the direct North African military pressure on the Umayyads at Cordoba, it was a blow to caliphal prestige.[13] Then, too, there was the ideologically still dominant, if otherwise debilitated, 'Abbāsid caliphate at Baghdad. Meanwhile, beyond the Islamic pale, in

---

[10] Connerton, *How Societies Remember*, 45.

[11] Kuhrt, "Usurpation, conquest, and ceremonial," 40.

[12] On the precept that the imamate is from the Quraysh, see W. Montgomery Watt, art. "Ḳuraysh," *Encyclopaedia of Islam*, 2d ed.

[13] See É. Lévi-Provençal, *Histoire de l'Espagne musulmane, Tome II: Le califat umaiyade de Cordoue (921-1031)*, new ed. (Paris: Maisonneuve/Leiden: E. J. Brill, 1950), 184-96 passim, and esp. 186-87.

Byzantium, Constantine VII Porphyrogenitus (913-59 CE) had just recently compiled his *De Ceremoniis* (Book of Ceremonies)[14]—not inconceivably a response to the increasing awe and threat of the Islamic east. Closer to home, in 347/958 the Fāṭimid general Jawhar had defeated the Umayyads in the Maghrib, and the Idrīsid prince Ḥasan ibn Qannūn (al-Ḥasan ibn al-Qāsim Gannūn),[15] whose dynasty itself claimed the imamate through its descent from ʿAlī ibn Abī Ṭālib,[16] shifted his allegiance from the Umayyads to the Fāṭimids. After al-Mustanṣir's first attempt to redress the situation in 362/972 met with defeat, he sent his renowned general Ghālib, who vanquished Ḥasan ibn Qannūn and brought him and the other Idrīsid lords and their sons as captives/hostages to Cordoba, where a spectacular victory celebration was held and where the Idrīsid princes were maintained for some time in guarded luxury.[17] In this respect, the ʿĪd ceremony must also be viewed as a triumph, or victory celebration, as indeed Ibn Ḥayyān states. The "ceremonial idiom"[18] is designed above all to convey "awe and fear," that is, to give expression to the ruler's power.

---

[14] Much work has been done on Byzantine ceremonial and the similarities with the Arabo-Islamic ceremonial are often striking. See Averil Cameron, "The Construction of Court Ritual: the Byzantine *Book of Ceremoniis*," in Cannadine and Price, *Rituals of Royalty*, 106-36; also Michael McCormick, *Eternal Victory* (Cambridge: Cambridge University Press, 1987), esp. chs. 4 and 5 on the Byzantine triumph. The classic in this field is Sabine G. MacCormack, *Art and Ceremony in Late Antiquity* (Berkeley: University of California Press, 1981).

[15] I will be giving the name as Ḥasan ibn Qannūn, as it appears in *Al-Muqtabis* and according to the standard Arabic transliteration. The name is normally given in Roman alphabet as Gannūn.

[16] See D. Eustache, arts. "Idrīs I" and "Idrīsids," *Encyclopaedia of Islam*, 2d. ed.

[17] Eustache, "Idrīsids"; Lévi-Provençal, *Histoire de l'Espagne musulmane* 2:190-95; Ibn Ḥayyān, *Al-Muqtabis*, 96-155, passim; García Gómez, *Anales palatinos*, 123-96, passim.

[18] For this term, see Paula Sanders, *Ritual, Politics, and the City in Fatimid Cairo* (Albany, N.Y.: State University of New York Press, 1994), ch. 2, "The Ceremonial Idiom," 13-38.

The result of this alignment of the Islamic calendrical festival of breaking the fast with the vanquishing of the Idrīsids is to identify the religious "rebirth" and "purification" with military-political victory and restoration. In ceremonial terms, it plays the role of the cosmic ritual combat between good and evil. Thus if the breaking of the fast marks the return to the normal, "secular" diurnal order of things after the "sacred" month of fasting, so too it becomes the celebration of the reestablishment of the proper legitimate Islamic rule, here Umayyad, after a period of Idrīsid insurrection, i.e., recognition of competing Fāṭimid claims. It is worth noting that throughout *Al-Muqtabis* Ḥasan ibn Qannūn is referred to as *al-mulḥid* (apostate), presumably for his having reneged on his Umayyad allegiance and recognized the Fāṭimids. What we see above all in the elaborate ceremonial is a ritual reestablishment or reaffirmation of the social, political, and religious hierarchy, the recreation of order after the preceding chaos.

The image of the caliph seated in majesty, flanked by his elite, ordering his (political) creation, certainly seems an *imitatio* of divine creation, and certainly it is to be understood from the meticulously orchestrated ranking, timing, and positioning that the social order mirrors the cosmic order. Here we might usefully invoke Connerton's term "the choreography of authority." He remarks:

> The importance of posture for communal memory is evident. Power and rank are commonly expressed through certain postures relative to others; from the way in which people group themselves and from the disposition of their bodies relative to the bodies of others, we can deduce the degree of authority which each is thought to enjoy or to which they lay claim. We know what it means when one person sits in an elevated position when everyone around them stands; when one person stands and everyone else sits; ... There will of course be disparities between cultures in the meanings ascribed to some postures, but, in all cultures, much of the choreography of authority is expressed through the body.[19]

[19] Connerton, *How Societies Remember*, 73-74.

Not only is the caliph al-Mustanṣir reaffirming his dominion through this ritual, but his subjects, for their part, are reaffirming their allegiance or paying homage both to the caliph and to the political and religious hierarchy of which he is the lynchpin. As each awaits the permission, gives the greeting, and takes his place, he is incorporating, that is, bodily enacting, his sub-ordination to the hierarchy.[20] Conversely, the failure to observe the ritual and protocol of the ceremony would amount to an act of insubordination, sedition (*fitnah*). In this respect Ibn Ḥayyān's detailed presentation serves to define the distribution of power and rank, and, with reference to the schema of other years, can provide the historian with a chart of the political rise and fall of groups and individuals.

The subduing of the forces of chaos is embodied in the ritual submission of the defeated Idrīsids to the Umayyad caliph. In such an event we see how inextricable are the social, political, military, and religious aspects of Arabo-Islamic rule. In ceremonial terms, we can observe ritualization or mythicization in the act: for the Idrīsid redoubt of Ḥajar al-Nasr was taken by the Umayyad forces under the general Ghālib on 21 Jumādā al-Ākhirah 363 (=19 March, 974) when Ḥasan ibn Qannūn, having just lost his city of al-Baṣrah to an Umayyad column, capitulated to the Umayyad general Ghālib. His submission and surrender were officially or ritually enacted on 29 Jumādā al-Ākhirah, 363 (= 27 March, 974) when, with Ghālib's assistance, he delivered the Friday sermon in the name of the Umayyad caliph al-Mustanṣir.[21] Now on the 'Īd al-Fiṭr, 1 Shawwāl, 363 (=25 June, 974) that surrender or submission is ritually reenacted as one of the elements in the iconography of power. The caliph's show of mercy in accepting the submission of the defeated enemy, i.e., sparing his life, is intended to express the concept that he holds power over life and death. We will argue below that the relation between the historical event and its poeticization is largely cognate to that between it and its ritualization in ceremony.

---

[20] See Connerton, *How Societies Remember*, 58-60.

[21] Lévi-Provençal, *Histoire de l'Espagne musulmane* 2:190-94, and see map, 2:192. D. Eustache gives the name of Ḥasan ibn Qannūn's redoubt as Ḥajar al-Naṣr instead of al-Nasr (Eustache, "Idrīsids").

Ibn Ḥayyān concludes his description of the lavish and festive celebration with the orators and poets who recited during it and finally gives us partial texts of some of the poems. I would like to discuss the first two of these with a view to substantiating and expanding upon my analysis of the ceremony itself. A few observations are in order before turning to the poetic texts.

First, I hope to elucidate the function of the *qaṣīdah.* In the context of ritual homage, as we have primarily defined the ceremony of the presentation of the ʻĪd greeting, we can remark that in an external sense the *qaṣīdah* as an object is itself one of the "royal insignia." The court poet's presentation of a *qaṣīdah* on the ʻĪd is an act of allegiance that is both politically and ritually obligatory[22] and, as a bodily performance, is part of the iconography of power. Furthermore, inasmuch as the *qaṣīdah* is one of the insignia of power, it constituted a field for rivalry between rulers, here, caliphs. As James Monroe writes of the poetry of the Cordoban caliphate,

> Concretely, what was now required was political poetry that would defend the Andalusian caliphate against the Abbasid, and later against the far more serious Fatimid challenge.... it led to a new kind of poetry designed to express the ideal of caliphal authority and to proclaim the unifying principle of Islam against the enemies of the state, both within and without.[23]

---

[22] See Suzanne Pinckney Stetkevych, "Abbasid Panegyric and the Poetics of Political Allegiance: Two Poems of al-Mutanabbī on Kāfūr," in Stefan Sperl and Christopher Shackle, eds., *Qasida Poetry in Islamic Asia and Africa* , 2 vols. (Leiden: E. J. Brill, 1996), 1:35-63 and 2:92-105; and "ʻAbbāsid Panegyric: The Politics and Poetics of Ceremony: Al-Mutanabbī's Īd-poem to Sayf al-Dawlah," in J. R. Smart, ed., *Tradition and Modernity in Arabic Language and Literature* (Surrey: Curzon Press, 1996), 119-43.

[23] James T. Monroe, "Hispano-Arabic Poetry during the Caliphate of Córdoba," in Gustave E. von Grunebaum, ed., *Proceedings of the Third Giorgio Lévi della Vida Memorial Conference* (Berkeley and Los Angeles: University of California Press, 1971), pp. 137-38. It should be noted that by "new" here, Monroe means for al-Andalus, for, as he points out in his discussion, the Neo-classical panegyric reigned in the Arab east in the fourth/tenth century just at the time of the Andalusian Umayyad caliphate, which was officially proclaimed in 317/929 (p. 136). See also Monroe's

Further, although we analyzed the ceremony as creating an intersection between profane and sacred time, ritually incorporating a historical military victory into the mythic and ritual liturgical calendar, the only way this can be perpetuated is through the vehicle of the *qaṣīdah.* For this is the difference between ceremony and poetry: the ceremonial associated with a calendrical festival carries with it the illusion that it is repeated the same every year. Those details that change are forgotten. Thus, for example, the defeat of Ḥasan ibn Qannūn will not be celebrated in future 'Īd ceremonies. The only way that particular victory can be transformed from an ephemeral exemplum to perduring "myth," i.e., be permanently incorporated into the dimension of sacred time, is for it to be commemorated in a *qaṣīdah.* And, in doing so, it becomes prototypical or paradigmatic in a broad Arabo-Islamic cultural context. Thus I would like to look at the *qaṣīdah* first as it functions as ritual of homage particular to a distinct historical moment and second as the vehicle or means of transforming and commemorating that event so that it becomes permanently valid and validating.

Part II

THE 'ĪD *QAṢĪDAH* OF ṬĀHIR IBN MUḤAMMAD AL-BAGHDĀDĪ, AL-MUHANNAD

The poem, or what of it Ibn Ḥayyān has preserved, opens by establishing the lineage of al-Ḥakam II al-Mustanṣir bi-Allāh coupled with divine election, the Umayyad claim being that the Quraysh are the elect for both Prophethood and the Caliphate [vv. 1-3]. Verse 1 invokes the imamate/caliphate of al-Mustanṣir in broad Islamic terms: he has been chosen [by God] as the ruler of "creation"—he is not merely a local emir. God is not explicitly named here, rather the word *raḥmah* (mercy) evokes him by his foremost epithets *al-raḥmān al-raḥīm* (the merciful, the most merci-

---

examples, pp. 136-38 and García Gómez, in "La poésie politique sous le califat de Cordoue," *Revue des Études Islamiques* n.v. (1949), 5-11.

ful) in such a way that the caliph's mercy is an embodiment of divine mercy. The formulation of legitimacy proffered in verse 3 is of interest in light of Crone and Hind's discussion of the eastern Umayyads' claims to legitimacy. Arguing that Umayyad legitimacy rested on inherited authority, Crone and Hinds write:

> Ultimately, they have inherited it from 'Uthmān, a friend and helper of Muḥammad's, who was chosen by a *shūrā* and raised up by God Himself, and who was thus a legitimate caliph wrongfully killed. In raising up Umayyad caliphs, God gives His deputy something to which He [sic, =he?] has a hereditary right.... In short, the Umayyad's are God's chosen lineage.[24]

The authors proceed to remark that with the enhancement of the concept of Prophethood and growing prominence of Muḥammad, the Umayyad claim is weakened and the claims of direct descent from the Prophet Muḥammad of the 'Abbāsids, 'Alids, and Fāṭimids, etc., gain strength.[25] In the case at hand, al-Muhannad, no doubt as a reaction to this, offers a somewhat ambiguous formulation: "He established Prophethood among their fathers" (*aḥalla al-nubuwwata ābā'ahā*) [v. 3] could be taken to expand the concept of the hereditary from the individual to the tribal. Inasmuch as the Umayyads are Qurashite, like the Prophet Muḥammad, their claim could be understood as based on kinship to the Prophet through their common descent from 'Abd al-Manāf; otherwise, referring to the Umayyads, it would simply mean that they were the community to whom the Prophet was sent, and thus be in accord with the widely held precept (in the form of a *ḥadīth* in the *Musnad* of Ibn Ḥanbal) that the caliphs, or imams, are from the Quraysh.[26] I believe, however, that the poet's ambiguity is intentional and that, although strictly speaking the second interpretation should apply to the Umayyads, the line is constructed to be verbally identical to the 'Abbāsid claims.

---

[24] Patricia Crone and Martin Hinds, *God's Caliph: Religious Authority in the First Centuries of Islam* (Cambridge: Cambridge University Press, 1986), 31-32.

[25] Crone and Hinds, *God's Caliph*, 31-32.

[26] See Watt, "Ḳurays̲h̲."

The subsequent verses [4-10] celebrate al-Mustanṣir's personal qualifications for the caliphate: tending his flock, attending to the untended —presumably meaning the subjugation of those that don't recognize his caliphate (like Ḥasan ibn Qannūn)—, generosity, piety: he is the consummation, the adornment, the very image of the caliphate. In terms of the concepts of hierarchy discussed above, both the cosmic and social order require that al-Mustanṣir hold the caliphate. It is then by this combination of divine election and personal moral suitability that he holds this position and therefore should receive the expression of homage and allegiance of verse 11.

Verse 11 constitutes the 'Īd greeting itself. Of note is the "May God bring him many more like them" which, like the British "Many happy returns of the day," particularly suits the calendrically repeated holiday, as well as the precarious caliphal aspirations. The ensuing verses [vv. 12-14] serve to connect the concepts of religious virtue and military success, the twin pillars of legitimate rule, and to make a transition from the greeting to the recounting of the victorious military campaign. Pertinent to the present discussion are vv. 14, 17, 22-24, which present the God-given dominion of the caliph, the submission of the enemy, the caliph's leading them into the fold of Islam, and, finally, the image of the caliph as redeemer. The poem closes invoking the caliph's combined might and generosity, especially forgiveness, and ends with a benediction (*du'ā'*) that the caliph ever triumph over his enemies and over time, i.e., be victorious and live forever.

The immediate function of this *qaṣīdah* as an act of political recognition and oath of allegiance to the legitimate Islamic ruler is clear enough. We should understand too from its beauty as a work of art that it is part of the lavish decoration and splendid ornament that contributed to the magnificent spectacle of the caliph's 'Īd and victory celebration, i.e., that it is part of the royal insignia and the iconography of power. The establishing of his legitimacy, the recounting of his virtues, the "ritual reenactment" of the battle in which the forces of chaos (=insurrection against divinely appointed caliph) are subdued by the forces of divinely ordained order, are all in evidence. Above all, the caliph's mercy in sparing the life of his enemy so celebrated in the poem reiterates the act of submission and its acceptance in the ceremony itself. In a broader sense, we should understand that the poet's presentation of his 'Īd greeting and homage—the *qaṣīdah*—is paradigmatic for all of the caliph's subjects, and, further, that it has the effect of providing a verbal exegesis of the nature of the ceremony of which it is part.

The further function of the *qaṣīdah* is even more dependent on its esthetic aspects, for it is only because of its literary quality that it was preserved at all. In large part, the poem's success lies in its depiction of al-Mustanṣir in Arabo-Islamic terms of broad appeal as the consummate Muslim ruler, for long after our interest in al-Mustanṣir has waned, the model of the divinely elected merciful conqueror-redeemer remains operative. The military campaign, too, is not at all, as such passages are traditionally called, a "battle-description." Rather, the historical event has been recast in a very familiar poetic idiom that has the effect of absorbing the particular event into an overarching mythic agon or ritual combat [vv. 18-21].[27] Just as the historical acts of defeat-submission-mercy were ritually reenacted in the ceremony so as to assume a mythic dimension as part of the iconography of authority, so in their poeticization they assume archetypal and mythopoeic dimensions cast in a literary-verbal, poetic form. The point of poetry, though, is that it offers perpetuity. Thus, whereas the momentary incorporation of the historical event into the 'Īd ceremony produces a fleeting intersection or identity of profane and sacred time, the poeticization of the event-produces-event becomes a permanent incorporation of the historical event into the poetic-liturgical cycle. In effect, then, the *qaṣīdah* becomes a suitable poem to be recited by all Arabo-Islamic subjects to their rulers on any 'Īd al-Fiṭr, to be valued by all who ascribe to or celebrate the values embodied in it and, ultimately, to be enjoyed by anyone who by culture or acculturation appreciates classical Arabic poetry.

[27] On this subject, see S. Stetkevych, "Pre-Islamic Panegyric and the Poetics of Redemption," 13-19.

In this regard we could compare the panegyric *qaṣīdah* in the Arabo-Islamic tradition to royal portraiture in the European tradition. Take, for example, Rubens' cycle of the life of Maria de' Medici. The painter, with precise instructions from the patroness, incorporates passing political-biographical events into a lasting artistic work by means of two transformations: first a conceptual transformation from the historical to the archetypal, mythical—Maria de' Medici as Juno, Mary, etc.—and then a material one from actually occurring events to the conventions and materials of painting. As one of the insignia of power, the cycle of paintings provides for the enjoyment and aggrandizement of the queen herself—its immediate courtly function. In this respect we must take into account the repression of actual events and their replacement by a mythic-heroic construct. In this case the somewhat pathetic life of Marie de' Medici—plagued by contempt for her mercantile roots, the indifference and infidelity of Henri IV, and the perfidy of her son Louis XIII, not to mention Richelieu—is transformed into one of triumphant glory. Further, the cycle functions ideologically to bolster concepts of European royalty and dominion by bonding them iconographically to the broader and deeper cultural and religious foundations. For example, "The Marriage Consummated in Lyons" presents Maria and Henri IV as Juno and Jove with their emblematic peacocks and eagle, respectively; "The Birth of Maria de' Medici" and "The Education of the Princess" further illustrate the subsuming of the biographical in the mariological and the mythological. Thus the royal painting cycle functions as a manifesto not only of Maria de' Medici's political program, but ultimately of the Christian humanism that is one of the foundations of modern European cultural identity.[28] It will therefore be valued by all who subscribe to European cultural concepts, even when these concepts have been apparently ideologically abandoned or transformed (as when monarchy and church

---

[28] On myth and politics in Rubens' Maria de' Medici Cycle, see Ronald Forsyth Millen and Robert Erich Wolf, *Heroic Deeds and Mystic Figures: A New Reading of Rubens' Life of Maria de' Medici* (Princeton, N.J.: Princeton University Press, 1989), here, esp. chs. 3, 4, and 8.

have been transformed into secular democratic European nationalism). Even a further ideological distancing from "Western values" yet allows for an appreciation of the powerful symbolic transformations and the technical material mastery of a great painter.

One major aspect of al-Muhannad's *qaṣīdah* remains to be attended to. As we have seen, the classical Arabo-Islamic panegyric *qaṣīdah* as a literary genre was transferred to al-Andalus as an integral element of the courtly ceremony and the insignia of authority of the cultural hegemony of the Arab conquerors and of Arabo-Islamic rule. It is noteworthy in this respect that al-Muhannad apparently hailed from the 'Abbāsid capital of Baghdad. In this respect we can thus say of the *qaṣīdah* in the Cordoban caliphate what Paula Sanders has said of the Fāṭimids:

> the Fatimids challenged the hegemony of the Abbasid caliphate, and they therefore had a stake in appropriating its most visible signs of authority. Fatimid insignia of sovereignty and protocol look very much like Abbasid insignia and protocol. The protocol of both caliphates asserted their claims to political and religious leadership of the community of believers as well as established the relative ranks of men at court who stood beneath the caliph.[29]

Just as there occurred an imitation and competition in terms of claims to Arabo-Islamic legitimacy and sovereignty, there occurred a similar imitation and competition in the ceremonies, symbols, and insignia that generate the appearance of legitimacy and sovereignty.

It is in light of these remarks that we should process the information that our poet hails from Baghdad, and further, as Iḥsān 'Abbās has noted, that our poem is a *mu'āraḍah* (imitation, competitive response) to a panegyric delivered by the 'Abbāsid court poet (otherwise renowned as an ascetic poet) Abū al-'Atāhiyah to the caliph al-Mahdī.[30] A brief compar-

---

[29] Sanders, *Ritual, Politics, and the City*, 7. See also p. 29 and ch. 2 "Ceremonial Idiom," pp. 13-37, esp. p. 37 on ritual as negotiation.

[30] Iḥsān 'Abbās, *Tārīkh al-Adab al-Andalusī: 'Aṣr Siyādat Qurṭubah*, 2d ed. (Beirut: Dār al-Thaqāfah, 1975), 104, where, however, he states that it was presented to Hārūn al-Rashīd, whereas the other sources give al-Mahdī. 'Abbās addresses the issue of *mu'āraḍah* throughout his book. On the influence of Abū al-'Atāhiyah and

ison between Abū al-ʿAtāhiyah's original and al-Muhannad's *muʿāraḍah* will reveal the purpose of this "imitation."[31]

In contrast to al-Muhannad's *qaṣīdah*, Abū al-ʿAtāhiyah's *qaṣīdah* is short (11 verses) almost to the point of being epigrammatic and quite lyrical, and comes to us as well in a humorous anecdotal context quite at odds with Ibn Ḥayyān's formal description of the Cordoban ceremony. In the *Kitāb al-Aghānī*, for instance, we read that one day the caliph al-Mahdī held an audience for poets. Among them were Bashshār ibn Burd, Ashjaʿ al-Sulamī, a pupil and admirer of Bashshār's, and also Abū al-ʿAtāhiyah. As Ashjaʿ tells it:

> When Bashshār heard [Abū al-ʿAtāhiyah] speak, he said [to me], "O Akhū Sulaym, is this the one nick-named the Kufan? "Yes," I replied. "May God not reward with good him who brought us together with him!" returned Bashshār. Then al-Mahdī told Abū al-ʿAtāhiyah, "Recite!" Then Bashshār [muttered to me], "Woe to you! Is he going to begin and also be asked to recite before us!" "So it seems," said I, and Abū al-ʿAtāhiyah recited the first five verses of "Is my lady...." Then ... Bashshār said to me, "Woe to you, O Akhū Sulaym! I don't know which I am more amazed at: how weak his poetry is, or his reciting love poetry about the caliph's slave girl for the caliph to hear with his own ear/reciting it with the caliph's own permission!" Until he reached "There came to him the caliphate ..." and the five final verses, at which Bashshār, trembling with delight, said to me, "Woe to you! I can't believe the caliph isn't jumping from his throne with joy! ..."

[meter: *mutaqārib*]

1. Why is my lady then [so cruel to me]?
   Is she coy?
   And I must bear her coyness?[32]

Abū Tammām, etc., at this period, see esp. pp. 125ff.

[31] For a far-ranging and insightful discussion of *muʿāraḍah* and the poetics of imitation generally in the Arabo-Persian poetic tradition, see Paul Losensky, "'The Allusive Field of Drunkenness': Three Safavid-Moghul Responses to a Lyric by Bābā Fighānī," in S. Stetkevych, ed., *Reorientations*, 227-62.

[32] I have taken some liberty with the Arabic to achieve a more convincing English line.

2. And if not, why does she accuse me?
What crime did I commit?
May God send rain upon the ruins of her abode!

3. A slave-girl of the Imām—
has not love been lodged
inside her shirt?

4. She walked among the dark-eyed, short-stepped maidens,
contending with weighty buttocks
as she moved.

5. God has tried my soul with her,
and has tried her censurers
with blame.

6. As if before my eyes,
wherever I sojourn,
I see her likeness.

7. [She was] the Caliphate
[and] came to him, submissive,
trailing the train of her gown.

8. She was right only for him;
he only for her.

9. Should someone else desire her,
the very earth would quake.

10. Should the heart's daughters fail to obey him,
God would not accept their deeds.

11. And the Caliph, out of hatred for the word "no,"
hates whoever utters it.[33]

---

[33] Shukrī Fayṣal, ed., *Abū al-'Atāhiyah: Ash'āruh wa-Akhbāruh* (Damascus: Maktabat Dār al-Mallāḥ, 1964), poem no. 197, pp. 609-13. The anecdote is from Abū al-Faraj al-Iṣbahānī, *Kitāb al-Aghānī* (Dār al-Kutub ed., 4:33) as cited in Fayṣal, *Abū al-'Atāhiyah*, 609.

This *qaṣīdah* is striking for its charm—even humor—, brevity, and yet great panegyric power. With masterly concision Abū al-'Atāhiyah evokes all the essential conventions of the full panegyric in its two-part 'Abbāsid form. He opens, quite according to custom, lamenting his lost beloved, complaining of her coquetry, invoking God to shower rains upon the ruins of her abode [vv. 1-2]. In verse 3 the poet reveals just how illicit and forbidden this love is—she is the property of the caliph—and yet, even in the caliph's presence, continues to vaunt her charms [v. 4]—chief among them her buttocks so delightfully ponderous that they pull her back when she tries to walk forward—and finally to complain of the torments of the lovesick [vv. 5-6]. Inasmuch as the composition of *tashbīb* (erotic verse) describing a girl or woman was considered proof positive of carnal knowledge, as it stands so far, the expected—indeed obligatory—response of the caliph would be to call the executioner. But suddenly, in verse 7, the concubine with trailing gown led submissively to the caliph is revealed to be a metaphor for the caliphate itself. This metaphor is as powerful as it is charming, for it is now the entire *ummah* that submits to al-Mahdī in an image whose origins lie in the ancient Near Eastern *hieros gamos* (sacred marriage/ritual coitus). The sexual metaphor of caliph and concubine [vv. 7 and 8] then perfectly expresses the relation of domination and submission on the one hand, and, on the other hand, perfect mutuality (modern sexual politics would find these two entirely incompatible) that defines the relation of ruler to realm. So too does the tremendous rage of sexual jealousy serve as a superb metaphor for both the personal anger of the caliph and the cosmic rage, the earthquake, that others' designs on the caliphate would occasion [v. 9]. The metaphor of concubine for the caliph's subject remains operative in verses 10 and 11, where, first, obedience and submission to the caliph become an article of Islamic faith, without which one's good deeds are unacceptable to God; and finally, in what seems to mean the refusal of the caliph's sexual advances, the caliph, likewise, hates all that refuse to submit to him. The charm and power of this poem lie above all in Abū al-'Atāhiyah's establishing a metaphor through which sexual potency and domination serve perfectly to express political dominion and power.

When we compare Abū al-ʿAtāhiyah's original with the "imitation," what strikes us above all is how unlike they are. al-Muhannad's poem is clearly a *muʿāraḍah*: he adopts the rhyme and meter of the original, employs a high incidence of the same rhyme-words within the 28 verses of his poem that Ibn Ḥayyān has cited, and twice employs *taḍmīn*, the incorporation or quotation of an entire hemistich.[34] It is therefore quite clear that he expects his audience, especially the caliph al-Mustanṣir, to recognize the poem he is imitating. At the same time, his own poem is so different in style, structure, and subject matter that we do not sense that he is trying to "outdo" the master, but, rather, to evoke him. I would argue that this particular case of *muʿāraḍah*, then, strives not so much to compete as to identify— *qaṣīdah* with *qaṣīdah* and caliphate with caliphate. In this sense we can identify the incorporation of rhyme-words and whole hemistiches from Abū al-ʿAtāhiyah's poem into al-Muhannad's as a form of "appropriation of the insignia of power."

Part III

THE ʿĪD *QAṢĪDAH* OF MUḤAMMAD IBN SHUKHAYṢ

The second *qaṣīdah* cited by Ibn Ḥayyān for the ʿĪd al-Fiṭr celebration of 363 H is a strange concoction by Muḥammad ibn Shukhayṣ.[35] It would be difficult, indeed misleading, to discuss it without reference first to the issue of *muʿāraḍah*, for the poem is strikingly an imitation of the master panegyrist of the ʿAbbāsids, Abū Tammām. In a direct and technical sense, it is a *muʿāraḍah* of that poet's renowned panegyric *qaṣīdah* to the ʿAbbāsid caliph al-Muʿtaṣim, celebrating his conquest of the Byzantine city of ʿAmmūriyah/Amorium in the year 223/838.[36] It exhibits the same

[34] Rhyme words: Abū al-ʿA. v. 3 = al-Muhannad, v. 27; v. 7 = v. 2; *taḍmīn*: 2d hemistich v. 8 = 2d of v. 9; 2d hemistich of 9 of = 2d hemistich of v. 19.

[35] Lines from several of his poems are dealt with in García Gómez, "La poésie politique," 8-9.

[36] Abū Tammām Ḥabīb ibn Aws al-Ṭāʾī, *Dīwān Abī Tammām bi-Sharḥ al-Khaṭīb al-Tibrīzī*, ed. Muḥammad ʿAbduh ʿAzzām, 4 vols. (Cairo: Dār al-Maʿārif, 1951) poem

rhyme in *bāʾ*—although with a different end-vowel—and meter, *basīṭ*. It also, in so far as we can determine from the verses cited by Ibn Ḥayyān, is built according to the military victory ode structure that Abū Tammām employs in the ʿAmmūriyah *qaṣīdah* and many other well-known poems: that is, the poem begins with what we might term "archetypal" panegyric to the caliph, proceeds to a poetic presentation of the military campaign in which detailed historical referents are formulated as ritual agon between good and evil, and concludes with the reaffirmation of the "archetypal," a celebratory benediction (*duʿāʾ*) for the caliph's long life, prosperity, and, sometimes, a call for recognition or crowning of the heir apparent.[37] In addition, we find more particular themes and motifs from the ʿAmmūriyah poem: the supremacy of the sword over the book; military might over astrology; the use of astrological/astronomical terminology of rising, setting, overturning, shooting stars; the months of the year; the ripening of dates—all these evoked with Abū Tammām's diction, especially through the rhyme-word. To all this we can add imitations, what the classical Arab critics would have termed *sariqah* (plagiarism), of other well-known verses by Abū Tammām. For example, compare verses 25 and 26 of Ibn Shukhayṣ's *qaṣīdah* with the two opening verses of Abū Tammām's ʿAmmūriyah *qaṣīdah*:

1. The sword is more veracious than the book,
   its cutting edge splits earnestness from jest.

2. The white of the blade, not the black on the page,
   its broadsides clarify uncertainty and doubt.[38]

Likewise, verse 56 with a verse from the same poem:

35. The reversal of our fortunes brought forth
    from their unfortunate reversal auspicious issue.[39]

no. 3, 1:40-74. For a translation and analysis, see Suzanne Pinckney Stetkevych, *Abū Tammām and the Poetics of the ʿAbbāsid Age* (Leiden: E. J. Brill, 1991), 187-211.

[37] See S. Stetkevych, *Abū Tammām*, 108-235, passim.

[38] See references in note 36.

[39] See references in note 36.

And, verse 46 with a verse from Abū Tammām's *qaṣīdah* to the caliph al-Mu'taṣim on the immolation of his allegedly traitorous Persian general, al-Afshīn:

> 24. Fire's worshipper in life, its fuel in death,
> with the wicked he shall enter it.[40]

Finally, in a more general sense, we find the use of a distinctly Abū Tammāmian rhetorically ornate *badī'*-style in verses such as verse 50.[41] In other words, to the audience then, and for that matter to any Arab audience now, what we have here is an Abū Tammāmian panegyric composed by another poet for another *mamdūḥ*. In ceremonial terms, too, we can talk of its success in the translation and appropriation of insignia of sovereignty.

It should be clear from this and the preceding poem that, although in a general sense the panegyric *qaṣīdah* was one of the insignia of power, the Cordobans were also keen to compete for the prestige conferred by the great master-panegyrists of the east, Abū al-'Atāhiyah (perceived as such, although otherwise renowned as an ascetic poet), Abū Tammām, and, as we will see below, al-Mutanabbī. In aesthetic terms, however, the problem in the case of Ibn Shukhayṣ's poem is that the copy is so artfully achieved that it lacks sufficient authenticity. We can interpret this perhaps as a lack of political and poetic confidence, and sense in Cordoban caliphal culture the compensatory attitude of arrivistes. An analogy would be the beautifully constructed Florentine or Renaissance palaces of the American robber barons: however fine the craftsmanship and perfect the detail, there is something inherently inauthentic, i.e., unoriginal, about them. Ironically, then, although the power and beauty of this poem derive largely from its evocation of Abū Tammām's master- panegyric, that too is what prevents it from achieving its true greatness.

This having been said, we must nevertheless admit that Ibn Shukhayṣ has composed a poem of considerable power and artistry. In archetypal

[40] Abū Tammām, *Dīwān*, poem no. 72, 2:198-209; S. Stetkevych, *Abū Tammām*, 215.

[41] See S. Stetkevych, *Abū Tammām*, 3-106, passim.

and structural terms, he has successfully fused the seasonal cyclical pattern with the cycle of the military campaign to fit the Islamic lunar (and hence not meteorologically seasonal) calendar and the celebration of the ʿĪd. We can get a good grasp of this if we view the poem through the lens of Gaster's formulation of the "seasonal cycle" in ancient Near Eastern myth, ritual, and drama. Of the public ceremonies that usher in years and seasons which "represent the mechanism whereby ... society seeks periodically to renew its vitality and ensure its continuance" he writes:

> The activities fall into two main divisions which we may call, respectively, rites of Kenosis, or Emptying, and rites of Plerosis, or Filling. The former portray and symbolize the eclipse of life and vitality at the end of each lease, and are exemplified by lenten periods, fasts, austerities, and other expressions of mortification or suspended animation. The latter, on the other hand, portray and symbolize the revitalization that ensues at the beginning of the new lease, and are exemplified by rites of mass mating, ceremonial purgations of evil and noxiousness (both physical and "moral"), and magical procedures designed to promote fertility, produce rain, relume the sun, and so forth.[42]

The two divisions of Emptying and Filling he then subdivides:

> First come rites of *mortification*, symbolizing the state of suspended animation that ensues at the end of the year, when one lease on life has drawn to a close and the next is not yet assured. Second come rites of *purgation*, whereby the community seeks to rid itself of all noxiousness and contagion, both physical and moral, and of all evil influences which might impair the prosperity of the coming year and thereby threaten the desired renewal of vitality. Third come rites of *invigoration*, whereby the community attempts, by its own concerted and regimented effort, to galvanize its moribund condition and to procure that new lease on life which is imperative for the continuance of the topocosm. Last come the rites of *jubilation*, which bespeak men's sense of relief when the new year has indeed begun and the continuance of their own lives and that of the topocosm is thereby assured.[43]

---

[42] Gaster, *Thespis*, 23.

[43] Gaster, *Thespis*, 26.

Given that the *qaṣīdah* was presented at the ceremony of the 'Īd greeting, it is not surprising that its opening verses [vv. 1-7] correspond to the final section of Gaster's formulation, i.e., jubilation. The poet begins with the Islamic lunar calendrical cycle that has brought the fulfillment of hopes —presumably in the victory over Ḥasan ibn Qannūn as well as the 'Īd. In verse 3 the seasonal/agricultural, the astrological/astronomical, and the military spheres are aligned: ascending stars (of good fortune) have revived victory and fertility, perfidy and drought have died. This may entail a reference to the torrential rains of the month of Rajab/April of that year.[44] The poem then develops the "pathetic fallacy" describing the earth swaggering in amazement at the caliph's victory and putting forth its blooms. These delightful verses [5-7] should remind us of the origin of the much admired garden lyrics in the much maligned panegyric.[45]

The middle section of the poem, as cited in Ibn Ḥayyān, is devoted to the defeat and disgrace of the enemy. In terms of the seasonal pattern, this corresponds to the purgation and invigoration sections, the "purgation of evil and noxiousness" and "galvanizing the moribund condition to gain a new lease on life" respectively. We can understand it as well as a ritual reenactment of al-Mustanṣir's victory. Verses 8 through 17 describe the enemy's, Ḥasan ibn Qannūn's, futile attempt to flee from the caliph whose will and determination are embodiments of divine decree. Verses 18 through 24 present what we might in Arabic genre classification term *hijā'*, the public disgracing of the defeated enemy, much akin to the ritual humiliation of the defeated enemy of the Byzantine triumph.[46]

If the previous section describes Ḥasan ibn Qannūn's cowardice, this one challenges the claim to Hāshimite lineage, which in Arabo-Islamic

[44] Ibn Ḥayyān, *Al-Muqtabis*, 154.

[45] On the function of floral elements in panegyric, esp. of Ibn Darrāj, see James T. Monroe, *Risālat at-Tawābi' wa z-Zawābi': The Treatise of Familiar Spirits and Demons by Abū 'Āmir ibn Shuhaid al-Ashja'ī al-Andalusī* (Berkeley and Los Angeles: University of California Press, 1971), 8-10.

[46] See McCormick, *Eternal Victory*, 161-63.

terms constitutes a denial of the legitimacy of his hereditary claim to the imamate or caliphate. Although in an immediate sense this verse [18] is aimed at Idrīsid claims, within the broader political arena it constitutes a pot shot at the 'Abbāsids, the Fāṭimids, and assorted 'Alid pretenders. For Hāshim ibn 'Abd al-Manāf, the great grandfather of the Prophet Muḥammad, was the common ancestor of Muḥammad, 'Alī, and al-'Abbās, whereas the Umayyads claim descent from 'Abd al-Shams ibn 'Abd al-Manāf.[47] It should be noted that the poet does not deny the legitimizing role of heredity, but rather questions the authenticity of the genealogies in question. After denying the validity of Ḥasan's Hāshimite lineage, Ibn Shukhayṣ proceeds to describe his people as likewise unsuitable for the caliphate in other respects: they are morally blind, incapable of pious deeds, barbaric and uncouth. Their ancestors settled in a place of no learning or civility; they were savages associating with wild beast and concerned only with "slurping soup." All these terms are perceived as dialectically opposed to the true qualifications for the (Umayyad) caliphate: true lineage to the Quraysh, piety, civility and civilization [vv. 19-22].

Of particular interest for the legitimizing of the Cordoban Umayyads is verse 23 which refers to the murder in the year 35/656 of the third Orthodox caliph, 'Uthmān ibn 'Affān, through whom the Umayyads trace their caliphal claims and Qurashī descent, and of whom 'Alī ibn Abī Ṭālib was a staunch political opponent, in whose murder he was indirectly implicated, and whose murderers he protected.[48] In the political context of this poem, then, Ibn Shukhayṣ depicts the Idrīsid sedition against the Umayyads as a reiteration of the originary 'Alid abomination

[47] In fact, the hereditary claims of the dynasties are shrouded in obscurities and complications, and even the term Hāshimite appears originally to have referred to the supporters of the imamate of Abū Hāshim, the son of the 'Alid Muḥammad ibn al-Ḥanafiyyah. See B. Lewis, arts. "Hās̲h̲imiyya" and "'Abbāsids" and M. Canard, art. "Fāṭimids" (under genealogy of the Fāṭimids) in *Encyclopaedia of Islam*, 2d ed.

[48] See M. Hinds, art. "Mu'āwiya" and L. Veccia Vaglieri, art. "'Alī b. Abī Ṭālib" in *Encyclopaedia of Islam*, 2d ed.

of the murder of 'Uthmān, that is, he identifies a political cycle of Umayyad defeat and restitution with the seasonal cycle.

Against the false claims of Ḥasan ibn Qannūn the poet posits the truth of the spears and swords, i.e., of the victory of the authentic, legitimate caliph, which culminates in verse 37. Verses 38 through 47 then present the victorious military campaign. Of note is the appearance of the caliph as the star of good fortune (*ghurratu al-sa'di*) who spares his enemy's life. In seasonal terms this suggests a "new lease on life" for both Ḥasan ibn Qannūn and the Umayyad *ummah,* for *ghurrah* means, too, the new moon that appears at the beginning of the new lunar month, hence marking here the 'Īd al-Fiṭr. But *ghurrah* also means the radiance or numen of the caliph's face which then [v. 42], by dazzling his enemy's eyes, forms a virtual veil. Verses 43 and 44 demonstrate what would have happened had the caliph let down this veil of his mercy to reveal his awful power: bloodshed, the oppression of religion, free men enslaved, property plundered—i.e., the overturning of the decreed order of the topocosm. Verses 45 through 47 inform us that Ḥasan ibn Qannūn brought about his own demise: in a complex Abū Tammāmian *badī'* construction of combined *jinās* (root-play) and *ṭibāq* (antithesis), it was his own withholding of nobility—that is his renunciation of loyalty to the Umayyads to render allegiance to the Fāṭimids—that brought him to this sorrowful end [v. 45]. Again, in a virtual case of *sariqah* from Abū Tammām's renowned *qaṣīdah* on the immolation of his general al-Afshīn (cited above), the vehemence of his insurrection renders his soul kindling for hell-fire.

The final section that Ibn Ḥayyān cites [vv. 48-66] counters the chaos of insurrection with a celebration of the restoration of order, political and cosmic. It begins [v. 48] by addressing the caliph in terms that define the inter-relationship between Islam, military success, and the preservation of historical and cultural memory in the form of poems and orations. The following verse [49], following closely in the footsteps of the theme and diction of Abū Tammām's 'Ammūriyah *qaṣīdah,* stresses that the caliph's success is not the result of the astrologers' shooting stars, but his own resolute action in effecting divine decrees. In conquering Ḥasan ibn Qannūn's domain and then taking him captive, the caliph has, as Ibn Shukhayṣ puts it—again in an Abū Tammāmian *badī'* formulation—made him both plundered and plunder [v. 50]. In verse 51 the poet reminds us that in sparing his defeated enemy, the caliph has virtually given him life: he gave him something that cannot be given—his soul.

From verse 52 through 58 the poet invokes the loyalty and obedience of the caliph's liege-men, the bedouin (Arab) client-tribes, and the devotion of the army that conquers in al-Mustanṣir's name to urge the caliph on. Now that the entire dominion of the west is subject to him, he should turn his sights toward the oppressive and unstable domains of the east, to wit, Fusṭāṭ (it is of note that the poet uses the name of the pre-Fāṭimid city rather than recognize the Fāṭimid triumph implicit in the name al-Qāhirah, "the [city] triumphant" or "victorious") and Aleppo. García Góṃez, in his discussion of this verse and similar examples of poetic claims to Cordoban Umayyad rule of the Islamic heartlands, remarks that:

> Ces jugements sur les Etats musulmans autres que l'Espagne ne sont pas simples confidences rhétoriques, mais bien au contraire l'annonce de plans d'expansion umaiyade. Selon les poètes cordouans, les pays musulmans, pleins d'envie, regardent le calife cordouan victorieux, "ainsi que les femmes regardent par les fentes de leurs voiles" [Ibn Shukhayṣ].[49]

While, indeed, nothing in poetry is simple rhetoric, and we do know that in early 363/974 the Qarmaṭī al-Ḥasan al-A'ṣam launched an unsuccessful attack on Cairo[50] and that Aleppo was at this time subject to the Byzantines,[51] on the whole we would do best to understand these poetic claims and incitements to conquest in the Islamic heartlands not as concrete plans for Umayyad expansion, but rather as ideological statements. For all claimants to the caliphate, whether 'Abbāsid, Umayyad, or Fāṭim-

[49] García Gómez, "La poésie politique," 8.

[50] Canard, "Fāṭimids."

[51] M. Canard, art. "Ḥamdānids," *Encyclopaedia of Islam* 2d ed.

id, etc., shared the tenet that there was only one true orthodox Islam and only one legitimate caliph. Anyone who claimed the caliphate *ipso facto* claimed to be the sole legitimate ruler of Islamdom.[52]

Verses 59 through 66 provide a closure for the *qaṣīdah* that recapitulates the celebration of military victory, agricultural or vegetable fertility, and 'Īd al-Fiṭr of the opening section [vv. 1-7]. If, following the formulation of the seasonal pattern cited above, we take the Ḥasanid insurrection as an expression of *mortification* phase—disorder, the threat that the new lease on life (here the perpetuation of the Cordoban Umayyad dynasty) will not be obtained—and take the military campaign and its attendant hardships as the *purgation* phase—ridding the community of the moral contagion of political and religious insurrection—then we will take the military victory to mark the *invigoration* phase—the galvanizing of the community to procure a new lease on life and the guarantee of the continuation of the topocosm. The military political situation in this manner is aligned with and mythically incorporated into the agricultural (solar) seasonal cycle, so that the invigoration of the realm through military conquest is identified with agricultural or vegetable fertility. At the same time the military victory is also aligned with and mythically incorporated into the Islamic lunar calendar through its identification with the (moral) pollution → purgation → purification pattern of the fast and festival of Ramaḍān and 'Īd al-Fiṭr.

In brief, the closure, like the opening of the *qaṣīdah,* we can identify with the *jubilation* phase, the celebration of the renewal of the topocosm. The dominant feature here is the mythicization of the caliph's military campaign, and, through it, the perpetuation of the Umayyad house at Cordoba. Thus, verse 59 compares the caliph's radiant face to the fertile year, to be followed in verse 60 by a *du'ā'* (benediction) calling for the caliph's enduring might. Playing on the ritual gift-giving and greeting of the 'Īd, the conceit of verse 61 makes the caliph an 'Īd-gift that God "the

[52] On the authority of the caliphate, including references to poetry, see Crone and Hinds, *God's Caliph.*

Greeter" has bestowed upon Islam. Natural or vegetable fertility is invoked once more in verse 62 in which the bounties called down upon the caliph's victorious armies are described as a flood. Again, in verse 63, the magnanimity of the caliph is, according to poetic convention and fertility imagery, termed a generous rain. In verse 64 the entire project of the *qaṣīdah*—of mythicizing the military campaign in order to incorporate it into the seasonal/solar and Islamic/lunar calendrical cycles, thereby to ensure its perpetuity—is expressed with great concision: the mighty victory and prosperous fertile year which are being especially celebrated at this ʻĪd al-Fiṭr are what al-Mustanṣir's days will be named for [cf. v. 48]. The notion of pollution and purification is conveyed here by the word *qushubu* (new, polished, i.e., after having been rusty). In the closing couplet the poet moves from mythic and poetic perpetuity to a continuance, a "new lease on life," of a more pragmatic dynastic sort, in calling al-Mustanṣir to crown his son, i.e., to formally recognize him as his *wālī al-ʻahd* (successor).

Of the many functions the *qaṣīdah* can perform, several are most noteworthy in the context of the present study. First, particularly through Ibn Shukhayṣ's identification of the cognate patterns of the military campaign, the solar agricultural or vegetable calendar, and the lunar Islamic liturgical calendar, the *qaṣīdah* mythicizes and poeticizes the event, transforming it from the ephemeral to the cyclically perpetual. Further, with respect to the ceremony that Ibn Ḥayyān describes, the *qaṣīdah* serves an exegetical function. Then, too, the *qaṣīdah* itself, like the lavish decorations and extravagant spectacle, is one of the elements of the *jubilation*-phase. Finally, the net effect of all of these is the reaffirmation of legitimate Arabo-Islamic rule of which al-Mustanṣir is, by virtue of the *qaṣīdah*, both particular exemplar and general paradigm.

Part IV

THE *QAṢĪDAH* OF IBN DARRĀJ AL-QASṬALLĪ, 'ĪD AL-AḌḤĀ, 403/1013 [53]

The third *qaṣīdah* in our discussion arises out of quite different political circumstances. About forty years later than the other two, it is a product of the turbulent period of the disintegration of the Umayyad caliphate at Cordoba. In the most immediate sense, the calamitous downfall of the Umayyad house at Cordoba was precipitated by al-Ḥakam II al-Mustanṣir's son and heir, Hishām II, long the puppet of his 'Āmirid *ḥājib*s, when he named the last of these, 'Abd al-Raḥmān Sanchuelo, heir apparent in Rabī' al-Awwal, 399/Nov., 1008—much to the displeasure of other descendants of the Marwānid–Umayyad line. This sparked the *fitnah* or civil war that brought down the Umayyad house, led to the establishment of the *mulūk al-ṭawā'if*, "petty kingdoms," and paved the way for the Reconquista.

Hishām II's ill-advised act was followed by a coup d'état resulting in the caliphate of another Marwānid, Muḥammad ibn Hishām al-Mahdī (399/1009), and the capture and execution of Sanchuelo. Next, the *mamdūḥ* of Ibn Darrāj's *qaṣīdah,* Sulaymān ibn al-Ḥakam ibn Sulaymān, a great grandson of 'Abd al-Raḥmān III, with the backing of the Berbers and of Sancho García, Count of Castille, rose in rebellion. Sulaymān's forces arrived at Guadamellato on 11 Rabī' al-Awwal, 400/3 Nov., 1009 and two days later encountered and defeated al-Mahdī's Cordoban forces at Qantīsh. After briefly resuscitating Hishām II as caliph, Sulaymān had himself proclaimed caliph with the honorific al-Musta'īn (17 Rabī' al-Awwal, 400/ 9 Nov., 1009). This led to a civil war between Sulaymān with his Berber faction and his fellow Marwānid al-Mahdī. Only the southern provinces ratified the accession of Sulaymān, and, meanwhile, the Cordoban populace had become disaffected with the Berbers. Al-Mahdī went to Toledo where he continued to be recognized as the sole legitimate sovereign. Having secured the support of two Frankish counts, Ray-

[53] The poet's dates are given as 347/958–421/1030. Sezgin, *Poesie,* 699-700.

mond Borrell III of Barcelona and his brother Ermengaud (Armengol) of Urgel, he made for Cordoba. He was met by Sulaymān and his Berbers at 'Aqabat al-Baqar, northwest of Cordoba, where a fierce battle ensued on 5 Shawwāl, 400/22 May, 1010. Ermengaud was killed, Sulaymān fled, and the next day al-Mahdī and the Frankish troops took Cordoba. Pressed by his Catalan auxiliaries, whom he could not pay, al-Mahdī pursued the Berbers, only to be defeated and abandoned by the Catalans. Soon we find Hishām II reinstated in Cordoba, and al-Mahdī assassinated by Slavs of 'Āmirid loyalties. The Berbers and Sulaymān refused, however, to recognize Hishām II. This led to a prolonged and debilitating siege of Cordoba followed by especially brutal pillaging and rapine when the city ultimately capitulated, and finally by Sulaymān's victorious reentry on 27 Shawwāl 403/ 10 May, 1013.[54] Putting these historical facts together with the remarks of Ibn Ḥayyān that accompany the text in Ibn Bassām's *Al-Dhakhīrah* (quoted above) and the 'Īd topos of the opening and closing of the poem, Maḥmūd 'Alī Makkī dates the poem to the time of 'Īd al-Aḍḥā, i.e., 10 Dhū al-Ḥijjah, 403/June 1013, after Sulaymān's restoration to the caliphate in Shawwāl of that year.[55]

Ibn Ḥayyān's remarks are of particular interest to us for what they reveal about the relation of panegyric to courtly values and culture in general. First, the role of panegyric *qaṣīdah* in a ritual exchange of poem and prize is portrayed as a sacred trust upon which courtly culture is founded. The patron's failure to reward the poets according to custom and expectation leads to their dispersal and ultimately to the demise of culture in Cordoba and the rise of barbarity. With regard to the poem at hand, these remarks inform us that this was Ibn Darrāj's first panegyric to the caliph Sulaymān. As I have demonstrated elsewhere, the Arabic panegyric *qaṣīdah* can be expected to perform the function of declaration of allegiance, *mubāya'ah*, to the new patron, and the exchange of

[54] This is only the sketchiest of summaries of a very complex period. For the full and fascinating story, see Lévi-Provençal, *Histoire de l'Espagne musulmane* 2:291-326.

[55] Ibn Darrāj al-Qasṭallī, *Dīwān*, ed. Makkī, 51. The date is given as 26 Shawwāl, 403/9 May, 1013 in Lévi-Provencal, *Histoire de l'Espagne musulmane* 2:319.

poem and prize will thus be a ritual and contractual one that establishes a bond of fidelity and clientage between the two.[56] The sense of a declaration of a new allegiance, indeed of submission or surrender, should be particularly acute here, inasmuch as Ibn Darrāj had been a court panegyrist of the ʻĀmirids. In light of the contemporary political situation, we can expect as well in the poem at hand an emphasis on the restoration and legitimacy of the Umayyad Marwānid house.[57] The mythic and ritual patterns thus far introduced are all applicable to or extricable from this *qaṣīdah*, too.

The *qaṣīdah* opens proclaiming the restored Umayyad caliph Sulaymān to be like the ʻĪd among the days, thereby setting the stage for the mythicization and incorporation of the historical present—in this case the restoration of Sulaymān to the caliphate—into the lunar liturgical Islamic calendrical cycle, a process with which we are by now familiar.[58] It proceeds through verses 1 through 4 to describe his reign in mythic terms of renewal, return, rebirth. Nor is the political dimension left out, as in verse 2 the submission of the rebellious is listed among the forms of purification after pollution.

The next five verses [5-10] turn to the subject of the legitimacy of the Umayyad house. Especially effective here is verse 5 in which the Meccan/Qurashī origins of the Banū Umayyah are invoked and described as incubating until the promised time arrived. The verse is lent rhetorical force by its recalling through the phrase *maʻādi ayyāmin* (return of days) the words *al-ayyām* (days) and *ʻīd* (from the same root *ʻ-w-d* as *maʻād*) of verse 1 and then adding *jinās* (root-play) within the line in the word *mawʻūd* (promised) from the root *w-ʻ-d*. Thus the calendrical cycle is presented

---

[56] See S. Stetkevych, "Pre-Islamic Panegyric and the Poetics of Redemption," "ʻAbbāsid Panegyric and the Poetics of Political Allegiance," and "ʻAbbāsid Panegyric: The Poetics and Politics of Ceremony."

[57] An excellent study of panegyric with emphasis on the theme of restoration is James D. Garrison, *Dryden and the Tradition of Panegyric* (Berkeley and Los Angeles: University of California Press, 1975).

[58] Again on the association of *bayʻah* and the ʻĪd, see the examples from the poetry of Ibn ʻAbd Rabbih in ʻAbbās, *Tārīkh al-Adab al-Andalusī*, pp. 190-91.

as not merely repeating, but as fulfilling the promise of time, i.e., the divinely decreed Umayyad rule. The loyalty of the military and their devotion to the call—*da'wah* actually carries the sense of a religious claim/call—is then tied to the mythic association of the legitimate ruler and the prosperity of the land [verses 6 and 7]. This section culminates in a reaffirmation of loyalty to the hierarchy: the elevation of the patron to the caliphate, i.e., his proper position in the ordered ranks that form society [v. 8]; the familiar metaphor of dominion as a tent, now with loyal Berber tribes forming the tent ropes and pole [v. 9]; and finally the loyalty of those tribes in battle and in politics [v. 10]. In short, the two foundations of the Islamic (or for that matter any) proper polity: a system of ranks appropriately filled by members true to their bonds of loyalty and obligation.

This evocation of the ordered and prosperous Islamic polity is countered in verses 11 through 14 with a picture of the chaos that reigned before Sulaymān acceded to the caliphate, here referring to the events of 400/1009. The internecine nature of the struggle is expressed in a double-entendre of failed fertility in verse 11 where "cut bonds of kinship" can be read equally as "slit-open wombs." Verse 12 depicts social and especially military disorder resulting from the abomination of unsanctioned rule: the noble humbled to the base, slaves attacking free and noble kings, heroes fleeing in terror, guides loosing their way, shots missing their mark [vv. 12-14]. Sulaymān's restitution of order and prosperity is presented in verse 15 in terms of the rising new moon of good fortune. The word *ghurrah* conveys at once the image of the caliph's radiant countenance and the renewal symbolized by the rising of the new moon. In the Islamic lunar calendar this signals the new month and, in particular, is associated with the new moon of the month of Shawwāl that signals the end of the month of fasting, Ramaḍān, and the feast of 'Īd al-Fiṭr. Verses 16 through 31 refer to the battle at 'Aqabat al-Baqar in which, simply put, Sulaymān lost his caliphal seat at Cordoba to al-Mahdī. When viewed in light of the historical accounts of the struggle between the two scions of the Marwānid line, Sulaymān and al-Mahdī, these verses reveal a process of mythicization through which the *fitnah* or civil war between Muslim kinsmen has been transformed into a *jihād* or holy war between the legitimate Muslim ruler and the Christian infidel. This is accomplished above all by simply omitting any mention of al-Mahdī and his 30,000 Muslim troops, and concentrating instead on the Frankish counts with their 10,000.[59] The historical battle of Sulaymān against al-Mahdī is rendered into a ritual cosmic agon between good and evil, the roles played here by Islam and Christianity, respectively. Although names and places are specified, such specificity should not gull us into accepting the text as historically accurate, for the images are archetypal, mythical, and poetic, and the aims of the *qaṣīdah* are highly political. Thus, for example, in verse 17 the prosperity achieved by military victory is likened to agricultural fertility: harvest time has come and the crop is enemy heads. The description of the army in verse 21 is purely poetic convention in both image and diction. The victorious blades are Muslim as well as sharp [v. 25]; the Christian general marches his troops straight into hell-fire [v. 23]. Finally, the regeneration of life through military victory is again given vegetable expression as the poet asks why the shaft of the Khaṭṭī spear did not sprout in the caliph's hand [v. 30].

What is particularly noteworthy and curious here is not merely the poet's recasting of *fitnah* as *jihād*, but that in describing the events leading to Sulaymān's restitution to the caliphate at Cordoba, his loss is turned into a victory, and—no doubt with great sensitivity to the prevailing political climate—the brutal siege and reconquest of Cordoba is not mentioned at all.

The closing verses [vv. 32-34] contain a charming but complex conceit through which the poet seems to style his *qaṣīdah* a bride and the verse of praise in it her dowry. This leads to some ambiguity, perhaps intentional, between the bride and the dowry, and then a further metaphor of the *qaṣīdah*/dowry/bride as an exquisitely set necklace. The *qaṣīdah* as bride, a conceit known already from, e.g., Abū Tammām, implies its virginity, that is, its originality. The necklace metaphor is also a conventional one employed to convey not only the idea of rhyme and

---

[59] These are the figures given by Lévi-Provençal, *Histoire de l'Espagne musulmane* 2:313.

meter—the ordering (*naẓm*) of the *qaṣīdah*, by also its artistry, its uniqueness, and its lasting value and beauty. The closing verse begins with an 'Īd-greeting for the *qaṣīdah* itself, but it must be understood that the days of glory for the poem mean the perpetual glory of the *mamdūḥ*. Finally, Ibn Darrāj closes his *qaṣīdah* at once recapitulating the opening verse and declaring his submission and obedience: the caliph is, for those who obey him, the 'Īd among 'Īds.

Ibn Darrāj's *qaṣīdah* thus functions as a declaration of submission and allegiance to the Cordoban Umayyad house (with no hint that there might be other Marwānids to choose from), a confirmation of legitimacy of its rule in terms of lineage and military success, and the caliph's position vis-à-vis the Islamic topocosm. Once again, the incorporation of the ephemeral contemporary event into the recurrent Islamic liturgical cycle through the processes of mythicization and poeticization is nowhere more succinctly exemplified than in the metaphor of the opening (and closing) verses: "The days bore witness that you are their 'Īd."

At this point we cannot avoid mentioning the apparent source of this controlling metaphor, which is the *dāliyyah* in the meter *ṭawīl* of the master panegyrist of the east, al-Mutanabbī, to the Ḥamdānid emir Sayf al-Dawlah for 'Īd al-Aḍḥā, 342/953.[60] Not only does Ibn Darrāj, whose position in al-Andalus al-Tha'ālibī likens to that of al-Mutanabbī in Shām,[61] adopt al-Mutanabbī's extensive *jinās* (root-play, punning) on the word *'īd*, but his structuring the poem around a mythicized agon between Islam and Christianity seems also to derive from this model.[62]

---

[60] Aḥmad Abū al-Ṭayyib al-Mutanabbī, *Al-'Arf al-Ṭayyib fī Sharḥ Dīwān Abī al-Ṭayyib*, ed. and com., Nāṣīf al-Yāzijī, (Beirut: Dār Ṣādir/Dār Beirut, 1964) 2:179-85 (rhyme -*dā*). This poem is the subject of my "'Abbāsid Panegyric: The Politics and Poetics of Ceremony."

[61] Abū Manṣūr 'Abd al-Malik al-Tha'ālibī al-Naysābūrī, *Yatīmat al-Dahr fī Maḥāsin Ahl al-'Aṣr*, ed. Mufīd Muḥammad Qumayḥah (Beirut: Dār al-Kutub al-'Ilmiyyah, 1983), 2:119.

[62] Inasmuch as this pattern emerges more clearly in the 34-line version given by Ibn Bassām (who cites al-Tha'ālibī's remark 1:1:44) in *Al-Dhakhīrah* (1:1:50-53) than in the *Dīwān* version (pp. 51-57), we might credit Ibn Bassām's sense of *Formgefühl*

Although Ibn Darrāj's *qaṣīdah* is pleasantly Mutanabbian in style, we nevertheless perceive a comfortable sense of self-sufficiency in Ibn Darrāj's poem that distinguishes it from the anxious insecurity of the first two poems. We sense now that Andalusian poetry is standing on its own two feet. Nevertheless, we must recognize that throughout the period of the Cordoban caliphate and for some time thereafter, a key element in the appropriation of the insignia of power and authority from the Arabo-Islamic east was the appropriation specifically of the poetic voices of the great master panegyrists of the east, chief among them Abū Tammām and al-Mutanabbī.

Returning once more to Ibn Ḥayyān's introductory remarks to Ibn Darrāj's poem, perhaps we can deduce from the failure of the panegyric enterprise more about its power and function. The ritual exchange of panegyric *qaṣīdah* and prize now appears as paradigmatic of the social contract and the archetypal act of allegiance upon which the entire social and cultural enterprise of the Arabo-Islamic polity is founded. When this contractual ritual fails, as when in the caliph Sulaymān's case the *mamdūḥ* fails to produce the prize to which the presentation of the panegyric obligates him, the entire Arabo-Islamic cultural enterprise fails. Perhaps then it is not enough to say that the panegyric *qaṣīdah* was one of the Arabo-Islamic insignia of power, but rather, following Ibn Ḥayyān's line of reasoning, that the *qaṣīdah* and the exchange ritual of which it was part, was the very basis of that power.

---

for extracting from Ibn Darrāj's rather long and loose imitation of al-Mutanabbī's *qaṣīdah* a formally tighter and closer reflection of the original. This is particularly the case with his choice of closing lines that most resemble al-Mutanabbī's closure.

PHILOLOGIANS AND POETS IN SEARCH OF THE HEBREW LANGUAGE

ANGEL SÁENZ-BADILLOS *

Hebrew Language versus Arabic Language

During the Middle Ages, Hebrew, strictly speaking, was never a "language of power" in the sense of "political power" primarily because the Jews were a subject people and not an autonomous authority. Hebrew was not even the only language of the Jewish people, since in their daily life and cultural activities they employed Arabic or other languages of the lands in which they lived. The use of Hebrew as a spoken or a literary tongue was extremely rare, but for the Jews it represented a very old tradition and held particular significance since it was the language in which the Bible had been written. During centuries under Byzantine and Islamic rule that exiled and dispersed nation had preserved Hebrew as the language of the Torah and the liturgy, including the midrashic homilies on the Bible.

Nevertheless from the tenth century on, particularly in al-Andalus, philologians and poets decided to give new life to this language. Hebrew might have been a remnant of the past, but they tried to utilize it for cultural expression in re-examining the old biblical and rabbinic domains as well as in new cultural forms paralleling the impressive achievements of the majority language, Arabic. Under the pressure and challenge that Arabic presented, they were searching for ways to solve all the problems

* The preparation of this article has been possible thanks to a scholarship received from the Dirección General de Investigación Científica y Técnica of the Spanish Ministry of Education.

posed by this novel historical and cultural situation. In that sense the Bible served Jewish writers as a stylistic and linguistic model whose existence led to a certain confrontation with Arabic. This dispute was not free of national and religious pride and it dared Jewish writers to prove that Hebrew could also be a culturally significant language.

Philologians and poets were particularly affected by the problematic of the language. Jewish scholars educated both in Arabic and Hebrew cultures and interested in linguistics had no scientific philological tradition of their own. They could only admire the progress made in the systematic study of the language by Arab grammarians, who had been discussing such matters for many years. For Jews, even for socially integrated and arabized Jews, it was actually disturbing to concentrate their interest and research on the basic texts of a foreign religion. For writers willing to express themselves in a poetical way the tradition of the old Palestinian liturgical poetry in Hebrew was clearly poor in comparison to the rich production of a technically sophisticated Arabic poetry in the East and West. Just a few decided to write Arabic poetry in the language of the Qur'ān, a language which could only be acquired through extraordinary effort.

The new use of the Hebrew language was not promoted by an imposing Jewish personality nor did it follow a clear declaration of principles. Rather, it seems to have matured in the cultural atmosphere of the Caliphate of Cordoba. A few samples of short writings in Hebrew were known in the East in the fields of the Masoretic study of the Bible, grammar and poetry before the middle of the tenth century. But the full development of the renaissance of the Hebrew language took place in al-Andalus during the epoch of 'Abd al-Raḥmān III.

We do not know very much about the first stage of the renaissance of Hebrew. From Ezra Fleischer's studies we are aware that a whole group of Jewish poets writing in Hebrew was probably active in Cordoba before or at the same time that Ḥasdai ibn Shapruṭ's secretary Menaḥem ben Saruq started to write Hebrew poetry and prose.[1] His first activities at the

---

[1] See above all Ezra Fleischer, "*L^{e}-qadmoniot shirateinu bi-Sfarad – 'Iyyunim b^{e}-shirim*

service of Isaac ibn Shapruṭ were already in Hebrew, and the poems written for Ḥasdai (such as the introduction in verse to the letter sent to the King of the Khazars) were written in a language that is very different from Eastern liturgical poetry. But his decision to write *about* the "holy language" in the same "holy language" was still more important. Until that time Arabic had been the language used by Hebrew grammarians (except Aharon ben Asher). Menaḥem was thus the first medieval Jew to write an extensive philological work in Hebrew. It had to be a difficult decision for him for it entailed all kinds of problems. First he had to create a philological terminology in Hebrew. But he did not hesitate to do it. His rival Dunash ben Labraṭ was obliged to answer Menaḥem in Hebrew, and the other philological works written during the next decades by Jewish grammarians were also in Hebrew. The language was not pure Biblical Hebrew, but closer to it than to the language of the Midrash for instance. At the end of the tenth century and the beginning of the eleventh century Ḥayyūj and Ibn Janāḥ sought a more precise and technically exact expression and decided to write in Arabic. Abraham ibn 'Ezra' returned again to Hebrew in the twelfth century with the Jews of Italian or French communities in mind.

Great Jewish-Andalusian scholars of this epoch felt the necessity of employing their own national language in their literary activity. They could not continue to feel dependent on another people's culture since, as Menaḥem's disciples remembered, each nation has its own language and its own metrical system and the heritage of the Jewish people was not inferior to that of the most culturally sophisticated peoples.

From the middle of the tenth century every Jewish author first had to face the difficult choice of the language in which he wanted to write, that is "middle" Arabic or Hebrew. Was it possible to write poetry or prose in the language of the Bible, or, even more challenging, to deal with philological, philosophical or scientific questions in the language of David

w^{e}-piyyuṭim l^{e}-Rabbi Menaḥem ben Saruq," *'Asufot* 2 (1988): 227-69; "*L^{e}-toldot shirat ha-ḥol ha-'ivrit bi-Sfarad b^{e}-re'shitah,*" *Tarbut w^{e}-ḥevrah b^{e}-toldot Isra'el bi-yme ha-benayim, l^{e}-zekher Ḥ.H. Ben Saśon,* ed. R. Bonfil, etc. (Jerusalem: Merkaz Zalman Shazar, 1989), 197-225.

or Isaiah? Furthermore, to discuss linguistic problems of the biblical tongue parallel to the Arab grammarians' study of the language of the Qur'ān seemed to reduce Hebrew to the category of the other human languages. And was the "holy language" appropriate for writing poetry on secular themes? How could the poetical images and conventions of Arabic court poetry be expressed in that language or incorporated into the literary world of Biblical Hebrew? Or had Hebrew to be transformed in order to adapt itself to the new needs? Could they also employ the language of rabbinical writings or the peculiar language used by Palestinian Hebrew poets? The whole enterprise doubtless endangered the same holy language that it intended to renew. We do not know of much evidence of direct opposition to the use of the holy language in poetry; however, in view of the monumental change and the risks it represented it is easy to imagine that some extremely religious people and talmudic masters in al-Andalus reacted against such a usage of the "holy language."[2] In any case, Hebrew acquired a new literary vitality which also contributed to its usage in other areas of ordinary life.

I see three factors in the cultural and social climate of al-Andalus at this time which may have contributed to the renaissance of the Hebrew language: the sociological and intellectual climate created by the Caliph 'Abd al-Raḥmān III in Cordoba; the movement of the *shu'ūbiyyah*; and Karaism.

First of all, the Jewish community adapted itself to significant social change in the new atmosphere of Cordoba's court. The insistence of 'Abd al-Raḥmān III in creating an autonomous cultural life in al-Andalus

---

[2] Late evidence of that opposition: Abraham ben Nathan ha-Yarḥi, a halakhist of French origin who established himself in Toledo at the beginning of the thirteenth century, censures young authors who have written books on the love of women: "Their authors ought to suppress them...for they have appropriated biblical verses...and applied them to the shameful vices of women." *Perush Massekhet Kallah Rabbati*, ed. B. Toledano (Tiberias, 1906), 20, quoted by Bernard Septimus, *Hispano-Jewish Culture in Transition* (Cambridge, Mass.: Harvard University Press, 1982), 34.

was very important. He sought to strengthen the central power of the state by limiting the power of Arab aristocracy. He favored the middle classes and created a new nobility drawn from the various non-Arab peoples of his kingdom.[3] At the same time he fostered a new "national" culture independent of the traditional centers of the Muslim East. In his politics of tolerance and his various projects the Caliph found in the Jewish court-officer Ḥasdai ibn Shapruṭ an excellent collaborator. Ḥasdai enhanced the autonomy of Andalusian Jewish communities and loosened links with the East. Ḥasdai charged his secretary Menaḥem with the task of preparing a work on the Hebrew language, something that had been done already in Babylonia and North Africa but not in Muslim Spain. Menaḥem had previously served Ḥasdai's father as the family's secretary. What is new is that his function consisted in writing letters and poetry in Hebrew and not in Arabic: he is the first known Hebrew secretary in the Middle Ages. In probably another aspect of the same independent policy he appointed an eminent scholar, Moses ben Ḥanokh, as rabbi and dayyan of Cordoba's community. These were not isolated cases. A new class of Jewish courtiers was emerging in the city, courtiers faithful to their Jewish roots but ready to adopt the new way of life and its au currant cultural values. The members of this new social class felt the need to create a culture of their own and they adopted literary Hebrew as one of the signs of their identity.[4]

It has become common in this field of research to relate the process of the Hebrew renaissance to a broader cultural phenomenon: the reac-

---

[3] See James T. Monroe, *The Shu'ūbiyya in al-Andalus. The Risāla of Ibn García and Five Refutations* (Berkeley, etc.: University of California Press, 1970), 5f.

[4] See the presentation of this question in Ross Brann, *The Compunctious Poet: Cultural Ambiguity and Hebrew Poetry in Muslim Spain* (Baltimore and London: Johns Hopkins, 1991), 23ff. Concerning the language of the poetry, see Samuel M. Stern, "Arabic Poems by Spanish-Hebrew Poets," *Romanica et Occidentalia, études dédiés à la mémoire de Hiram Peri (Pflaum)*, ed. Moshe Lazar (Jerusalem: Magnes Press, 1963), 254: "...the chief motive in creating poetry in Hebrew was the love for the holy tongue and the desire to clothe the new most prominent expressions of the new ideals of Jewish society... in the forms of the national language..."

tion of the *shu'ūbiyyah* versus *'arabiyyah.* As is well-known, the prevailing opinion among some cultured Muslims was that the Arabs are the best of all nations, since the Arabian peninsula lies in the best possible clime, where God gave His messenger the revelation of the Qur'ān in the most select of languages, Arabic. Such a cultural ideology exalting the qualities of everything Arabic contributed to the internal unity of the empire. But peoples representing the multiplicity of cultures in the extensive Islamic domain reacted against that pan-Arabist tendency, stressing the value of their own national cultures (*shu'ūbiyyah*). As has been said, it was a struggle to determine the destiny of Islamic culture as a whole. In the East (already in the eighth or ninth century) the protected peoples proclaimed the superiority of non-Arab peoples vis-à-vis the Arabs. In the tenth century al-Andalus experienced a similar movement.[5] Among the defenders of nationalistic values were Jewish authors who, despite their admiration for Arabic culture, could match and oppose their historical Holy Land to Arabia, their Torah to the Qur'ān, and Hebrew to Arabic. Moses ibn 'Ezra', who highly esteemed Arabic literature, held up Hebrew poetry to the classical and renowned Arabic poetry.

> In each instance, I shall adduce one example from Arabic poetry and then compare it with a verse from the Holy Scriptures, so that people should not despise them and think that these figures are utterly unknown to us, and that the Arabic language is the only one that has piquant proverbs and wonderful expressions and that the Hebrew language is devoid of all these.[6]

---

[5] For the *shu'ūbiyyah* movement and its literary manifestation, above all in the East, cf. I. Goldziher, *Muhammedanischer Studien* (Halle, 1889), I:147ff.; *Muslim Studies,* transl. C. R. Barber and S. M. Stern (London: George Allen & Unwin, 1967–71), I:137ff.; for its social significance see H. A. R. Gibb, *Studies on the Civilization of Islam* (Boston: Beacon Press, 1962), 62ff.; for its echo in al-Andalus, cf. Monroe, *The Shu'ūbiyya,* 5ff.

[6] *Kitāb al-muḥāḍarah wal-mudhākarah* 116b [ed. Abraham S. Halkin, (Jerusalem: Mekize Nirdamim, 1975), 220-21; ed. Montserrat Abumalham, (Madrid 1985), I:239; II:249]. See Neḥemiah Allony, "*T^{e}guvat Rabbi Mosheh ibn 'Ezra' la-'arabiyyah' b^e-Sefer ha-diyyunim w^e-ha-siḥot (Shirat Isra'el)*," *Tarbiz* 42 (1973): 97-112; "The Reaction of Moses ibn Ezra to 'Arabiyya," *Bulletin of the Institute of Jewish Studies* 3 (1975): 19-

The reality of the Jewish reaction to *'arabiyyah* is clear enough, but for the period we are considering there is no conclusive evidence of *shu'ūbiyyah* in al-Andalus. Even if both movements went in similar directions I do not think that reaction to *'arabiyyah* is the only explanation for the interest shown by Jewish philologians and poets in the revitalization of the Hebrew language. It is just part of the picture, one of the relevant elements that contributed to the process.[7] For instance, the origins of Hebrew philology during the Middle Ages can be traced to the Karaite sect and its influence on all of Jewish culture. The first known philologian is one of the most distinguished representatives of the Rabbanite, anti-Karaite version of Judaism, Saadia Gaon. But he was probably not the first Jew interested in the grammatical study of Hebrew. A Karaite list of philological terms prepared in the eighth century (published by Neḥemiah Allony) confirms the central role played by the sectarians in establishing the new science of the language. Karaites concentrated their concerns on the written Torah. This focus created the need for investigating the most intricate details about the "Holy Language," in

40. See also Norman Roth, "Jewish Reactions to the *'Arabiyya* and the Renaissance of Hebrew in Spain," *Journal of Semitic Studies* 28 (1983): 63-84, with extensive bibliography in both articles. Neḥemiah Allony cites some interesting texts written by Jacob ben Eleazar of Toledo (c. 1170–1230) in reaction to *'arabiyyah.* See Allony, "The Reaction," 37f., and also his edition of *Ya'aqov ben El'azar, Kitāb al-Kāmil* (Heb.) (Jerusalem: American Academy of Jewish Studies, 1977), 6ff.

[7] Joshua Blau, *The Emergence and Linguistic Background of Judaeo-Arabic. A Study of the Origins of Middle Arabic* (Jerusalem: Ben-Zvi Institute, 1981), explains the process of adoption of Judaeo-Arabic by the Jews of the Islamic world. He presents the main reasons why they nevertheless wrote poetry in Hebrew, insisting on the "basic dichotomy between the analytical Middle Arabic dialects as against synthetic Classical Arabic... The Jews spoke Middle Arabic. Being much less attracted by the ideal of *'arabiyya,* the veritable Arabic language, than their Muslim fellow citizens, they generally attained only a limited mastery of Classical Arabic... their superficial knowledge did not suffice for writing poetry" (22f.). And Blau completes the picture by offering several more reasons, underlining the difficulties that the Jews found in the use of Classical Arabic and the psychological barrier to adopting foreign ideas. However, he does not explain the simultaneous use of Hebrew in al-Andalus for poetry and philology.

the same way as their Muslim counterparts used to study the language of the Qur'ān. But we do not know any Karaite author who wrote extensively about linguistics before Saadia's work. In any case, the contributions to the knowledge of the Hebrew language made by Karaite scholars during the tenth century are very significant. The presence of a considerable number of members of this sect in the Iberian peninsula from the tenth to the thirteenth century is well documented.[8] By the way, the attribution of some philo-Karaite tendencies to Menaḥem ben Saruq is not new, and I consider it well-founded, as I have tried to explain elsewhere.[9]

Medieval Ideas about the Origin of Language

One of the first questions that a medieval linguist asks himself concerns the origin of language. Is language a consequence of human nature, something taught by God to the first man or to the Prophet(s), or is it the result of human convention? All those basic views, already formulated in late antiquity, were known among Arabs and Jews in the Middle Ages.

For Greek philosophers alternative opinions about the origin of language are defined by the terms *physei* ("by nature") / *thesei* ("by convention"), to which the old theory of language as a divine gift was frequently added.[10] Muslim thinkers discussed this question at length. In principle, the words of the Qur'ān (II, 31) complementing a verse in Genesis (2:19), "He taught to Adam all the names," caused many religious thinkers to

---

8 Cf. I. Loeb, "Les Caraïtes en Espagne," *Revue des Études Juifs* 19 (1889): 206-9. Gershom D. Cohen, ed. *A Critical Edition with a Translation and Notes of The Book of Tradition (Sefer ha-qabbalah) by Abraham ibn Daud* (Philadelphia-London: Jewish Publication Society of America, 1967), XLVIff.; D. J. Lasker, "Karaism in Twelfth-Century Spain," *Journal of Jewish Thought & Philosophy* 1,2 (1992): 179-95.

9 See the Introduction to my edition of Menaḥem's *Maḥberet* (Granada: Universidad de Granada, 1986).

10 So in Plato's *Cratylon*; cf. J. C. Rijlaarsdam, *Plato über die Sprache. Ein Kommentar zum Kratylus* (Utrecht: Bohn, Scheltema and Holkema, 1978). About the problem among the Greeks, cf. W. S. Allen, "Ancient Ideas on the Origin and Development of Language," *Transactions of the Philological Society of London* (London: Blackwell, 1948), 35-60.

adopt the idea that language was revealed. But, of course, this was not a unanimous opinion.[11] The different positions maintained by Muslim thinkers have been presented in a very systematic and precise way by B. G. Weiss,[12] who distinguishes six main theories about the origin of language, i. e., the three known fundamental conceptions (the "naturalist" theory; the "conventionalist" theory; and the "revelationist theory") and combinations of them. ʿAbbād ibn Sulaymān (d. 864), for instance, maintained the first position, according to which language has its origin in a natural affinity between expressions and the things they signify. Abū Hāshim (d. 933) defended the conventionalist theory, maintaining that language is a social convention, the result of an arbitrary choice of names made by men. Abū al-Ḥasan al-Ashʿarī (d. 935/36) represented the revelationist theory, arguing that language was originally revealed by God, who gave names to everything. Other Muslim thinkers sought compromises, merging these theories.[13]

At the beginning of the eleventh century in al-Andalus Ibn Ḥazm represents a rather traditionalist position, although open to compromise: language is the result of divine inspiration, but human convention plays a role in the origin of the multiplicity of languages:

> It is therefore demonstrated that language owes its origin to divine teaching and instruction. But at the same time we do not deny that common agreement of men has originated the innovation of many languages, after having had only one, thanks to which they knew the essences of things, their modalities and definitions.[14]

---

[11] On the question of the origin of language according to Arab writers, cf. Miguel Asín Palacios, "El origen del lenguaje y problemas conexos, en Algazel, Ibn Sina e Ibn Ḥazm," *Al-Andalus* 4 (1936–39): 253-81; R. Arnaldez, *Grammaire et théologie chez Ibn Ḥazm de Cordoue* (Paris: J. Vrin, 1956), 37ff.; H. Loucel, "L'origine du langage d'après les grammairiens arabes," *Arabica* 10 (1963): 188-208, 253-81; 11 (1964): 57-72, 157-87.

[12] "Medieval Muslim Discussions of the Origin of Language," *Zeitschrift der Deutschen Morgenländischen Gesselschaft* 124 (1974): 33-41.

[13] Weiss, "Medieval Muslim Discussions," 34f.

[14] *Kitāb al-iḥkām fī uṣūl al-aḥkām* (Cairo, 1952–55), I:29 ss., quoted by Asín Palacios, "El origen," 276.

In general terms most Mu'tazilites were distinctly conventionalist, while the traditionalist defenders of the "uncreated Qur'ān" maintained the revelationist position. Ash'arites interpreted Divine Speech as an abstract quality and declared (end of the eleventh century) that both positions were plausible and that there was no conclusive solution to the problem.

What was the opinion of Jewish philologians and poets? The question did not seem to be as important for Hebrew philologians as for their Muslim colleagues, but sometimes we find in medieval authors traces of a certain interest in defining their positions in favor of the conventionalist or the revelationist theories. In the first generations of Hebrew linguists the question was usually not discussed, but the general consensus saw language as a gift of God to man. Among Muslim thinkers the most traditionalist and religious people adopted the revelationist position while the more liberal ones were conventionalist. The naturalist view of language, which was well represented among early Arabic philologians, was not very common among Jewish writers, at least in its purest form. Only Abraham Abulafia combined this theory with a more general conventionalism.

The fact that during the tenth and eleventh centuries most Hebrew philologians perceived language to be a divine gift did not mean that they adopted the revelationist position, since it was not specified if the gift consisted in the faculty of speech or in the language itself. The former was probably true in most cases. According to Menaḥem, God is the "Creator of language,"[15] by which he very likely means the faculty of language.[16] Similarly Jonah ibn Janāḥ states: "Praise to the eternal God who created man and taught him logic and speech and instructed him how to exalt His divinity and proclaim His unity with them."[17] And Abra-

[15] *Maḥberet*, 1*.

[16] The conviction that Hebrew is a holy language inspired by God could be the basis of his opposition and that of his disciples to comparative linguistics, as practiced in Rabbanite and Karaite circles.

[17] *Sefer ha-riqmah*, Introd. Ed. Wilensky-Téné. (Jerusalem: Academy of the Hebrew

ham ibn 'Ezra' declares in the introductory poem of his *Sefer ṣaḥot*: "He puts language in the mouth and science in the heart..."[18]

By contrast, Judah ha-Levi's *Kuzari* upholds the typical revelationist attitude in medieval Judaism:

> The language created by God, which He taught Adam and placed on his tongue and in his heart, is without any doubt the most perfect and most fitted to express the things specified, as it is written: "And whatsoever Adam called every living creature, that was the name thereof" (Gen. 2,19). This means that it deserved such name which fitted and characterized it. This show the excellence of the 'holy tongue' as well as the reason why the angels employed it in preference to any other.[19]

Different still is the position of Maimonides and some of his disciples. Their views represent the clearest defense of the conventional character of the Hebrew language. According to Maimonides, primeval humanity lived in one place and spoke a single language.[20] Commenting on Genesis 2:20 he adds:

> Among the things you ought to know and have your attention aroused to is the dictum: "And the man gave names, and so on" (Gen 2,20). It informs us that languages are conventional and not natural, as has sometimes been thought.[21]

Language, 1964), 8. Joseph Qimḥi expresses the same view in the Introduction to his *Sefer ha-galuy*. See *Sepher ha-galuj von R. Joseph Kimchi*, ed. H. J. Mathews (Berlin, 1887), 1ff.

[18] See *Sefer Ṣaḥot de Abraham ibn 'Ezra*, edición crítica y versión castellana C. del Valle (Salamanca: Universidad Pontificia, 1977), 1 (99). Nevertheless, in the same book he goes on to establish a parallel between the basic movements of the world and the Hebrew vowels, or between the planets and the vowels, a view that seems close to a "naturalistic conception" of language.

[19] *Kuzari*, transl. Hartwig Hirschfeld, (Brooklyn, N.Y.: P. Shalom Pub., 1969), 229 [IV, 25].

[20] *The Guide of the Perplexed*, transl. Shlomo Pines (Chicago and London: The University of Chicago Press, sec. impr. 1969), 613f. [III, 50].

[21] *The Guide of the Perplexed*, II, 30, pp. 357f. He maintains similar conventionalist theories in several passages of his works, see Isadore Twersky, *Introduction to the Code of Maimonides* (New Haven-London: Yale University Press, 1980), 324ff.

Naḥmanides, the great spiritual leader of the Catalonian communities in the middle of the thirteenth century and a well-known kabbalist, opposed the Maimonidean view. He thought that to consider Hebrew language a convention (like all other languages) was tantamount to denying the divine character of the Torah. In his *Essay on the Internal Character of the Torah* Naḥmanides objects to those who consider the holy language a matter of human agreement:

> The reason there can be nothing conventional about its language, as some of the leaders of the preceding generations said, is that if we were to say that the language of the Torah is conventional like all the rest of the languages, we would be denying the gift of the Torah, which was given to us totally by the hand of the Almighty.[22]

But even among kabbalists different opinions are possible: for most of them the Hebrew language is a divine gift. Others, as in the case of Abraham Abulafia, maintain that it is a natural language—*the* natural language, which was chosen by God due to its special qualities and chosen by the Prophets for communicating the divine message:

> Know that for any conventional language to have arisen there had to have been an earlier language in existence. For if such a language did not precede it there couldn't have been mutual agreement to call a given object by a different name from what it was previously called, for how would the second person understand the second name if he doesn't know the original name, in order to be able to agree to the changes?[23]

Hebrew is the "mother of all languages," from which all the other languages derive:

> Know that the mother of all conventional languages is the natural Hebrew language. For it is only by means of a natural language that all the conventional languages arose. And this served as the elementary matter for all of them. Such is also the case regarding natural writing

[22] *Kitvei R. Mosheh ben Naḥman*, ed. C. B. Chavel (Jerusalem: Mosad Ha-Rav Kook, 1964), II:467.

[23] *Sefer 'or ha-sheqel*, according to Moshe Idel, *Language, Torah, and Hermeneutics in Abraham Abulafia* (Albany: State University of New York Press, 1989), 14.

> out of which all other written language arose. This is likened to the first created human form, from whom all other human beings were created...[24]

Commenting on the words of the Book of Genesis Abulafia writes:

> "And the entire land was of one language and one speech": this verse instructs us as to the nature of language, each of which, according to our tradition, has its origin in the sacred language, which is the Mother of all Languages.[25]

Regarding the other languages Abulafia agrees with Maimonides and maintains that they were created by human convention. Those languages imitate Hebrew:

> The other languages are likened to Hebrew as an ape, who upon observing the actions of a human being wants to do likewise, and like a person who visually appears to another, through a mirror, and he mimics his actions and does not attempt to add or diminish from them—but [still] they are not human.[26]

Joseph ibn Gikatilla, Abulafia's disciple, has a different, more traditional position with respect to the first language:

> And it is necessary for us to believe that the language of the Torah is not a result of convention as some illustrious rabbis of previous generations had thought. For if one were to say that the language that the Torah employs is a result of convention, as is the case with the other languages, we would end up denying the [Divine Revelation] of the Torah, which was in its entirety imparted to us from God... And if the language of the Torah is, originally, conventional like all other languages... it [Hebrew] would be like all other languages.[27]

As Moshe Idel observes, the difference between Abulafia and Ibn Gikatilla is that for Abulafia the Hebrew language (in contrast to all other languages) is the natural language chosen by God, and not a gift of God. Only the form of the letters comes directly from the Creator:

---

[24] *Liqquṭei ḥamiṣ*, ms. Oxford 2239, 125b. According to Idel, *Language*, 14.

[25] *Sefer mafteaḥ ha-ḥokhmot*. Ms. Moscú 133, 16b. See Idel, *Language*, 14.

[26] *Sefer 'Imrei Shefer*, quoted by Idel, *Language*, 21.

[27] *Ma'amar 'al p^enimiyut ha-Torah*, publ. by Gershom Scholem, *Kiryat Sefer* 6 (1930): 111f., quoted by Idel, *Language*, 11f.

> For whereas all languages exist by convention, the forms of the letters of the Hebrew language are Divine.[28]

The Excellence and Temporal Weakness of Hebrew Language

The question of the origin of language is closely connected to the identity of the primeval language and the derivation of the plurality of languages from the first one. Most Muslim writers did not pretend that the primeval language was Arabic: many thought it was Syriac. They probably followed various Near Eastern traditions on this point; some Christian authors thought that Aramaic (specifically the Syriac dialect) was the language of Creation. The same view is recorded in the *Talmud Bavli* (*Sanhedrin* 38b). But in al-Andalus most Jewish philologians maintained that Hebrew was the first language of humankind, as it was the language of the Torah that was formulated before the creation of the world. Of course, this is a Jewish answer to identical statements made by Muslim thinkers about Arabic as the language of the Qur'ān.

Some Arab authors, such as Ibn Ḥazm, defended the fundamental unity of Syriac, Hebrew, and Arabic, but maintained that the distinctions among the three "dialects" was due to phonetic alterations in the language as spoken by members of different social groups in diverse countries.[29] For Jews, this question was directly related to the idea of the primeval language and the particular excellence of Hebrew.

For medieval Jewish philologians and poets it was beyond dispute that Hebrew was the continuation of that first language of humankind. Solomon ibn Gabirol (middle of the eleventh century) gave expression to the idea of the excellence of the Hebrew language in a didactic poem. He presented Hebrew as the first and most select of tongues:

> Know therefore the superiority of the Hebrew language, that surpasses
> the language of all peoples.

---

[28] *Sefer Gan Na'ul*, ms. Munich 58, fol. 333a. As Moshe Idel points out: "Abulafia, like Maimonides, uses the terms *Divine* and *natural* interchangeably," *Language*, 16.

[29] Cf. Asín Palacios, "El origen," 262f.

> Heavenly inhabitants give praises in it day after day to The One who covers Himself with light as a robe.
> It was from ancient times the language of all living beings...
> In it was given the fire of the Torah...[30]

A century before Ibn Gabirol, Menaḥem ben Saruq opened his biblical dictionary with the following words:

> With the help of the Creator of the language I shall begin to follow the steps of the most cultivated language, and to explain the most excellent of the tongues and the summit of all beautiful expressions, a language refined in the crucible, more elated than any other of the tongues of the other peoples upon Earth from the time that the nations separated from one another, each one with its own language.[31]

Jonah ibn Janāḥ says: "... [God] made the language of the Hebrew people unique with every kind of excellence among all the languages, and he gave in it His holy Torah and He explained in it His sacred commandments"[32] He maintains—and after him other Hebrew writers from al-Andalus—that, according to the *Talmud Bavli* (*'Eruvin* 53a), the inhabitants of Judea were superior to other Jews because of their language. Since the Jews of al-Andalus are their descendants, they too have excelled as guardians of the Hebrew language. However, Ibn Janāḥ also finds the same community guilty of neglecting the study of Hebrew.[33]

In his well-known apologetic work the *Kuzari* (beginning of the twelfth century) Judah ha-Levi presented an elaborate justification of the superiority of Hebrew, despite its present situation of apparent inferiority. The Khazar king asks:

---

[30] *'Anaq*, verses 38-40 and 44. See *Solomon Ibn Gabirol. Secular Poems* (Hebr.), ed. Ḥ. Brody and J. Schirmann, (Jerusalem: The Schocken Institute, 1974), 170. See my article "El 'Anaq, poema lingüístico de Šĕlomoh ibn Gabirol," *Miscelánea de Estudios Arabes y Hebraicos* 29. 2 (1980): 17f. Similar ideas were maintained by Arabic scholars about Arabic. Saadia mentioned most of them in his Hebrew introduction to the *'Egron*.

[31] *Maḥberet*, 1*.

[32] *Sefer ha-riqmah*, 8.

[33] *Sefer ha-riqmah*, 10f.

> Is Hebrew superior to other languages? Do we not see distinctly that the latter are more finished and comprehensive?

To which the Jewish rabbi replies:

> It shared the fate of its bearers, degenerating and dwindling with them. Considered historically and logically, its original form is the noblest. According to tradition it is the language in which God spoke to Adam and Eve, and in which the latter conversed. It is proved by the derivation of Adam from *adamah, ishshah* from *ish*... This is supported by the evidence of the Torah. The whole is traced back to Eber, Noaḥ and Adam. It is the language of Eber after whom it was called *Hebrew,* because after the confusion of tongues it was he who retained it. Abraham... employed Hebrew as a specially holy language and Aramaic for everyday use. For this reason Ishmael brought it to the Arabic speaking nations, and the consequence was that Aramaic, Arabic and Hebrew are similar to each other in their vocabulary, grammatical rules, and formations. The superiority of Hebrew is manifest from the logical point of view if we consider the people who employed it for discourses, particularly at the time when prophecy was rife among them, also for preaching, songs and psalmody. It is conceivable that their rulers such as for instance, Moses, Joshua, David, and Solomon lacked the words to express what they wished, as it is the case with us today, because it is lost to us?...[34]

The Khazar king is not ready to accept the superiority of Hebrew. He maintains that other languages surpass Hebrew in metrically constructed songs arranged for tunes but the rabbi finds an answer for this assertion too.

For a poet and grammarian such as Abraham ibn 'Ezra' Hebrew was greater than all the languages of the other nations, since it was the first.[35] Other Jewish authors, such as al-Ḥarizi, emphasized the high distinction of the language which is due not only to the fact that God spoke in it to

[34] *Kuzari* II, 67f., pp. 124ff. For an interpretation of this passage, see Brann, *The Compunctious Poet,* 109ff.

[35] Cited by Ezra Fleischer from the introduction to *K^eli n^eḥoshet,* "*L^e-'inyan shir ha-p^etiḥah shel R. Abraham ibn 'Ezra' l^e-ferusho l^e-sefer 'Iyyov,*" *Lĕshonenu* 36 (1972): 315.

His prophets (and He could not chose for Himself a deficient language),[36] but also to its intrinsic qualities:

> The holy language cannot be compared with any other because of the purity of its words and beauty of its metaphors.[37]

Why is Hebrew called "the holy language"? The question is not posed during the first centuries in al-Andalus, when its old rabbinic designation was simply accepted. But in the twelfth and thirteenth centuries some of the leading figures of Judaism felt the need for an explanation. The approaches are diverse according to the psychological and religious attitudes of the writers. Maimonides maintains that language is one of the faculties that have been given to human beings and that distinguishes them from animals. For that reason, he continues, it should not be employed in an inappropriate way, as, for instance, in obscene expressions. According to him, Hebrew is called the holy tongue "for in this holy language no word at all has been laid down in order to designate either the male or the female organ of copulation, nor are there words designating the act itself that brings about generation, the sperm, the urine, or the excrements."[38] Joseph ibn Kaspi, a follower of Maimonides, states that Hebrew is the holy language because it is in general terms a correct language.[39] Naḥmanides does not accept Maimonides' opinion but gives his own explanation: Hebrew is the holy language because the words of the Torah and the Prophets were pronounced in Hebrew, which is the language of creation and in which God speaks to his prophets and to his community.[40]

---

[36] *Taḥkᵉmoni.* Ed. Kaminka (Warsaw, 1899), 18.

[37] Al-Ḥarizi, *Taḥkᵉmoni,* 18.

[38] *Guide of the Perplexed,* III, 8, p. 435.

[39] *'Asarah kᵉlei kesef,* ed. I. Last, (Pressburg, 1903), II, 17.

[40] "I hold that this is the same reason why our Rabbis call the language of the Torah 'the sacred Language', because the words of the Torah, and the prophecies, and all words of holiness were all expressed in that language. It is thus the language in which the Holy One, blessed be He, spoke with His prophets and with His congregation... In that tongue He created His world...," *Comment. to Exod.* 30,13, transl. Ch. Chavel (New York: Shilo Publishing House, 1973), 518f.

Despite the excellence of Hebrew, most philologians and poets allege that the Jewish people has forgotten its language. Solomon ibn Gabirol claims:

> Their tongue is alien to Hebrew and is not acquainted with Jewish speech.
> A part of them speak Edomite and a part the language of Qedar, which is obscure.[41]

Moses ibn 'Ezra' writes:

> Due to the length of the exile and the long time we were in it the Hebrew language was lost... Only a remnant of 24 books has survived from the Hebrew language, which include exclusively the most indispensable parts of the language...[42]

We can find two different positions regarding the decline of Hebrew: for most of the writers the Jewish people is held responsible for having forgotten an important part of their covenant with God; and the exile is a divine punishment. However some Jewish scholars, among them Abraham ibn 'Ezra', consider it something unavoidable, a historical fact without particular Jewish responsibility.[43] The result is the same: the most perfect of languages, once an elegant and fully expressive medium, has been forgotten and is now lacking, poor and restricted. According to Menaḥem's disciples the limitation of the Hebrew language is due to the exile and only on account of divine mercy has a remnant of the language not been lost. Those holding this view believe that if the Jews were in their original country they would control all the minutiae of their tongue.[44] Moses ibn 'Ezra' alludes to the culpability of the forefathers:

---

[41] *'Anaq*. See my article, "El 'Anaq," 15f. Regarding Saadia's opinion, see A. S. Halkin, "The Medieval Jewish Attitude toward Hebrew," *Biblical and Other Studies*, ed. A. Altmann (Cambridge, Mass.: Harvard University Press, 1963), 233-48, and in particular 235f.

[42] *Kitāb al-muḥāḍarah wal-mudhākarah*, 28a [ed. Halkin, 52-3; ed. Abumalham, I:57; II:57].

[43] As observed by Twersky, *Introduction*, 326f.

[44] *Teshuvot Talmidei Menaḥem*, ed. S. Benavente (Granada: Universidad de Granada, 1986), 20.

> Our ancestors and forefathers were censured on behalf of their negligence, or better, their guilt, because they did nothing to assure their language nor to care about their Hebrew, and they were not able to polish their language nor to record in it their facts nor to remember in it their history or traditions.[45]

In the thirteenth century the kabbalist Abraham Abulafia states:

> Due to our dispersion among many nations, with varied languages, we have forgotten our own language, its clarity and precision, which is nearly lost among the majority of our population. And if not for the continued writing of books, it would have been completely lost... Had we preserved the Holy Tongue we would have been more worthy, and the majority of our nation would have been wise and understanding and knowledgeable in our language.[46]

Some Jews were in principle opposed to using Hebrew in particular fields of discourse. They thought that to do so represented an ultra-nationalistic position, and that from the point of view of praxis Arabic was much richer in possibilities than Hebrew.[47]

Most of those involved in translating Arabic texts into Hebrew starting with Moses ibn Gikatilla, and above all the Ibn Tibbon family, tried to be realistic: it does not help to cry and lament for the actual state of the language. According to Ibn Gikatilla the fact is that even the grammarians had to employ Arabic for describing the Hebrew language, because Arabic is much clearer and everyone can understand it.[48] Judah ibn Tibbon recalls that most of the Babylonian Geonim wrote in Arabic and he adds:

> They did it because it is the language people understood, and also because it is an adequate and rich language for every subject and for every need, for every speaker and every author; its expression is direct,

---

[45] *Kitāb al-muḥāḍarah wal-mudhākarah,* 27a [ed. Halkin, 50-1; ed. Abumalham, I:55; II:55].

[46] *Sefer 'oṣar 'Eden ganuz,* quoted by Idel, *Language,* 25.

[47] See Halkin, "The Medieval Jewish Attitude," 235f.

[48] *Sh^eloshah Sifrei diqduq,* ed. J. W. Nutt (London and Berlin: Asher and Co. 1870. Repr. Jerusalem, 1968), 1.

> lucid, and capable of saying just what is wanted much better that can be done in Hebrew, of which we possess only what has been preserved in Scripture and is insufficient for the needs of a speaker. It is simply impossible to express the thoughts of our hearts succinctly and eloquently in Hebrew as we can in Arabic, which is adequate, elegant and available to those who know it.[49]

Justifying those Jewish writers who chose Arabic, these translators were at the same time justifying their own work and their practice of creating new Hebrew words from the Arabic works they were translating. Such efforts provoked a reaction from other Jewish scholars. For al-Ḥarizi, the language that was "the true lady" has become a "servant." The Jews prefer Arabic and do not consider valuable their own language:

> From ancient times pious men all over the world were rejoicing with the holy language. Today, violent, wicked men of our own people are piercing it with the point of their tongue .... She claims: "your sons have despised me and have embraced the language of foreign peoples .... Their heart was seduced seeing the precious poetry born from Hagar the Egyptian, Sarah's slave, while Sarah had no children.[50]

According to al-Ḥarizi the Jews are not well versed in their language and think it is insufficient for their needs:

> Every nation is concerned about its speech and avoids sinning against its tongue, whereas our tongue which was a delight to every eye is considered a brother of Cain...[51]

Even as late as the fifteenth century Profiat Duran attributed deficiencies in the interpretation of the Bible to Israel's neglect of Hebrew, with pernicious consequences in his time.[52]

---

[49] Introduction to his translation of Baḥya ibn Pakudah's *Duties of the Heart: Sefer Torat ḥovot ha-l^{e}vavot.* Targum ḥadash, Sh. Yerushalmi (Jerusalem: M^{e}orei Israel, 1972), 8; similar words in his translation of Ibn Janāḥ's *Sefer ha-riqmah*, 4-6. See Halkin, "The Medieval Jewish Attitude," 239.

[50] Al-Ḥarizi, *Taḥk^{e}moni*, Introduction.

[51] That is, *Hevel*, "nothing." Al-Ḥarizi, *Taḥk^{e}moni*, Introduction.

[52] *Ma'aseh 'Efod*, 7.

The Search of the Philologians

Philologians and poets were equally interested in the renaissance of the Hebrew language, but, of course, they had their own concerns and methods for contributing to its rebirth. The philologians were concerned first and foremost with describing the linguistic characteristics and lexicon of Biblical Hebrew. Why did Jewish linguists suddenly turn their attention to the Hebrew language? They could not ignore the influence of Arabic grammar and lexicography long since established in the eighth and ninth centuries. With such models in mind, the Jews of the tenth century started caring about their own language. It is worth recalling that the well-known academies of Kufa and Basra were founded by passionate defenders of Arabic cultural values, and that for them the study of the Arabic language represented the best means of diffusing the main ideas of *'arabiyyah*.[53] Jewish grammarians could not be bound by such objectives, but felt stimulated to learn the methods of the Arabic grammarians and to apply them to the language of the Torah, the most precious treasure of Judaism.

What was their "corpus" of information? The traditional basis for the study of the Arabic language was the Qur'ān, the *ḥadīth* or the Prophet's oral tradition, and the so-called pre-Islamic poetry.[54] By comparison the Jews had the biblical text which was presented by some linguists, such as Ḥayyūj, as evidence of ancient Israelite speech rather than as a revealed text, that is, a text uttered by God. The oral tradition of the Jews, corresponding to the traditions of the Prophet, was preserved in a different language according to the rabbis themselves. What we call today Rabbinic Hebrew was recognized in the Talmud as a separate linguistic entity distinct from the language of the Torah.[55] The language of traditional Hebrew liturgical poetry, the Oriental *piyyuṭ*, was not a linguistic

---

[53] See Gibb, *Studies*, 62.

[54] Cf. al-Suyuṭī, *Al-'Iqtirāh*, 14.

[55] The attitude of medieval writers towards Rabbinic Hebrew deserves a study of its own.

model comparable to that of early Arabic poetry. I would even say that the criticism of medieval philologians such as Abraham ibn 'Ezra' is evidence of the embarrassment felt by those linguists when comparing their own poetic tradition to that of the Arabs. Other extra-biblical texts were not known at that time so that the biblical text was the only basis for Hebrew philology.

What was the first goal that Jewish grammarians had in mind, to understand and explain the Bible or to convert Hebrew into a living language? Ḥayyūj began his grammatical writings by underlining the danger posed to the Hebrew language by those who did not know its secrets. He stated that he was searching "to learn from the words of the first Hebrew people who were born in that language and grew up in its ways and fixed its limits."[56] These ancient Hebrew speakers, *ha-'ivrim ha-qadmonim*, knew the mysteries of the language: "...to all those to whom God gave science in their hearts and enlightened their minds for learning the language of the first Hebrew speakers, since we do not know their secret."[57] These are probably the same secrets that Moses ibn 'Ezra' considers revealed by God to the Andalusian Jewish community, heir of the Jerusalem community.[58] But Ḥayyūj's attitude is not the most common one among Hebrew philologians. Ḥayyūj is probably the only true linguist among Jewish grammarians of the classical period. For the rest of them, understanding the Bible is the primary goal of their philological work. That linguistics served as the basis for exegesis explains many of the fierce debates of the period.

For Arabic grammarians mainly interested in the interpretation of the Qur'ān the unusual forms and apparent irregularities of the language constituted a very complicated question. How did Hebrew linguists react to the same problem found in the Bible? The efforts of Saadia and other grammarians to find the meaning of the *hapax-legomena*

---

[56] *Sheloshah Sifrei diqduq*, 3-4.

[57] *Sheloshah Sifrei diqduq*, 99.

[58] *Kitāb al-muḥāḍarah wal-mudhākarah*, 29a-b [ed. Halkin, 54-55; ed. Abumalham, I:60-61; II:60-61].

could show the degree to which they were occupied with the same problems as their Arabic contemporaries. Most Hebrew grammarians (except for the school of Menaḥem) employ comparative methods for dealing with these difficult words. Of course, that brings us to a more general question of the philologians: can and should Hebrew, the holy language, be compared to cognate languages? Saadia established the grounds for comparative study of the Hebrew language. His positive attitude was followed by most Hebrew philologians in the Arabic-speaking world, even by Karaite authors such as David ben Abraham al-Fāsī. The same is true in al-Andalus, where only Menaḥem and his disciples were opposed to comparative grammar, probably based on ideological, that is, religious reasons: to compare could mean to reduce the category of the "holy language" to that of the rest of the conventional languages.[59]

Many of the first philologians did not have any problem writing in Arabic about the Hebrew language. For them Arabic was the most suitable language for dealing with Hebrew linguistics. The technical terminology already existed and it was easier to apply to Hebrew the schemes employed by Arabic grammarians. Hebrew, by contrast, was not equipped to handle those detailed matters. Aharon ben Asher employed Hebrew in his work. Saadia tried to use Hebrew too in the first, more simple edition of the *'Egron*, but in the second edition he wrote in Arabic. Arabic was thus the accepted language among Jewish grammarians until Menaḥem decided to write in Hebrew, creating a new and original terminology for this purpose.[60] At the end of the tenth century, Ḥayyūj reverted again to Arabic in his definitive works on Hebrew verbs.

If the Qur'ān was the archetype of *al-faṣāḥah* (the purity and eloquence of the language) for Arab grammarians, Hebrew philologians sought in the Bible the model of *ṣaḥot ha-lashon*. This term, usually translated by scholars of Biblical Hebrew as "correction" of the language, was

[59] See, for instance, *T^eshuvot Talmidei Menaḥem*, 54*f., 88.

[60] See my article "En torno al Mahberet de Menahem ben Saruq," *Miscelánea de Estudios Arabes y Hebraicos* 25.2 (1976): 11-50, and the Introduction to my edition of the *Maḥberet.*

understood by medieval grammarians as a reference to an expression's biblical purity parallel to the Arabic concept.[61]

In al-Andalus the first grammarians and poets employed a language very close to the biblical model, but they sometimes introduced words taken from Mishnaic Hebrew, arabisms, or neologisms as necessary. The so-called "biblical purism" appears only in the eleventh century and finds its most representative expression in *Kitāb al-muḥāḍarah wal-mudhākarah* of Moses ibn 'Ezra'. For him, Hebrew writers were not authorized to freely expand the attested forms of the language even if the remnants of Biblical Hebrew were scarce. For instance, Ibn 'Ezra' discouraged using the principle of *qiyās* or "analogy" developed in the Arab school of Basra in order to complete the forms of verbs or nouns that could not be found in the Bible:

> Everything you find in it [the text of the Bible], use, and when you cannot find something, do not apply analogy. Go where the language goes and stop where it stops, as an imitator, not a creator, a follower, not an inventor.[62]

With respect to Rabbinic Hebrew, Andalusian grammarians did not always agree about its nature and proper usage. Menaḥem and his disciples essentially avoided the use of Mishnaic Hebrew for illuminating difficult forms of Biblical Hebrew. But the rest of the philologians followed Saadia's practice and referred to Mishnaic Hebrew without any problem. Menaḥem himself rejected the forms innovated by the rabbis that do not observe the rules of correct grammar.[63] But Ibn Janāḥ, not being such a "purist," considered it permissible to employ such forms in Hebrew. When Maimonides decided to write his *Mishneh Torah* in Rabbinic Hebrew, he wrote: "I deemed it advisable not to compose this book in

---

[61] See Shelomo Morag, "*Re'shit ha-millona'ut ha-'ivrit we-ha-'aravit,*" *Molad* 3 (26) (1970–71): 575-82; Ilan Eldar, "*'Askolat ha-diqduq ha-'andalusit: tequfat ha-re'shit,*" *Pe'amim* 38 (1989): 24, with bibliography about the question.

[62] *Kitāb al-muḥāḍarah wal-mudhākarah,* 107b-108a [ed. Halkin, 202-3; ed. Abumalham, I:220-21; II:225-26]. As a poet Ibn 'Ezra' occasionally violated his own prescription and utilized some Mishnaic forms and words.

[63] Such as *taramti* (from the root *rwm*), see *Maḥberet,* 20*.

the language of the Prophetic Books, since that sacred language is too limited for us today."[64] Instead, he chose the language of the Mishnah, since he considered that in this way he could be understood by more people. He probably had in mind Talmudic scholars.[65]

Until Abraham ibn 'Ezra' wrote his well-known criticism against Kallir, the most relevant representative of Palestinian *payyeṭanim*, philologians paid little attention to the language of *piyyuṭ*. According to Ibn 'Ezra', Kallir and the other liturgical poets of that school did not always follow the rules of grammar and introduced many grammatical mistakes in their compositions.[66]

The Poets' Search

The poets' interest in the Hebrew language coincided with the grammarians' in some respects, but they had their own motivations, problems, and perspectives. Andalusian poetry was one of the most important signs of the revival of Hebrew. It is noteworthy that Andalusian Hebrew philology and poetry began at the same time, and in many cases philologians were poets while poets were usually well-versed in the intricacies of Hebrew. The ability to write poetry was not at all incompatible with concern about language. We can probably add that the new type of poetry that begun in al-Andalus could only originate on the basis of the excellent knowledge of Biblical Hebrew attained by the poets of the school.

As is well-known the Andalusian Jewish poets search for a pure biblical language is one of the main characteristics of their literary tradition. That search was only possible thanks to the new grammatical knowledge of the Bible. The sociological change among a class of Andalusian Jews and their quest for a new way of expressing their own culture could help explain this phenomenon, as we have said. In any case, here was one of the most important differences between the new Hebrew poetry and the

[64] *Sefer ha-miṣwot,* Introduction.

[65] See Twersky, *Introduction,* 330.

[66] See the annotated text published by Joseph Yahalom, *Poetic Language in the Early Piyyuṭ* [Heb.] (Jerusalem: Hebrew University, 1985), 183-96.

payṭanic poetry that immediately preceded it: the new Andalusian secular poetry abandons the freedom and obscurities employed by the *payy^{e}ṭanim* and chooses a language whose principle feature is that it aims to be as close as possible to Biblical Hebrew. As one of the last poets of Christian Spain says:

> the language of their poems was pure gold,
> while the language of the others was lead and copper.[67]

What does the biblical text and language represent for a Jewish poet? Hebrew poets of al-Andalus transformed the Hebrew Bible into a source of poetic creativity. They employed its language, sometimes twisting it, freely exploring the limits of the expressions. The poets interpreted many debated biblical passages in their own way. They had to show a particularly fine philological knowledge, for instance, when using the *tajnīs* technique, that is playing with the different meanings of the same rhyming word. At the same time they were able to introduce themselves and their readers to a new literary world full of biblical characters and situations. As Ross Brann describes it, the Hebrew Andalusian poet "looked to the Hebrew Bible for lexical, stylistic and figurative models, while his studied intimacy with it brought his own verse to life"; poets use biblical language as "decorative emulation, rhetorical-artistic allusion, and historical typologizing."[68] Of course, the employment of other languages, such as Aramaic, Arabic, or Rabbinic Hebrew was not excluded. Andalusian Hebrew poets felt free to write in any language. But compositions in those other languages are relatively scarce and most of the poets decided to write exclusively in Biblical Hebrew. This biblicizing style became one of the basic characteristics of this school of poetry.

The pronunciation of Hebrew found in Andalusian poetry conformed to Tiberian usage, perhaps with some Spanish peculiarities. It has been suggested by some scholars that the writers also employed other systems of pronunciation, such as the Babylonian. But the evidence in favor

[67] Solomon ben Meshullam de Piera, *The Diwan*, ed. S. Bernstein (New York: Alim Publication, 1942), I:33 [#16, v. 18].

[68] Cf. Brann, *The Compunctious Poet*, 25, 39.

of this theory does not seem to be conclusive. We cannot be sure that during the Golden Age Hebrew poets ever followed traditions for the pronunciation of Hebrew other than the Sephardic one described by the grammarians of their time.[69]

For the Andalusian Hebrew poets fidelity to biblical patterns and language did not preclude introduction of some innovations. It is true that some poets were open to such changes while others were opposed. The first and most obvious among innovations, as Menaḥem's disciples declared, were those related to the new Hebrew prosody introduced by Dunash. The interfering effect of the new prosody on the language illustrates what has been called "exigencies of meter," and in many cases we can see traces of metrical influence in the language of the poetry.[70]

The revolutionary inclusion of the images, motifs, and metaphors of Arabic poetry in the universe of the neo-Biblical Hebrew language represented another important type of innovation. In the new poetical world created by the Hebrew poets technical terms and conventional motifs had to be expressed in the national language, but in the process of adaptation loanwords and calques from Arabic were unavoidable. In this way, the poets enriched the language of their tradition.[71]

---

[69] See the relatively recent debate between Joseph Yahalom, "*Re'shitah shel ha-sh^eqilah ha-m^eduyyeqet ba-shirah ha-'ivrit,*" *Lĕshonenu* 47 (1983): 25-61, and Ezra Fleischer, "*B^eḥinot ba-'aliyat shiṭot ha-sh^eqilah ha-m^eduyyaqot ba-shirah ha-'ivrit,*" *Lĕshonenu* 48/9 (1985): 142-62.

[70] See my study "Los discípulos de Mĕnaḥem sobre la métrica hebrea," Homenaje al Prof. F. Pérez Castro. *Sefarad* 46 (1986): 421-31. About its effects on the language, see Esther Goldenberg, "*Doḥaq ha-shir b^e-torat ha-lashon ha-'ivrit bi-yme ha-benayim,*" *Hebrew Language Studies presented to Professor Zeev Ben-Hayyim,* ed. Moshe Bar-Asher, etc. (Jerusalem: Magnes Press, 1983), 117-41.

[71] See my book *A History of the Hebrew Language* (Cambridge: Cambridge University Press, 1993), 219ff. See the article by Arie Schippers, "Arabic and the Revival of the Hebrew Language and Culture," *Joden onder de islam. Een cultuur in historisch perspectief. Jews under Islam. A Culture in Historical Perspective,* ed. Julie-Marthe Cohen (Amsterdam-Zwolle: Jodds Historisch Museum & Waanders Uitgevers, 1993), which I did not receive until after this article was prepared.

REPRESENTATION AND IDENTITY IN MEDIEVAL SPAIN:

BEATUS MANUSCRIPTS AND THE MUDEJAR CHURCHES OF TERUEL

D. FAIRCHILD RUGGLES *

THE IBERIAN PENINSULA in the medieval period was poised geographically between two very different worlds—Christian Europe and Islamic North Africa. Modern historians place the Iberian peninsula either in "Islam" or "Europe" (terms which are not equivalent and which reflect a modern rather than medieval conceptualization), invariably locating it on the periphery of either culture. Northern Spain is almost never considered part of mainstream medieval European culture because it was small, relatively poor, geographically isolated, and "corrupted" by proximity to Islam. At the same time, al-Andalus (the Muslim-ruled kingdom of southern Spain), except for a brief and stunning golden age in the tenth century, is not held to represent the values of the Islamic central lands. For these reasons as much as any, the Iberian peninsula has been marginalized in medieval studies.

Politically, the Christian kingdoms and al-Andalus were separate domains with ever-changing configurations; what separated them was not a border (although such a fictitious line has been drawn by historians for the sake of map-making) but a zone of contested space.[1] They shared the

* Warm thanks to Professor Barbara Abou-El-Haj of Binghamton University for her lengthy and valuable comments on the penultimate version of this paper. The mudejar material in this paper was presented at College Art Association in 1991 in the session "The Preservation of the Past," chaired by Frederick Asher. I am grateful to him and also to Ross Brann for the opportunity to develop it further.

[1] For a discussion of the frontier as a political, geographical, and imaginative concept, see Thomas Glick, *Islamic and Christian Spain in the Early Middle Ages* (Princeton, 1979), 58-65.

fact that they were far away from capital cities such as Rome and Aachen or Baghdad and Damascus. Both were in constant contact with other peoples who were in at least one significant respect—religion—very different from themselves.

It is in situations just such as these that concepts of cultural identity are confronted and reconciled, for the question of who we are is to a large extent answered by determining who we are not. On the Iberian peninsula, however, the problem was complex, for although there were three religions, they lived in each other's pockets: al-Andalus had a huge population of Christians and a smaller though significant population of Jews; the northern kingdoms of Asturias, Aragon, and Leon were home to Mozarabic (that is to say, culturally Andalusian) Christians who had emigrated from al-Andalus; and from the eleventh century onward, as the Christian-held territory expanded, more and more Muslims lived under Christian rule. Moreover, religion is not the only factor determining identity, nor it is perhaps the strongest. Among three religious groups we can distinguish ethnicity as a category—Arabs, Berbers, Asturians, Catalans, and Basques, to name a few—and class. The elite Jews, Muslims, and Christians who frequented the royal courts of Christian or Muslim rulers may have had more in common with each other with respect to education, wealth, and social fraternization than with ordinary laborers of their same religion.

Clearly cultural identity is more complex than merely sameness and difference; there lurks the question of agency. On what basis is identity formed, and for or by whom? For many decades a small group of scholars have debated the formation of the Mozarabic and Romanesque art in northern Spain, using terms such as cultural "influence," a term implying passive reception, and "appropriation," which acknowledges active selection and rejection. Meyer Schapiro first articulated the problem in his seminal essay of 1939, "From Mozarabic to Romanesque in Silos," in which he emphasized the local conditions that made reception of French influences possible or allowed the continuity of native Visigothic traditions.[2] He stated that "new forms may emerge beside an older art

---

2 Schapiro, "From Mozarabic to Romanesque in Silos," *Art Bulletin* 21 (1939):

not simply as a development from it, but also as its very negation, and the old may persist beside the new in affirming an opposed or declining culture."[3]

In 1965 Otto-Karl Werckmeister addressed the question of the reception of Islamic influence and published a list of motifs from Islamic art used by Christian Spanish artists[4] that he updated in subsequent essays. He asks, "In a deliberately antagonistic culture, where art was often used for creating images and symbols of triumphant power on both sides" to what extent did the borrowing of Islamic and Visigothic forms by Christian artists reflect the political ideology of different groups of ecclesiastical leaders?[5]

More recently Jerrilynn Dodds has weighed into the debate. She argues that the active selection of artistic motifs and architectural forms is a self-conscious act of appropriation in which the church, the state, and other groups may respond independently to Islamic culture. She notes that admiration for Islamic culture and reconciliation directed the use of Islamic motifs as often as hostile antagonism.[6] The acknowledged issue at stake is not merely the formation of cultural identity in the Middle Ages, but its contemporary identity as well.[7]

312-74; reprinted in Meyer Schapiro, *Romanesque Art* (New York, 1977), 28-101.

3 Schapiro, "From Mozarabic to Romanesque in Silos," 29-30.

4 Otto-Karl Werckmeister, "Islamische Formen in spanischen Miniaturen des 10. Jahrhunderts und das Problem der mozarabischen Buchmalerei," in *Settimane di Studi del Centro Italiano di Studi sull'Alto Medioevo,* XII (Spoleto, 1965) *L'Occidente e l'Islam nell'alto Medioevo,* 933-67.

5 Otto-Karl Werckmeister, "Art of the Frontier: Mozarabic Monasticism," in *The Art of Medieval Spain, A.D. 500-1200* (New York, 1993), 121.

6 Jerrilynn D. Dodds, "Islam, Christianity, and the Problem of Religious Art," in *The Art of Medieval Spain, A.D. 500-1200* (New York, 1993), 27-37, and *Architecture and Ideology in Early Medieval Spain* (University Park, Pa., 1990).

7 P. E. Russell, "The Nessus-shirt of Spanish History," *Bulletin of Hispanic Studies* 36 (1959): 219-25; Thomas Glick and O. Pi-Sunyer, "Acculturation as an Explanatory Concept in Spanish History," 11 (1969): 136-54; Dodds, *Architecture and Ideology,* 2.

This debate centers on the formation of the Mozarabic and Romanesque styles of painting and architecture. In the present paper, I will take up the question of the cultural frontier, comparing earlier artistic appropriations and representations of Islam with those of a later period when the Spanish Gothic coexisted with an alternative form of architecture that today is called *mudejar.*[8] The fact that these different styles flourished at the same time in regions close to one another confirms that style was neither aggressively imposed by a dominant culture nor passively received, but was elective.

In the production of Christian art of the north from the tenth to the mid-fourteenth centuries, the representation and visual allusion to Islamic al-Andalus changed from rejecting it as the enemy to reinventing it as the historic self. This visual realm contains a dialogue between northern, Christian-dominated culture and southern, Islamic culture that is markedly different from that in the written texts. Dodds has pointed out that the polarization between Christianity and Islam evident in the religious writings of medieval Christian Spain was not paralleled in secular cultural life.[9] Christian responses to Islamic culture were complex and variable. In the ninth and tenth centuries, Christian ecclesiastical and political leaders admired the Islamic world of palatine luxury, yet feared it as alien and potentially corrupting.[10] Illustrating this point are the early Beatus

---

[8] The term "mudejar" was coined by José Amador de los Ríos in 1859 to replace, or at least to elaborate upon the broader stylistic terms Mozarabic and Plateresque (Amador de los Ríos, *El estilo mudéjar en arquitectura,* ed. and introduction by Pierre Guenoun [Paris, 1965]). For the Muslims themselves, the terms used by Christians in the primary documents are, variously, *moros de paz* in the twelfth century, *moros* and *sarraceni* in the fourteenth century, and *moriscoes* in the sixteenth century (Angel Novella and Victoria Ribot, "Los mudéjares en Teruel," in *Simposio internacional de mudejarismo, III Actas [Teruel, 1984]* [Teruel, 1986], 245-49; John Boswell, *The Royal Treasure: Muslim Communities under the Crown of Aragon in the Fourteenth century* [New Haven, 1977], 3; María Luisa Ledesma, *Los mudéjares en Aragón* [Tema aragones, 3] [Saragossa, 1979], 3-6).

[9] Dodds, "Islam, Christianity, and the Problem of Religious Art," 27-37.

[10] Dodds, "Islam, Christianity, and the Problem of Religious Art," 30-32.

Commentary manuscripts and various church reliquaries. By the thirteenth and fourteenth centuries, Andalusian Islamic culture was no longer held at arm's length but embraced as indigenous and quintessentially "Spanish." Islamic art was then integrated into northern Spanish culture and even into the architecture of its churches, as demonstrated by the *mudejar* churches of Teruel in Aragon.

The Beatus is a commentary on the Apocalypse (the last book in the Christian Bible), written in 776 by an Asturian monk named Beatus of Liébana, as an elaboration of an earlier text. That more copies of it have survived in medieval Spain than the bible itself attests to its popularity, and today 32 whole or partial manuscripts exist from the ninth through thirteenth centuries, an astounding quantity. Equally as remarkable is the size and luxuriousness of the manuscripts: they generally measure well over a foot in length and are densely illustrated with a rich cycle of pictures that represent scenes from the text. There is considerable debate as to whether the illustrations are descended from a single, lost archetype, which Wilhelm Neuss dated to c. 785 CE[11] and John Williams to c. 380–85,[12] or based on two editions,[13] or even three.[14] The oldest extant manuscript is a one-page fragment from Silos (Silos, Bib. del Mon. de Santo Domingo, frag. 4), dated on the basis of paleography to the end of

---

[11] Wilhelm Neuss, *Die Apokalypse des hl. Johannes in der altspanischen und altchristlichen Bibel-Illustration* (Münster in Westfalen, 1931), 3 vols., I:81-111.

[12] Williams, *The Illustrated Beatus,* 5 vols. (London, 1994), I:31-39, 50.

[13] Léopold Delisle "Les manuscrits de l'Apocalypse de Beatus conservés à la Bibliothèque Nationale et dans le cabinet de M. Didot," in *Mélanges de paléographie et de bibliographie* (Paris 1880), 137.

[14] First put forth by Henry Sanders, ed., *Beati in Apocalipsin Libri Duodecim* (Papers and Monographs of the American Academy in Rome, VII) (Rome 1930), XV; adapted by Peter Klein, *Der ältere Beatus-Kodex Vitr. 14-1 der Biblioteca National zu Madrid. Studien zur Beatus-Illustration und der spanischen Buchmalerei des 10. Jahrhunderts* Hildesheim-New York, 1976. For a detailed discussion of Beatus manuscript genealogies, see Williams, *Illustrated Beatus,* I:21-27.

the ninth century, one century after Beatus's original text.[15] The next oldest surviving manuscript is the copy in the Pierpont Morgan Library (M. 644), consisting of 300 folios and dated on the basis on pictorial style and paleography to 940–45 (figs. 1 and 2). It is believed to have been made at the Tábara monastery for the monastery of San Miguel de Escalada and illustrated by the monk Maius.[16] The other surviving copies of the Beatus manuscript from the second half of the tenth century are the Vitrina Beatus (Madrid, Bib. Nac. MS Vit. 14-1) and a later Vitrina fragment (Madrid, Bib. Nac. MS Vit. 14-2, ff. 1-5), the Valladolid Beatus (Valladolid, Bib. de la Univ., MS 433), the Tábara Beatus (Madrid, Arch. Hist. Nac., Cod. 1097B), the Girona Beatus (Museu de la Cat. de Girona, Num. Inv. 7[11]), the Urgell Beatus (Museu Dio. de la Seu d'Urgell, Num. Inv. 501), part of the San Millan Beatus (Madrid, Real Aca. de la Hist., Cod. 33), and the Escorial Beatus (Escorial, Bib. del Mon., Beatus and II.5).[17]

The function of the original commentary for Iberian Christians of the eighth century and thereafter has yet to be satisfactorily explained. Maius, copyist and illustrator of the Morgan Beatus, wrote: "I have painted a series of pictures from the wonderful words of its stories so that the wise may fear the coming of the future judgment of the world's end."[18] But as Williams has noted, the fact that the Beatus commentary continued to circulate and be copied after the millennium, when Maius and his contemporaries expected the world to end, proves that this was not its only meaning.[19] Its original apocalyptic meaning was eventually

---

[15] Williams, *Illustrated Beatus,* II:18, referring to Anscari Mundó, "Notas para la historia de la escritura visigótica en su período primitivo," in *Bivium: homenaje a Manuel Cecilio Díaz y Díaz* (Madrid, 1983), 176-96.

[16] For a discussion of the evidence supporting a mid-tenth-century date, see Williams, *Illustrated Beatus,* II:21-33.

[17] Williams, *Illustrated Beatus,* I:10.

[18] Williams, *Illustrated Beatus,* II:21.

[19] Williams, "Purpose and Imagery in the Apocalypse Commentary of Beatus of Liébana," in *The Apocalypse in the Middle Ages,* ed. Richard Emmerson & Bernard McGinn (Ithaca, N.Y., 1992), 217-33.

overshadowed by another one that reflected the contemporary struggle for dominance between the Christians and the Muslims.

The Apocalypse presents St. John's fantastic vision of the triumph of God's people over those who offer false prophecies and claim false authority. Clearly such a text had particular meaning for Christian leaders who intended to triumph over their enemies: namely Muslims and Christians following incorrect doctrine.[20] When Beatus of Liébana wrote, the kingdom of al-Andalus extended from the peninsula's southern shore to north of Saragossa, Toledo, and Merida, and the Umayyad emir 'Abd al-Raḥmān I (r. 756–88) was consolidating Muslim strength in order to push further north. While the written text of the Beatus manuscript does not explicitly state that al-Andalus is the enemy, tenth-century manuscript copies such as the Morgan Beatus suggest this in the visual imagery.

There are a number of references to Muslims and Islamic culture in the Morgan Beatus. One illustration, "The Whore of Babylon" (Morgan f. 194v) depicts a woman seated Islamic-style on cushions. The sexual licentiousness here attributed to a Muslim, identified as such by a crescent moon in her headdress, was probably a reference to the "soft" lifestyle of the Muslims.[21] When the Morgan Beatus was made in the mid-tenth century, Cordoba was famed for its handsome palaces with numerous reception halls giving onto extensive gardens with perfumed gardens, fruit trees, and singing fountains.[22] Poets and musicians performed there at the court of 'Abd al-Raḥmān III (912–61), which was acclaimed

[20] It is possible that Beatus intended his commentary to contribute to the struggle for dominance between a group of Asturian Christians and the see of Toledo in Muslim-ruled al-Andalus. However, as Williams has recently pointed out, it could not have been aimed specifically at the Archbishop Elipandus, for he did not begin to teach the heretical doctrine of Adoptionism until several years after Beatus wrote his commentary ("Purpose and Imagery," 217-33).

[21] Williams, "Purpose and Imagery," 217-33.

[22] For a description of Cordoban palaces, see Ruggles, *Landscape, Gardens and Vision in Islamic Spain*, forthcoming from Penn State Press, and "The Gardens of the Alhambra and the Concept of the Garden in Islamic Spain," in *Al-Andalus: The Arts of Islamic Spain*, 162-71.

for its literary brilliance. The comfortable standard of living enjoyed by farmers, merchants, and the aristocracy in prosperous, sunny al-Andalus was sufficiently attractive to pose a serious threat to Christian culture.[23] Indeed as early as 854 the bishop of Cordoba wrote that the young Christians of Cordoba were "intoxicated with Arab eloquence," and that while they could write grandiloquent Arabic poetry and learnedly discuss rhetoric, "the Latins pay so little attention to their own language, that in the whole Christian flock there is hardly one man in a thousand who can write a letter to inquire after a friend's health intelligibly."[24]

"The Destruction of Babylon" (Morgan f.202v) (fig. 1) shows a rich palace decorated with horseshoe arches, stepped merlons, precious vessels, and floral and geometrical designs. The horseshoe arches, which are often identified as Islamic,[25] may in other contexts (such as the Church of San Miguel de Escalada) refer to Visigothic models:[26] thus their presence in this miniature is not necessarily an Andalusian reference. But the emphasis on colorful non-figural decoration does indeed indicate that an Islamic palace is represented. Although figures are commonly represented in Islamic secular art—for example, Madīnat al-Zahrā' had a large sculpture of a woman over one of its principal gates[27]—buildings like the Mosque of Cordoba and various Cordoban palaces were better known for imaginative vegetal motifs, complex geometrical patterns, and ornamental epigraphy realized in stone, stucco and brilliant mosaics. Dodds has remarked that the Morgan manuscript's "Destruction of

[23] See E. Lévi-Provençal, *Histoire de l'Espagne Musulmane,* 3 vols. (Paris, 1953), III:397-451; María Rosa Menocal, *The Arabic Role in Medieval Literary History* (Philadelphia, 1987), chapter 2.

[24] Translated W. Montgomery Watt with Pierre Cachia, *A History of Islamic Spain* (Edinburgh, 1965), 56.

[25] Williams, *Early Spanish Manuscript Illumination* (New York, 1977), 19-20; *Illustrated Beatus,* I:148.

[26] Dodds, *Architecture and Ideology,* 50-52.

[27] Al-Rāzī, *Anales palatinos del califa de Córdoba al-Hakam II,* trans. E. García Gómez (Madrid, 1967), 68 and 153; Ibn Ḥayyān, *Al-Muqtabis fī akhbār bilād al-andalus,* ed. A. A. El-Ḥājjī (Beirut, 1965), 50-120.

THE DESTRUCTION OF BABYLON

The Pierpont Morgan Library, New York
M. 6444, f.202v

Figure 1

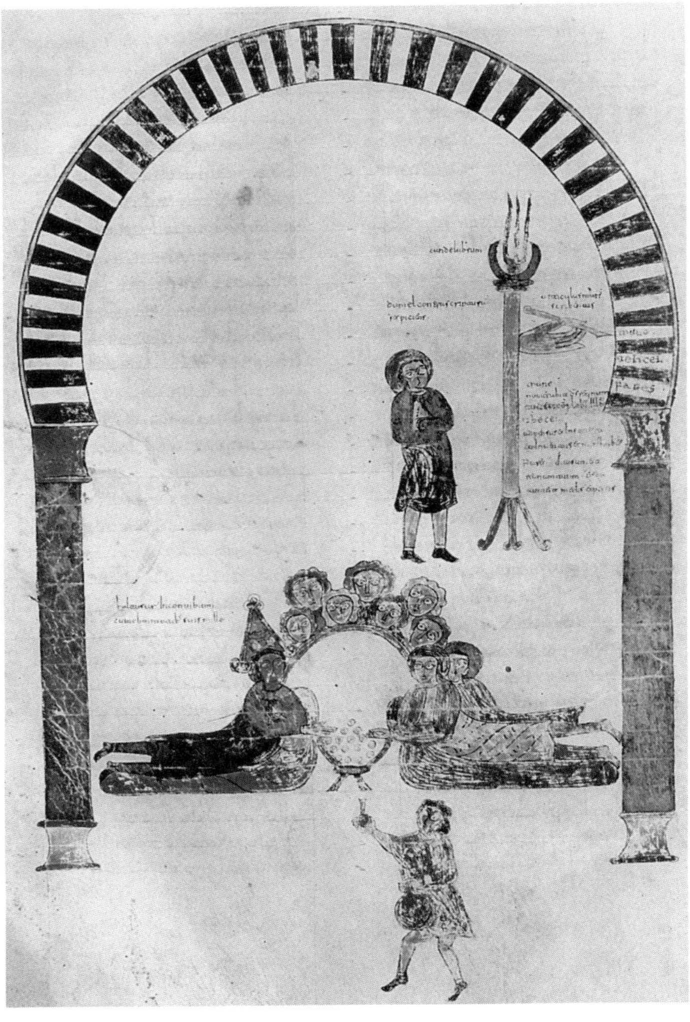

BALTASSAR'S FEAST

The Pierpont Morgan Library, New York
M. 6444, f.202v

Figure 2

Babylon" shows what aspects of Islam were the most seductive and to be resisted.[28] The underlying message is that Islam, like Babylon, is doomed for its sins.

The scene of "Baltassar's Feast" (Morgan f.255v) (fig. 2) is from St. Jerome's Commentary on the Book of Daniel, included at the end of some Beatus manuscripts beginning at least as early as the middle of the ninth century.[29] In the Book of Daniel (5:1-5), Baltassar was an impious king of Babylon, slain because he profaned the golden vessels from the temple of Jerusalem by drinking with them to false gods. The image shows the moment when, while he was feasting and drinking in the company of his sons, wives and concubines, a disembodied hand mysteriously appeared and wrote his fate on the walls of the palace. The Prophet Daniel is at the right, interpreting the words to Baltassar.

A pointed visual association was made between Baltassar and the Umayyad caliphs of Cordoba, for Baltassar reclines in the Islamic style on the floor under a distinctive arch of red and white voussoirs. This was either an allusion to the Cordoba Mosque, a monument well known to Muslims and Christians alike and absolutely identified with the Umayyad dynasty of Spain,[30] or to one of the Umayyad palaces in the outskirts of Cordoba. These included the huge al-Nā'ūrah palace, in existence already since at least 867,[31] and the palace-city Madīnat al-Zahrā', founded some five or ten years before the Morgan Beatus was made. Medieval historians described Madīnat al-Zahrā' as a center of scholarship and the arts, and the setting of splendid and elaborate festivities.[32] The red-and-

---

28 Dodds, "Islam, Christianity, and the Problem of Religious Art," 30.

29 However, Williams acknowledges that there is no proof that the ninth-century Daniel commentaries were illustrated (*Illustrated Beatus,* I:26).

30 Williams, "The Beatus Commentaries and Spanish Bible Illustration," in *Actas del simposio para el estudio de los códices del "Comentario al Apocalipsis" de Beato de Liébana* (Madrid, 1980), I:212-27.

31 Ruggles, *Gardens, Landscape and Vision in Islamic Spain,* chapter 3, forthcoming.

32 For a description of the palace, see Antonio Vallejo, "Madīnat al-Zahrā': The Triumph of the Islamic State," in *Al-Andalus: The Art of Islamic Spain,* 27-39.

white arches in the reception hall (fig. 3) were associated with the caliph because they framed the place where he sat in state during official receptions at which Muslims, Jews, and Christians from al-Andalus, Europe, and the Mediterranean were entertained.[33] Whether in the mosque or palace, red-and-white arches were an unmistakable reference to the Umayyad rulers of al-Andalus.

THE SALON RICO AT MADINAT AL-ZAHRA'
Figure 3

[33] Receptions for the Byzantine embassy were held September and October 949 at Madīnat al-Zahrā', specifically in the hall overlooking the gardens (Salon Rico). Many other receptions were held there earlier for Muslim vassals, European traders such as the merchants from Amalfi in 941–42, and Christian emissaries bargaining for peace after campaigns at Saragossa and Pamplona (936–37) and Barcelona and Huesca (939–40). For sources, see Rosario Castejón, "Madīnat al-Zahrā' en los autores árabes," *al-Mulk* 2 (1961–62): 119-56.

In both these pictures of Babylon, the Visigothic and Islamic references were ideologically constructed. However, it was not only in the Beatus commentary that such allusions were made; Werckmeister has shown similar references to Islam in the illustrations of the Bible of San Isidoro (Leon), dated 960, where Philistine horsemen are represented riding in the Sasanian and Islamic style.[34] In idealizing the Visigothic past or casting the confrontation with al-Andalus in biblical terms, the past was envisioned in accordance with the present struggle.[35]

The scene of Baltassar's Feast is duplicated in the Tábara Beatus copy of 970 (f. 143), illuminated by Magius and Emeterius, and in the Girona Beatus of 975 (f. 253v), illuminated by Emeterius and the nun Ende; and it is repeated on a different scale in the Valladolid Beatus of 970 (f. 204), illuminated by Obeco.[36] In these early copies of the Beatus there are two related yet separate languages operating: one is the text written by Beatus himself and copied again and again with minimal change, and the other is the visual language of the illustration cycle which was perfected early on and likewise remained remarkably constant. Lacking the original, we cannot know what the first illustrations looked like, but at some point along the way the Beatus acquired an additional level of discourse which was visual and enhanced one of the meanings of the text. The new level of discourse was anti-Muslim. The verbal text made no mention of Islam; yet the visual pointed clearly toward it.[37]

---

[34] Werckmeister, "Islamische Formen in spanischen Miniaturen," 948-67; and "Art of the Frontier," 122.

[35] For the development of this theme, see Werckmeister's discussion of a tenth-century manuscript, "Das Bild zur Liste der Bistümer Spaniens im *Codex Aemilianensis*," *Madrider Mitteilungen* 9 (1968): 399-423.

[36] See Williams, *Illustrated Beatus*, II: fig. 256 (Tábara Beatus), and II: fig. 232 (Valladolid Beatus).

[37] It was not unique in this respect: large jewelled triumphal crosses that overlaid the meaning of Christ's ultimate victory over death with the contemporary victory of the Christian kingdoms over al-Andalus were common in Asturian art of the ninth and tenth centuries. Examples are the Cross of Victory (Oviedo), and three relief pan-

For its anti-Muslim stance, the Beatus commentary has been called the Book of the Reconquest, but while it had assumed that meaning by the tenth century, it is unlikely to have had such a meaning in the eighth century when composed because, as Williams has explained, the Beatus was written when Christian/Islamic conflict was minimal.[38] For example, in 776 Cordoba's old Visigothic church, San Vicente, had not yet been demolished to build the Great Mosque which was the first permanent mosque built in al-Andalus. The Reconquest did not mobilize, and anti-Islamic statements did not appear in written sources until the ninth century, and even then the animosity was by no means unilateral or constant.

The Morgan, Tábara, Girona, and Valladolid copies of the Beatus commentary date to the period 940–75 when the Umayyad rulers of Spain were at the height of their power. 'Abd al-Raḥmān III ruled, having assumed the title of caliph in 929. His kingdom enjoyed enormous wealth (far greater than that of Asturias-Leon) with access to the North African gold trade and a prospering economy based on agriculture and Mediterranean commerce. Successful military campaigns were pushing the borders of al-Andalus further and further northward, and diplomacy and maritime strength in the Mediterranean were bringing the Maghreb's western coast under submission. Moreover, the rate of conversion to Islam veered sharply upwards in Cordoba in the tenth century so that for the first time Muslims outnumbered Christians.[39] As the political, economic, military, and demographic strength of Islam increased, a resurgence of Christian identity among Andalusian Christians began in the mid-ninth century with the Cordoba martyrdom movement and emigration of monks from al-Andalus to the north, and continued into the

---

els from the Church of San Martín in Oviedo, reproduced in *The Art of Medieval Spain, A.D. 500-1200* (New York, 1993), 118, 137, 146-47.

[38] Williams, "Purpose and Imagery in the Apocalypse Commentary of Beatus of Liébana," 228.

[39] Richard Bulliet, *Conversion to Islam in the Medieval Period* (Cambridge, Mass., 1979).

next century. The Beatus commentary from the first held an explicit meaning for Christians as the representation of Christ's triumph over evil; by the mid-tenth century when the Muslims of al-Andalus embodied that evil, it acquired an implicit meaning for the Reconquest and became, in Werckmeister's words, "a quintessential expression of a distinct northern Spanish cultural identity."[40]

But if Islam was the enemy, how then do we explain the existence of so many Islamic objects in the church treasuries of the north? The Girona Cathedral, Braga Cathedral, the monastery of Santo Domingo at Silos, the monastery at Leyre, the Real Colegiata de San Isidoro in Leon, and even Saint-Jean in Liège, among others, owned precious containers and textiles of Islamic manufacture that were used as reliquaries; some are boxes or pyxides of exquisitely carved ivory or inlaid silver, others are wood revetted with silver or ivory and lined with costly silk textiles.[41] Most of them were obtained in the eleventh century or afterward. They were made for Muslim patrons and in some cases even bore inscriptions glorifying the military strength of the prince-patron, such as the ivory casket for al-Manṣūr's son, called "Sword of the Realm" for his victory at Leon.[42] But once obtained by the abbey of Leyre in Navarre, where it served as a reliquary for two Christian martyrs from al-Andalus, the object acquired the meaning of Christianity's ultimate victory over Islam and military defeat of the Muslims: a triumph spiritual and political, but surely not cultural.[43]

The answer is not as simple as a direct correlation between military ascendancy and artistic reception, as Schapiro, Werckmeister, Klein, and Dodds have taken great pains to demonstrate. The convoluted histories

---

[40] Werckmeister, "Art of the Frontier," 125.

[41] See Renata Holod, 190-91, 198-201, Manuel Casamar Pérez, 208-9, and Cristina Partearroyo, 226-28, 229, in *Al-Andalus: The Art of Islamic Spain*; and Marilyn Jenkins, 94 and 97, and Stefano Carboni, 98-99, in *The Art of Medieval Spain, A.D. 500-1200.*

[42] Werckmeister, "Art of the Frontier," 121-22.

[43] Dodds, "Islam, Christianity, and the Problem of Religious Art," 32.

of these numerous "cross-over" objects are symptomatic of the complex relationship between Christianity and Islam. There are two explanations for Islamic objects used thus in the service of Christianity. One is that with regard to beautiful things the artistry of Islam was admired even while its precepts were reviled. The second is that the act of appropriating of these pieces began to symbolize the church's ascendance over Islam.[44] Both interpretations are acceptable. What is important is that, despite service to the Christian Church, the objects did not lose their identity as Islamic, for many of them had prominent Arabic inscriptions and depicted recognizably Andalusian scenes such as musicians and princes seated cross-legged on raised daises. Clearly while owners of these objects may have had theological objections to Islam, it did not prevent them from appropriating its material culture. The concurrent admiration for Islamic art as evident in the reception of the reliquaries, and vilification of its religion as evident in the Beatus manuscripts, typifies the variety of Christian responses to Islam in the tenth and eleventh centuries.

In the middle of the eleventh century, the rulers of the northern kingdoms began to affiliate themselves more self-consciously with Christian Europe, particularly with France, the closest neighbor. A relationship between Navarre and Cluny had been established by Sancho of Navarre (r. 1004–35) who became an associate of the order and invited Cluniac monks to his monastery at San Juan de la Peña.[45] Ferdinand I and Alfonso VI of Leon-Castile, in 1062 and 1077 respectively, gave enormous gifts of land and gold to Cluny in return for perpetual masses.[46] The benefits for Cluny were matched by profits made by southern French nobles in Spain (in the trade of precious metals, agricultural

---

[44] Werckmeister, "Art of the Frontier," 122.

[45] R. A. Fletcher, *Saint James's Catapult: The Life and Times of Diego Gelmírez of Santiago de Compostela* (Oxford, 1984), 29-30.

[46] The relationship betrween Leon and Cluny is discussed in O. K. Werckmeister, "Cluny III and the Pilgrimage to Santiago de Compostela," *Gesta* 27 (1988): 103-12, and J. Williams, "Cluny and Spain," *Gesta* 27 (1988): 92-101

goods, and trade tariffs).[47] As a result of these ties, the French came to Spain as artisans, merchants, as royal queens, and as members of the clergy (in Toledo, Braga, and Valencia).

The internal tide of political power turned in the north's favor after the Umayyad caliphate collapsed in 1010, and Christian kings began capturing large portions of Islamic territory. The kingdoms of Leon and Castile, united under Fernando I in 1037 and again under Alfonso VI in 1072, were more formidable together than either had been individually. The small taifa kingdoms that replaced the unified Umayyad kingdom squabbled incessantly and proved vulnerable to assault. Some, like Toledo and Valencia, were soon conquered; others became vassals to Castile-Leon, paying tribute (*parias*) with gold from Africa. These tribute monies from al-Andalus allowed Fernando I to become a major patron of the powerful Cluniac order, and through Cluny to win papal approval for the Reconquest.[48] Indeed Cluny's new church (Cluny III) could not have been built without the anticipation of Leonese funds—an example of the interdependence of the three societies.

At the same time, the cathedral of Santiago de Compostela, already an important pilgrimage shrine at the end of the tenth century,[49] sought to attract pilgrims from Spain and France to the shrine of St. James. One means of doing so was through relics, and the bishop of Compostela did not hesitate to steal relics from other churches to bolster the sanctity of his own.[50] For its church building campaigns it competed variously, in a complex web of allegiances, for Cluniac support as well as against Cluny

---

[47] Schapiro, "From Mozarabic to Romanesque in Silos," 49-50.

[48] The primary documents do not indicate that the pope regarded the war against al-Andalus as a true crusade until 1123; the Spaniards do not appear to have thought of them as crusades until 1147–48, according to Fletcher, *Saint James's Catapult*, 297-98.

[49] The reasons are both external (the pan-European increase in pilgrimages between 950–1150) and internal (the bishop's deliberate program to reform the monastic discipline and economics of the cathedral chapter at Compostela) (Fletcher, *Saint James's Catapult*, 82, 163-91).

[50] Fletcher, *Saint James's Catapult*, 115, 185-86.

for royal funds. The pilgrimage route to Compostela from France included stops along the way to visit intermediary cities such as Leon to which the relics of Isidore of Seville were brought in 1063[51] and where a hostel for pilgrims was established in 1084, and Burgos where altars were dedicated to St. James and St. Nicholas, the patron saints of travelers.[52] Such objects and actions suggest a deliberate program on the part of the ecclesiastical leaders of each church to attract the pilgrims that brought important revenues and prestige.[53]

Christian Spanish kings, seeking to unify the Spanish church and gain the support of ecclesiastical authorities in France and Italy in their crusade to regain the peninsula, adopted the Roman rite soon after 1070 and suppressed the old Visigothic-Mozarabic church liturgy. The suppression of Mozarabic rite met with resistance in many quarters, and indeed, it was never completely prohibited because, even while the Christian Spanish kings (Castile-Leon) were trying to impose a centralized—and more controllable—church organization upon their kingdoms, they recognized that their claim to authority rested in part on this tie to the Visigothic past. It was through their identification with the Visigoths that the Asturian kings beginning with Pelayo (r. 718–37), who supposedly launched the Reconquest, had first established their dynastic legitimacy as the Christian heirs to Spain. But, rewriting history for the sake of present political convenience, Pope Gregory VII sent a letter to Alfonso VI in 1074 insisting upon Rome's claim upon the peninsula to the exclusion of the Visigothic dynasty and stressing the preeminence of St. Paul, rather than St. James, in converting Spain to Christianity.[54] The

---

51 Peter Linehan, *History and the Historians of Medieval Spain* (Oxford, 1993), 174; Bernard Reilly, "Medieval Spain, A.D. 500-1200," in *The Art of Medieval Spain, A.D. 500-1200*, 2-11.

52 Serafín Moralejo, "On the Road: the Camino de Santiago," in *The Art of Medieval Spain, A.D. 500-1200*, 179.

53 Moralejo, "On the Road," 179. But Barbara Abou-El-Haj has shown that such programs were not unilaterally welcomed by the townspeople, and cites examples of resistance in her article "The Audiences for the Medieval Cult of Saints," *Gesta* 30 (1991): 3-15.

54 Linehan, *History and the Historians*, 173.

embattled parties—clergy clinging to the Mozarabic rite, the Roman papacy, the Burgundian Cluniac order, and the Leonese kings Fernando and Alfonso—were well aware of the usefulness of the past in defining present theological and political interests.

The conflict was not only theological and political, but cultural as well. Just as one liturgy was substituted for another, royal and ecclesiastical patrons of the arts imposed their taste for the more international Romanesque in place of horseshoe arches and geometrically self-contained building units—hallmarks of Visigothic architectural style. This preference for the Romanesque was self-conscious and mandated by ecclesiastical authorities; for instance in 1091 a council in Leon mandated that the Mozarabic script style be replaced by French script (generally called "letra fransisca") in Spanish Christian service books.[55]

The release from cultural insularity offered by associations with France and the Roman church in the tenth and eleventh centuries posed problems for the integrity of Leonese-Castilian Christian culture in the thirteenth. From beyond the Pyrenées emerged a new threat: the increasing dominance of the French in church and state. As earlier a faction of the clergy loyal to the Mozarabic rite had protested the imposition of the Roman rite by Alfonso VI, Abbot Hugh of Cluny, and the pope, now there were instances of resistance to French culture. To maintain Spain's own identity distinct from that of France, ironically it was Islamic art that offered a vocabulary of difference. Whereas earlier the attitude toward Islamic art in northern Spain had been either rejection on the grounds of religion or worldly decadence, or appropriation as booty and the sign of conquest, it eventually provoked an altogether different response: the direct imitation of Islamic models in Christian architecture.

[55] Schapiro, "From Mozarabic to Romanesque in Silos," 60.

The Islamic provinces such as Aragon that had been along the frontier with Christian Spain were naturally the first to succumb to the Reconquest. The Muslim aristocracy and high administrative officials left these provinces immediately, but rural Muslims and sectors of the urban population stayed. So tenacious was this community that even in the fourteenth century, Muslims in Valencia outnumbered Christians.[56] The Muslims were a sizeable portion of the population in Aragon as well, and their exodus would have seriously disrupted the economy. They formed the sector whose livelihood depended upon long-term stability, engaged in agriculture, commerce, textile production, and manufacturing and construction industries such as brick-making, ceramics, woodworking, and masonry. Boswell's documentary study of the *mudejar* community of Aragon has shown that of these occupations, commerce was the most common in Aragon, followed by construction.[57] Although relatively free in the thirteenth century, gradually more and more Muslims were enslaved on the land until by the mid-fourteenth century free Muslims for the most part were only to be found in the cities working as merchants and artisans, and their movement was subject to restrictions.[58] Emigration was discouraged because such artisans played an important role in architecture, building palaces and churches for the new Christian patrons. Using familiar methods and materials, these Muslims, known today as *mudejares*, from the Arabic *mudajjan*, meaning "one who remains," produced a distinctive style of art also called *mudejar*.

In the Aragonese city of Teruel, conquered by Alfonso II in 1171, the *mudejars* were protected by royal edicts (the Fueros de Teruel) that guaranteed certain rights such as the maintenance of a Muslim court of law, practice of religion, and freedom of movement including emigration.[59]

---

[56] Boswell, *The Royal Treasure*, 7.

[57] Boswell, *The Royal Treasure*, 56-57.

[58] Boswell, *The Royal Treasure*, 41-42; Francisco Roca Traver, "Un siglo de vida mudéjar en la Valencia medieval," *Estudios de Edad Media de la Corona de Aragón* (Saragossa) 5 (1952): 115-20.

[59] Angel Novella and Victoria Ribot, "Los mudéjares en Teruel," 245-51.

In 1365, Aragon had a mudejar population of approximately 235,000. That population dwindled between the twelfth and fifteenth centuries as a result of the plague, emigration, and probably conversion; however,

THE CHURCH OF SAN PEDRO, TERUEL
Figure 4

even as late as 1495, when a census was taken, Muslims made up eleven percent of Aragon and ten percent of Teruel's population.[60]

SAN MARTÍN TOWER, Teruel
Figure 5

[60] Boswell, *The Royal Treasure*, 7; María Luisa Ledesma, *Los mudéjares en Aragón*, 8-9.

There were several churches built by mudejars in Teruel in the late thirteenth and early fourteenth centuries, of which the remains of four survive. The first is the present cathedral, Santa Maria del Mediavilla, begun in the late thirteenth century, its tower built in 1257–58. The second is the Church of San Pedro (fig. 4) which replaced an older Romanesque church; its present structure was begun c. 1319; the apse was begun in 1383 and consecrated in 1392.[61] The brick tower at its west end is a tall, free-standing, rectangular block, built over the street with a large archway. The surface of the tower is treated with simple panels of interlaced arches, bricks set in a sawtooth pattern, framed ajimez (paired) windows, and green glazed ceramic tile that was the specialty of the potters of Teruel.

The Tower of San Martín (fig. 5), constructed in 1315–16, was built in the area that had been the intra-muros Muslim quarter after the conquest.[62] It too consists of an independent structure, a tall rectangular block with an arched passageway at ground level. Its four facades are decorated with bands and panels of green and white glazed tile. The ceramic is either cut mosaic fashion or inserted as plugs, some resembling shallow platters affixed to the surface. There are repeating bands of brick laid in a sawtooth pattern that creates a sharp contrast of light and shadow. Elsewhere bricks placed in relief form elaborate screens; in one panel the bricks weave a fabric of eight-pointed stars and Greek crosses, and in another interlacing polylobed arches make a blind arcade supported by green and white ceramic cylindrical "columns." The entire surface of the majestic tower is crisply textured, colorful, and gleams in the sunlight.

The fourth tower is from the Church of El Salvador, begun soon after 1277. The church was replaced in the seventeenth century, but its

---

[61] The exterior of San Pedro was badly restored in 1901 according to Gonzalo M. Borrás Gualis, "El arte mudéjar en Teruel y su provincia," in the series *Castillas Turolenses* 3 (1987). I am grateful to Isabel Rojas Serrano for having directed me toward this and other sources on mudejar architecture.

[62] Ledesma, *Los mudéjares en Aragón*, 10.

tower, which is dated on the basis of style to the time of San Martín, still survives and is clearly the latter's mudejar twin.[63] Both San Martín and San Salvador towers were built on a square plan consisting of two con-

MOSQUE OF HASAN, RABAT
Figure 6

[63] Borrás Gualis, "El arte mudéjar en Teruel," 52.

centric towers united by stairways, the central tower being divided into separate floors. In this they resemble the Almohad minaret in the congregational mosque of Seville (1184–95), today known as the Giralda and serving as a belltower for a late Gothic cathedral.

All four of the Teruel towers are decorated in the style of the larger but similarly decorated Almohad minarets in the Mosque of Hasan in Rabat (fig. 6) (1195–96), the Kutubiyya Mosque in Marrakesh (fin. by 1197), and the mosque of Seville. The Rabat and Seville minarets are of brick (although stone was available to the architects), and the Marrakesh minaret is of stone. All three are tall, solemn rectangles, their facade decoration is limited to panels of geometrical and interlaced ornament in low relief. The Almohad buildings derive their decorative vocabulary of blind polylobed interlacing arches from the *maqṣūrah* screen surrounding the *miḥrāb* of the Cordoba Mosque. The leap from Cordoba to the Almohad minarets is enormous (although not unmediated), for arches that were architectonic and weight-bearing in the Cordoba *maqṣūrah* are translated into flat, surface designs in the Almohad context. This leap from structure to ornament is architecturally far more significant than the transformation from mosque minaret to church tower, yet the ideological leap was greater in the latter.

The Teruel towers look remarkably like Almohad minarets. Why did the Teruel patrons choose an overtly Islamic vocabulary for the decoration of their churches? Particularly in the towers which were signs announcing visually and aurally the presence of the church and Christianity, much as the minaret serves as a visible sign of Muslim presence and domination?[64] A possible answer is that Teruel was a divided place, the elite consisting of a church hierarchy and the lower class consisting of mudejar workers. The church may simply have employed the most skilled artisans who happened to be mudejars and who built using the

[64] Jonathan Bloom, *Minaret: Symbol of Islam* (Oxford, 1989); for a discussion of the first minaret in Spain, see Bloom, "Mosque Towers and Church Towers in Early Medieval Spain," in *Künstlerischer Austauch: Akten des XXVIII. Internationalen Kongresses für Kunstgeschichte (Berlin, 15.-20. Juli 1992)* (Berlin, 1993), 361-71.

techniques and in the style inherited from their fathers. According to this limited explanation, the mudejar churches of Teruel were completely traditional and were the result of artisans working without direction from the churches' patrons. It assumes that artisans did not travel, whereas the opposite is true: for instance, we know that a master architect named Yuçaf de Huzmel came from Saragossa to work on the apse of Teruel's cathedral in c. 1335.[65]

Another proposal is that mudejar architecture, which used brick instead of more expensive stone (which was scarce in Aragon anyway), was an architecture of necessity, adopted in a time of economic crisis because brick was cheap and locally available.[66] However, Aragon's economic woes, brought about by the agricultural failures of 1325–50, occurred after the mudejar style had already been employed in Teruel for some time. This explanation assumes that medium determines architectural design and leads us back to the theory that the church had no choice but to employ Muslim artisans. Ultimately both of the above explanations assume passivity on the part of the patrons; that through sheer inertia, they ended up with mudejar-style churches. While the idea of the Andalusian-Islamic style being foisted upon innocent church authorities by their workers is attractive, it is not persuasive. Artisans from Romanesque cathedral sites could have been invited to Teruel, and the patrons of San Pedro and San Martín could have chosen an architectural style that was more appropriately Christian.

For example, the Leon Cathedral, an episcopal see and an important station along the pilgrimage road, was rebuilt in its present form during the second half of the thirteenth century, and finished just about the time that the Church of San Pedro was begun. The Leon Cathedral is

---

65 G. M. Borrás Gualis, "Alarifes mudéjares aragoneses," in *Gran enciclopedia aragonesa* (1981), IX:2374-75.

66 L. Corral Lafuente and J. C. Escribano Sánchez, "La crisis económica en el origen de la arquitectura mudéjar aragones," 51-65, and María Agueda Castellano, "El mudejar en los castillos españoles…" 20, in *II Simposio international de mudejarismo: arte. Actas [Teruel, 1981]* (Teruel, 1982).

a fine example of French Gothic with flying buttresses, a nave and transept supported on tall piers rising to groin vaulting, the walls opened up with stained glass windows, and tripartite portals on the west and south sides with sculptured tympana that advise the visitor to prepare for the Day of Judgment and accept the salvation offered by Christ through his Church. Leon is almost a copy of Reims Cathedral, and it makes sense for this important monument on the French-dominated Santiago pilgrimage trail to be built in a French Gothic style. But architectural style did not simply flow southward in the wake of the waves of devout pilgrims; it was deliberately embraced by kings and ecclesiastical leaders because the relationship with French monastic orders was already strong and because France had become Europe's arbiter of style.

However, the question is not why the Leon Cathedral was built in the Gothic style, but why Teruel's churches were not. Between Islamic mudejar architecture and French Gothic, the patrons in Teruel had a choice which was exercised in favor of the mudejar. Clearly, the selection of architectural style was not arbitrary; style had meaning, communicating as a language communicates, and here mudejar style announced an identity. Oddly enough, whereas Gothic was employed at Leon because it was French, in Teruel mudejar was employed because it was *not* French. Despite Islamic roots, it was recognized as more Spanish than the imported Gothic style. In Teruel—not patronized by Cluny, not on the pilgrimage trail, and lacking a major cathedral the size of Leon or Burgos—the discourse had shifted from one of religion, to one of regionalism and cultural identity. The shift was by no means confined to Teruel: French architectural influence was waning throughout Spain by the end of the thirteenth century as an appropriately Spanish style was sought.

Mudejar was a style adopted elsewhere in Spain, too, the best known example being the Alcazar of Pedro I in Seville, built in 1364 on the foundations of an Islamic palace (fig. 7). He invited artisans from Granada to replicate the Alhambra's lovely courtyards (fig. 8) with slender arcades and lacy stucco in his Sevillian palace. Far from trying to Christianize or subdue the Islamic decorative vocabulary, Pedro appears to have revelled in its Islamicness even to the extent of allowing his workmen to place inscriptions in Arabic praising the building and its patron. There were compelling reasons for adopting the vocabulary of the Islamic palace, for the Alhambra had set the standard for luxury and magnificence in fourteenth-century Spain. Such deliberate copying occurred easily in the realm of secular palatine architecture where there was a common identity in royal luxury. This explanation does not suffice for church architecture where one might expect a glaring conflict on the grounds of religion, but there the discourse centered on the issue of self-definition. Mudejar art was perceived as Andalusian (a regional qualification) rather than Muslim.

ALCAZAR, SEVILLE
Figure 7

By the late thirteenth century Islam no longer posed a grave threat to the Christian kingdoms. After the Battle of Las Navas de Tolosa in 1212, the remaining Islamic kingdoms of Valencia, Murcia, Granada, and Almeria were subjugated through treaties, and to survive, each proved willing to betray the others. The Castilian policy of diplomatic divide and conquer was successful. Christianity was in ascendance, and the one remaining Islamic province was now a tolerated neighbor. As a result of the Reconquest, Christian kings ruled formerly Islamic territories with large Muslim populations in which the Christian and Jewish populations were heavily Arabicized. By the fourteenth century, Islam

ALHAMBRA'S COURT OF THE LION'S, GRANADA
Figure 8

was not a foreign presence, and its arts—already appropriated in the tenth century—were now assimilated because Islamic (or mudejar) art served to identify Spanish culture vis-à-vis that of the French.[67]

The changing response to Islam in the illustrations of the Beatus commentary and the mudejar architecture is best explained by two relationships: that between the northern kingdoms and al-Andalus, and that between northern Spain and France. Whereas in the tenth century Islam was a worrisome foe, the balance eventually tipped the other way. As the Christian kingdoms gained strength, supported by the Roman Catholic church and powerful French monastic orders, the old association with the Visigothic past was exchanged for an association with Andalusian Islam which by then was thoroughly domesticated. Islamic art was Spanish.

---

[67] Geneviève Barbé makes a similar point regarding the selection of style in sixteenth-century Aragon. Whereas private palaces were generally Italianate, public buildings were mudejar because the latter was, by then, an expression of Aragonese patrimony ("Mudejarismo en el arte aragones del siglo XVI," in *Simposio internacional de mudejarismo, I Actas [Teruel, 1975]* [Madrid, 1981], 166).

TEXTUALIZING AMBIVALENCE IN ISLAMIC SPAIN:

ARABIC REPRESENTATIONS OF ISMĀ'ĪL IBN NAGHRĪLAH

ROSS BRANN *

DESPITE ITS REPUTATION as a highly tolerant society and its romanticized popular image as an interfaith utopia, Muslim Spain of the High Middle Ages was repeatedly torn by tribal and ethnic social cleavages, and socio-economic struggles and factional rivalries among Andalusian-Arabs, Berbers, the *ṣaqāliba*, and Mozarabic Christians. For their part the Jews prospered materially under Muslim rule and apparently ranked among the most acculturated and politically complacent groups in the society. They readily accepted Muslim political and cultural hegemony and, until the rivalries between the *taifa* kingdoms of the eleventh century, seem to have had no stake in the various internecine disputes among Muslims. Associations between Muslims and Jews in al-Andalus nevertheless seem to have been charged on occasion and, it appears, marked by contradiction. On the one hand were extended periods of calm and tolerance; on the other were sporadic outbreaks of tension, reaction, and deteriorating relations between the two communities.

Research on this complex relationship has primarily relied upon the "direct testimony" of historical chronicles, *adab* and travel literature, legal codes and responsa, literary polemics, documentary materials pertaining to Spain preserved in the Cairo Genizah,[1] and to a lesser extent upon

* Research for this essay was made possible by fellowships from the National Endowment for the Humanities and the John Simon Guggenheim Memorial Foundation. The author wishes to thank both institutions for their generous support.

[1] On the extent of *genizah* materials pertaining to Spain, see S. D. Goitein, *A Mediterranean Society: The Jewish Communities of the Arab World As Portrayed in the Documents of the Cairo Geniza* [six vols.] (Berkeley: University of California Press, 1967–1993),

information culled from imaginative narratives and poetry. Have these various documentary and literary sources been exhausted or if we ask different questions of them can they legitimately be read in new ways? Apart from their significance as primary materials for the political, social and cultural history of al-Andalus the texts which have come down to us are insufficiently utilized as sources for exploring the nuances of how the Muslims and Jews of al-Andalus thought of and lived with one another during the High Middle Ages. In the words of Brian Stock:

> Accounting for what actually happened is now recognized to be only part of the story; the other part is the record of what individuals thought was happening, and the ways in which their feelings, perceptions, and narratives of events either influenced or were influenced by the realities they faced.[2]

If we apply to medieval texts post-structuralist methods and insights critical to literary study such as Antonio Gramsci's that power is the power to represent we are likely to generate new readings of the sources —readings which emphasize the *construction of social meaning* and the reciprocal way in which texts both reflect and shape the attitudes of the society in which they are produced. Issues of power relations among social groups, for example, are frequently played out in textual representations of individuals and events, crisscrossing the imaginary textual boundary between the supposedly objective and the allegedly subjective, the "real" and the "imaginary."[3] Again, to cite Stock's keen formulation of the two orders of the textual experience:

1:70. On business partnerships among Jews and Muslims in Spain, see *A Mediterranean Society*, 1:428.

[2] Brian Stock, "History, Literature, and Medieval Textuality," *Yale French Studies* 70 (1986): 7.

[3] As explained by the critic W. J. T. Mitchell, "Representation," *Critical Terms for Literary Study,* edited by Frank Lenticchia and Thomas McLaughlin (Chicago: University of Chicago Press, 1990), 15: "representation...can never be completely divorced from political and ideological questions; one might argue, in fact, that representation is precisely the point where these questions are most likely to enter a (literary) work. If literature is a "representation of life" then representation is exactly the place where "life," in all its social and subjective complexity, gets into the literary work."

> The historical is not isolated from the literary as fact and representation. The two aspects of the textual experience are multidimensional, and the objectivity of the alleged events spills over into the alleged subjectivity of the records, perceptions, feelings and observations.[4]

Whereas the fabulous aspects of Latin and Arabic accounts of the Muslim conquest of Spain have been recognized[5] the literary construction of the Jew and Muslim in Hispano-Arabic and Hispano-Hebrew historiography, *adab* literature, narratives and poetry has yet to be studied. We may thus re-read Arabic (and Hebrew) annalistic and literary sources *as texts,* reconsidering what they choose to report (and not to report) and examining *how* they relate, that is, their discursive language, narrative and rhetorical strategies, and their historically contingent relationship to other forms of cultural discourse.

How then did Muslim and Jewish literary intellectuals represent members of one another's community? The slavishly fawning lyrics of the Hispano-Arabic poet al-Munfatil in praise of Samuel ibn Naghrīlah,[6] for example, or the positive representation of Jewish courtiers and intellectuals such as Ḥasdai ibn Shapruṭ or Abū al-Faḍl ibn Ḥasdai in Ṣā'id al-Andalusī's (b. 1029) *Ṭabaqāt al-umam* seem completely at odds with the notorious attacks on the Jews produced by 'Alī ibn Ḥazm (d. 1064) and Abū Isḥāq of Elvira (d. 1067) devised during nearly the same time and in the same place. For their part, Hebrew and Judeo-Arabic texts from the period oscillate between a willingness to represent trenchant Muslim foes in a negative light as in Ibn Naghrīlah's (d. 1056) poetic portrayal of

---

4 Stock, "History, Literature and Medieval Textuality," 16.

5 See Roger Collins, *The Arab Conquest of Spain, 710-797* (Oxford: Basil Blackwell, 1989), 17-18; 23-36, and 'Abdulwāḥid Dhanūn Ṭāha, *The Muslim Conquest and Settlement of North Africa and Spain* (London and New York: Routledge, 1989), 84-93.

6 Ibn Bassām Al-Shantarīnī, *al-Dhakhīrah fī maḥāsin ahl al-jazīrah,* 8 vols. ed. Iḥsān 'Abbās (Beirut: Dār al-Thaqāfah, 1979), part 1 vol. 2:761-65. This text and the tradition transmitted in Ibn Bassām's own name are analyzed in my work-in-progress, *Power in the Portrayal: Representations of Muslims and Jews in Islamic Spain.* For a preliminary discussion of this text, see Ross Brann, "Imáges de judios en la literatura hispano-árabe," in *La Sociedad medieval a través de la literatura hispano judia,* eds. R. Izquierdo and A. Sáenz-Badillos (Toledo: Universidad de Castilla – La Mancha, forthcoming 1997).

the 'Abbādids of Seville and a deep-seated reluctance to portray Muslims in any light, almost to the point of silence.

For purposes of this paper, part of a larger project devoted to mapping literary reflections of power relations among Jews and Muslims in al-Andalus, I would like to concentrate on the figure of Samuel the Nagid, known in Arabic historiography as [Abū Ibrāhīm] Ismā'īl ibn Naghrīlah [993–1056]. Rabbinic scholar, Hebrew poet and grammarian, and arguably the most significant Jewish cultural mediator of the eleventh century, Ibn Naghrīlah was also a highly skilled *kātib*, who began a gradual rise through the ranks of the state chancery around 1020 to prominence at the court of Zirid Granada. As a consequence of the unique range of his literary and scholarly activities and his political savvy and opportunism Samuel's stature grew along parallel tracks in two distinct domains, the Muslim civic sphere and the specifically Jewish social and cultural milieu. In the latter Ibn Naghrīlah came to assume the eminent role of Nagid, the unofficial head of the Jews of al-Andalus,[7] whereas in the former he functioned as the highest fiscal (*jibāyat al-māl*; revenue collection) and administrative official of the Banū Zīrī from 1038 until his death in 1056. Ibn Naghrīlah may have served Granada in some military capacity as well. According to the forty-one so-called "war poems" and their Arabic superscriptions preserved in his *dīwān* the poet accompanied the army of Granada on some twenty expeditions, although the nature and extent of his involvement, unattested in any Arabic source, are open to question.[8]

Ismā'īl ibn Naghrīlah, the Nagid, is thus an ideal subject for a study of Arabic representations of Jews in Muslim Spain on account of his sin-

---

[7] According to Abraham ibn Daud, *Sefer ha-Qabbalah*, ed. and trans. Gerson D. Cohen (Philadelphia: Jewish Publication Society, 1967), 56 [*Book of Tradition*, 74], the title was apparently conferred upon him around 1027.

[8] The texts and superscriptions may be found in Dov Yarden (ed.) *Dīwān sh*ᵉ*mu'el ha-nagid* [Vol. 1, *Ben T*ᵉ*hillim*] (Jerusalem: Hebrew Union College Press, 1966), 3-145. See Hayyim Schirmann, "The Wars of Samuel the Nagid" [Hebrew] reprinted in *Studies in the History of Hebrew Poetry and Drama* [2 vols.] (Jerusalem: Mossad Bialik, 1979), 1:149-89, and Angel Sáenz-Badillos and Judit Targarona Borras, *Šĕmu'el ha-Nagid, Poemas I: Desde el Campo de Batalla Granada 1038-1056* (Cordoba: Ediciones El Almendro, 1988).

gular importance as a protean figure to the Jews of that land during the eleventh century, the influence he achieved and political power he wielded within al-Andalus, and the variety of Arabic (and Hebrew) texts in which he is mentioned. If (as noted above) these texts have been handled as direct historical testimony on Ibn Naghrīlah's role in the affairs of Muslims and Jews respectively,[9] how has the attitude of the texts toward Ibn Naghrīlah been assessed by modern readers? Conventional wisdom is divided on this question. Several scholars emphasize that Ibn Naghrīlah was highly regarded by the Arab chroniclers of Spain especially for his "modesty, prudence, and munificence"[10] and that "Muslim writers...speak of Samuel with great respect."[11] Reading the same sources others conclude that Muslim writers (with the notable exception of Ṣā'id al-Andalusī) speak of Ibn Naghrīlah with enmity and contempt.[12] Clearly, the construction of Ibn Naghrīlah in Hispano-Arabic literature can be seen as unstable and complex rather than as determined and unambiguous.[13] The problem lies in the texts as much as between the readers.

---

[9] David J. Wasserstein, "Samuel ibn Naghrīla ha-Nagid and Islamic Historiography in al-Andalus," *al-Qanṭara* xiv (1993): 109-25, recently showed how investigation of the historical Ibn Naghrīlah has proceeded along strictly divided linguistic and cultural lines. Wasserstein insightfully calls for a new inclusive approach to Ibn Naghrīlah that would utilize all of the available sources.

[10] See Amin T. Tibi (trans.), *The Tibyān: Memoirs of 'Abd Allāh b. Buluggīn Last Zīrid Amir of Granada* (Leiden: Brill, 1986), 206. In this respect Ismā'īl is typically contrasted with his son Yūsuf who is portrayed as conceited and arrogant. See Henri Pérès, *La poésie andalouse en arab classique au xie siècle*, 2nd ed. (Paris: Adrien-Maisonneuve, 1953), 270.

[11] Sarah Stroumsa, "From Muslim Heresy to Jewish-Muslim Polemics: Ibn al-Rāwandī's *Kitāb al-Dāmigh*," *Journal of the American Oriental Society* 107 (1987): 769. So too Arie Schippers, *Spanish Hebrew Poetry and the Arabic Literary Tradition: Arabic Themes in Hebrew Andalusian Poetry* (Leiden: E. J. Brill, 1994), 54, who writes: "Muslim sources speak favourably of Samuel han-Nagid."

[12] For example see S. M. Stern, "Two New Data About Ḥasdai B. Shapruṭ" [Hebrew] *Zion* 11 (1946): 143 [n. 6], and Neḥemya Allony, "Songs of Zion in the Poetic Works of R. Shmuel Hanagid" [Hebrew], *Sinai* 68 (1971): 212-15.

[13] See the various lines of verse concerning Ibn Naghrīlah assembled by Pérès, *La poésie andalouse en arab classique*, 268-73.

Ṣā'id al-Andalusī — *Ṭabaqāt al-umam*

Let us now turn to the representative texts, first a brief passage found at the close of the final chapter (Chapter 14 devoted to the Banū Isrā'īl and their descendants the Jews) of Ṣā'id b. Aḥmad al-Andalusī's universal history of science and culture, *Ṭabaqāt al-umam*. Ṣā'id al-Andalusī, it should be noted, was a *qāḍī* in Toledo and, according to the testimony of *Ṭabaqāt al-umam*, a historian of science committed to the transconfessional search for truth.[14]

The seemingly insignificant and laconic passage in *Ṭabaqāt al-umam* presents Ibn Naghrīlah in a completely positive light. He is introduced by his *kunya* Abū Ibrāhīm, a sign of respect:[15]

> Of those (experts in Jewish law) who lived in al-Andalus, we have Abū Ibrāhīm Ismā'īl ibn Yūsuf al-Kātib, known by the name of al-Ghazal, who worked in the service of al-'Amīr Bādīs ibn Ḥabbūsh al-Ṣanhājī, the king of Granada and its provinces. *He was the director* [*mudabbir*] *of the state. He knew the Jewish laws and how to defend and protect them more than any other Jewish scholar of al-Andalus.*[16] [emphasis mine].

The text notes Ibn Naghrīlah's pre-eminent administrative (i.e., political) position within Islamic Granada, passing over it without protest.

---

[14] On this attitude as manifested in Baghdad during the High Middle Ages and the inclusion of non-Muslim minorities in the intellectual and cultural life of the age, see Joel L. Kramer, *Humanism in the Renaissance of Islam: The Cultural Revival during the Buyid Age* (Leiden: E. J. Brill, 1986), 75-86.

[15] See Ignaz Goldziher, *Muslim Studies*, [2 vols.] ed. S. M. Stern; trans. C. R. Barber and S. M. Stern (London: George Allen and Unwin Ltd., 1967), 1:242.

[16] Ṣā'id ibn Aḥmad al-Andalusī, *Ṭabaqāt al-umam*, ed. Louis Cheiko (Beirut: al-Maṭba'ah al-Kāthūlīkiyyah lil-Ābā' al-Yasū'iyyin, 1912), 90; *Science in the Medieval World*, trans. Sema'an I. Salem and Alok Kumar (Austin: University of Texas Press, 1991), 82. Compare the translations of Joshua Finkel, "An Eleventh Century Source for the History of Jewish Scientists in Mohammedan Land (Ibn Ṣā'id)," *Jewish Quarterly Review* 18 (1927): 54, "Abū Ibrāhīm's mastery of the Talmud and his skill for its vindication were such that none of his predecessors in Spain ever displayed" and Moshe Perlmann, "Eleventh-Century Andalusian Authors on the Jews of Granada," *Proceedings of the American Academy for Jewish Research* 18 (1948–49): 271, "He was learned in the law of the Jews and understood how to prevail in disputes on its behalf and to rebut its opponents."

More revealing is the observation of Samuel's distinctive role within Jewish society: he is identified as one who not only possesses expert knowledge of religious law but also as one who strives successfully to "protect and defend" its application and observance. The text thus projects a uniquely important value of *Islamic* behavior onto a Jewish communal leader and religious scholar operating within the context of his own religious community: Ibn Naghrīlah corresponds to the image of a just Muslim ruler whose obligation to uphold Islamic law defines his legitimacy in the eyes of God and Muslim society![17]

Is it a coincidence that such an image turns up in an eleventh-century Hispano-Arabic text even though the subject in question is a non-Muslim? The record of the various *mulūk al-ṭawā'if* in observing and maintaining Islamic law was continuously called into question by Muslim jurists, scholars and literati. Many writers go so far as to accuse the party kings of breaking faith with Islam, particularly for their excessive materialism, their association with *dhimmīs* and habit of elevating non-Muslims to positions of authority.[18] Such charges were by no means unique to eleventh-century al-Andalus. Similar criticism was sounded in the Muslim East regarding the ruler's betrayal of Islamic values in showing preferences to Jews and Christians.[19] Because appointment of non-Muslims

---

[17] On the ruler's obligation to uphold the *sharī'ah* and the nomenclature used to describe various types of rulers in Islam, see Bernard Lewis, "Usurpers and Tyrants: Notes on Some Islamic Political Terms," in *Logos Islamikos: Studia Islamica in Honorem Georgii Michaelis Wickens*, ed. Roger M. Savory and Dionisius A. Agius (Toronto: Pontifical Institute of Mediaeval Studies, 1984), 259ff.

[18] Several prooftexts for this pious complaint are discussed in David Wasserstein, *The Rise and Fall of the Party Kings: Politics and Society in Islamic Spain, 1002–1086* (Princeton: Princeton University Press, 1985), 280. So too 'Alī ibn Ḥazm, "*Al-Radd 'alā ibn al-naghrīlah al-yahūdī*," in *Rasā'il ibn ḥazm al-andalusī*, 4 vols. ed. Iḥsān 'Abbās (Beirut: al-Mu'assasah al-'arabiyyah lil-dirāsāt wal-nashr, 1980–83), 3:41; 67, on which see below. For a faint echo of a complaint about Ḥasdai ibn Shapruṭ who served as a physician and diplomat at the court of 'Abd al-Raḥmān III, see the line of verse preserved in Ibn Rushd's (d. 1198) *Talkhīṣ kitāb arisṭūṭālīs fil-shi'r*, trans. Charles E. Butterworth, *Averroes' Middle Commentary on Aristotle's Poetics* (Princeton: Princeton University Press, 1980), 115, and Stern, "Two New Data about Ḥasdai B. Shapruṭ," 141.

[19] See the account of the Caliph al-Ma'mūn's experience with an influential but

to high government office was a persistent source of complaint,[20] the image of Ibn Naghrīlah as upholder of [Jewish] holy law *and* "director of the [Islamic] state" serves as a doubly ironic comment on the Islamic scene.

Ibn Ḥayyān — *al-Iḥāṭah fī akhbār gharnāṭah (Ibn al-Khaṭīb)*

A more fully drawn portrait of Ibn Naghrīlah emerges in a tradition reported by the great Hispano-Arabic historian Abū Marwān Ibn Ḥayyān al-Qurṭubī (987/8–1076). It is transmitted in *al-Iḥāṭah fī akhbār gharnāṭah,* a chronicle of Granada compiled by the fourteenth-century Andalusi scholar Ibn al-Khaṭīb (1313–1375):

> This cursed man was a superior man, although God did not inform him of the right religion. He possessed extensive knowledge and tolerated insolent behavior with patience. He combined a solid and wise character with a lucid spirit and polite and friendly manners. Endowed with refined courtesy, he was able to utilize any circumstances to flatter his enemies or to disarm their hatred with his kind conduct. He was an extraordinary man. He wrote in both languages: Arabic and Hebrew. He knew the literatures of both peoples. He went deeply into the principles of the Arabic language and was familiar with the works of the most subtle grammarians. He spoke and wrote classical Arabic with the greatest ease, using this language in the letters which he wrote on behalf on his king. He used the usual Islamic formulas, the eulogies of God and

---

brazen Jew and similar stories transmitted by Ghāzī ibn al-Wāsiṭī (thirteenth century), "*Radd 'alā ahl al-dhimmah wa-man taba'ahum,*" ed. and trans. by Richard Gottheil, "An Answer to the Dhimmīs," *Journal of the American Oriental Society* 41 (1927): text, 396; trans., 429-30. On public opposition to Jewish officials in Fatimid Egypt, see Walter J. Fischel, *Jews in the Economic and Political Life of Mediaeval Islam* (London: The Royal Asiatic Society, 1937), 88-89, and Goitein, *A Mediterranean Society,* 2:374ff. On *dhimmī* public service in general, see Arthur S. Tritton, *The Caliphs and their Non-Muslim Subjects: A Critical Study of the Covenant of 'Umar* (London: Oxford University Press, 1930; reprinted London: Frank Cass, 1970), 18-36, and now Mark R. Cohen, *Under Crescent and Cross: The Jews in the Middle Ages* (Princeton: Princeton University Press, 1994), 65-68.

[20] Bernard Lewis, *The Jews of Islam* (Princeton: Princeton University Press, 1984), 28ff.

> Muḥammad, our Prophet, and recommended to the addressee to live according to Islam. In brief, one would believe that his letters were written by a pious Muslim. He was excellent in the sciences of the ancients, in mathematics as well as astronomy. Also in the field of logic he possessed ample knowledge. In dialectics he even prevailed over his adversaries. Despite his lively spirit he spoke little and reflected much. He assembled a beautiful library. He died on the 10th of Muḥarram, 459 A.H. The Jews decorated his coffin and bowed in deference (as it passed by). They held fast to him in their anguish and mourned him publicly.[21]

Apart from its perfunctory reference to Samuel's "accursed" religious identity, the *Iḥāṭah* like *Ṭabaqāt al-umam* casts Ibn Naghrīlah in an uncommonly favorable light. The text attributes to him every conceivable trait of a noble and aristocratic character: refined manners, disarming resourcefulness in dealing with associates and enemies, linguistic skill and eloquence, and literary and scientific knowledge and learning such as were valued in al-Andalus and all of medieval Islam.

Ibn Ḥayyān's depiction of Ismā'īl is at least as significant for what it neglects to report as for what it relates. The tradition transmitted in his name by Ibn al-Khaṭīb alludes to but makes no explicit mention of Ibn Naghrīlah's pivotal role in the political and financial administration of Zirid Granada. In this respect the text can be said portray Ibn Naghrīlah as a "mere" court secretary, a singularly gifted and important one to be sure, but certainly not as a central actor in the exercise of the power of the Islamic state. This striking omission is rectified and balanced by the previous source reported by Ibn al-Khaṭīb, a brief citation from *al-Bayān al-mughrib* by Ibn 'Idhārī al-Marrākushī. Ibn 'Idhārī identifies Ibn Naghrīlah as an essential figure in the exercise of power in Zirid Granada. As though it were a case in point of the harm which comes to Islam when a non-Muslim attains such a position the text reports that Ibn Naghrīlah and the lower-level Jewish functionaries who accompanied his designa-

[21] Ibn Ḥayyān quoted by Lisān al-Dīn ibn al-Khaṭīb, *Al-Iḥāṭah fī akhbār gharnāṭah*, 2 vols. ed. Muḥammad 'Abd Allāh 'Inān (Cairo: al-Khanjī Bookshop, 1973), 1:438-39, partial trans. Schippers, *Spanish Hebrew Poetry and the Arabic Literary Tradition*, 54-55.

tion as *wazīr* amassed wealth and displayed arrogant behavior toward the Muslims.[22]

'Abd Allāh b. Buluggīn, the last *amīr* of Zirid Granada (r. 1073–90), takes a completely different approach to portraying Ibn Naghrīlah in *al-Tibyān*. In sharp contrast to Ibn 'Idhārī's renegade Jewish *wazīr* 'Abd Allāh's revisionist historical memoir makes Ismā'īl out to be a perspicacious political operator who conducts his affairs responsibly in the interests of the ruler and the state. Moreover Ibn Naghrīlah accepts working in accordance with the sensibilities of Muslims and within the limits circumscribed for *dhimmī* subjects by Islamic law. 'Abd Allāh asserts with complete assurance that

> Abū Ibrāhīm was a Jewish *dhimmī* who would not lust after power... Abū Ibrāhīm, however, was not accorded any power over Muslims in any issue whether right or wrong.[23]

Based on the poetic account of the Nagid's military exploits in his *dīwān* and the extent of his political and financial functions described in other Arabic sources, it appears that the *Tibyān* aims to minimize Ibn Naghrīlah's role in the affairs of state in order to salvage Bādīs' ('Abd Allāh's grandfather) sullied reputation as a pious Muslim.[24]

To return to Ibn Ḥayyān: The *Iḥāṭah* presents Ibn Naghrīlah as the veritable embodiment of courtly virtues and secretarial skills. Most sig-

---

[22] Ibn al-Khaṭīb, *al-Iḥāṭah*, 1:438, and Ibn 'Idhārī al-Marrākushī, *al-Bayān al-mughrib fī akhbār al-maghrib*, ed. E. Lévi-Provençal (Beirut: Dār al-Thaqāfah, 1930; reprinted 1967) 3:264. When Yaddayr schemed to depose his cousin Bādīs (1038) Ibn Naghrīlah came to the aid of the new *amīr*. He foiled the plot, bringing down the (Muslim) conspirators as a result. The Nagid describes his and Granada's final reckoning with Yaddayr (1041) in two very long poems, "*She'eh mini 'amiti we-ḥaveri*," *Dīwān shemu'el ha-nagid*, 1:31-34 [#7] and "*Levavi ham be-qirbi*," 1:35-38 [#9]. These lyrics are noteworthy for the way in which they establish a correspondence between the poet's personal adversaries and the enemies of Israel, that is, the Jews. The literary construction of Muslims in the Nagid's poetry will be studied in my monograph-in-progress on representations of Muslims and Jews in Islamic Spain.

[23] *The Tibyān*, 55-56.

[24] *The Tibyān*, 211; Lisān al-Dīn ibn al-Khaṭīb, *A'māl al-a'lām fī man būyi'a qabl al-iḥtilām min mulūk al-islām*, ed. E. Lévi-Provençal (Beirut: Dār al-Makshūf, 1956), 232. The *Tibyān*'s portrayal of Yūsuf ibn Naghrīlah is another matter.

nificantly Ibn Naghrīlah is lauded for his exquisite use of the appropriate formulas of Islamic piety in his correspondence on behalf of the Zirids.[25] What with the words of the inimitable Qur'ān flowing from his stylus if not literally from his lips, Samuel's Jewishness is something of a marvel to behold, nearly more apparent than real. Signs of Ibn Naghrīlah's cultural otherness are limited to his knowledge of Hebrew language and literature. Reference to any form of behavior contrary to Islam and abhorrent or incomprehensible to Muslims is suppressed. Much like the image of the noble Moor in the *Poema de Mio Cid* (c. 1207)[26] the figure of Ibn Naghrīlah in *al-Iḥāṭah* is less a Jew than a Jew inscribed in the text, an emblem of an idealized *dhimmī* who is a Muslim in all but name.[27]

---

[25] The legendary vignette [preserved by Abraham ibn Daud, *Sefer ha-qabbalah,* 54-55; *The Book of Tradition,* 72-73, and for which S. M. Stern, "The Life of Samuel the Nagid" [Hebrew], *Zion* 15 (1950):135-38, identified a Hispano-Arabic parallel in a tale of how al-Manṣūr's eloquence and stylistic gifts hastened his ascent to power] concerning Samuel's accidental "discovery" in a Malagan spice shop is a significant illustration of the ecumenical importance of the rhetorical ideal of life, and for the Jews of Spain expert knowledge of Arabic. Saadia ibn Danān (15th century), "*Ha-ma'amar 'al seder ha-dorot,*" in Zvi Hirsch Edelmann (ed.), *Ḥemdah genuzah* (Koenigsberg: Gruber and Guphrat, 1856), 29a = Judit Targarona, "*Ha-ma'amar 'al seder ha-dorot* de Se'adyah ibn Danan: Edición, Traducción y Notas," *Miscelanea de Estudios Arabes y Hebraicos* xxxv (1986): 96, furthermore relates that the Nagid composed a seven-line panegyric in seven languages ("each verse in a different language") for the *amīr* Ḥabbūs. So too the famous "ethical will" of Judah ibn Tibbon to his son: "you know that the great men of our people attained their greatness and many virtues only because of their ability in writing Arabic. You have already seen what the Nagid, of blessed memory, said about the greatness he achieved through it...The achievement of his son as well was due to it"; trans. Israel Abrahams, *Hebrew Ethical Wills* [2 vols.] (Philadelphia: Jewish Publication Society, 1926), 1:59.

[26] Here I have benefited from reading Israel Burshatin, "The Moor in the Text: Metaphor, Emblem, and Silence," in Henry Louis Gates, Jr. (ed.), "*Race, Writing, and Difference* (Chicago and London: University of Chicago Press, 1986), 117-39.

[27] It should also be noted that the date given by Ibn Ḥayyān for Ibn Naghrīlah's death is none other than the tenth of Muḥarram, a Muslim holy day (*'Āshūrā'*) and the most sacred day in the Shī'ī liturgical calendar. Ibn Ḥayyān's tradition may belong among the (Sunnī) texts linking the Shī'ah with the Jews. See now Steven M. Wasserstrom, "The Shī'īs Are the Jews of our Community": An Interreligious Comparison Within Sunnī Thought," *Israel Oriental Studies* 14 (1994): 297-324.

ʻAlī Ibn Ḥazm—*al-Fiṣal fil-milal; al-Radd ʻalā ibn al-Naghrīlah al-yahūdī*

The figure of Samuel ibn Naghrīlah is also a subject in a text, possibly two texts, by ʻAlī ibn Ḥazm [994–1064], the outstanding Hispano-Arabic literary intellectual of the eleventh century. The texts present a fundamentally different portrait of Ibn Naghrīlah than either Ṣāʻid b. Aḥmad al-Andalusī or Ibn Ḥayyān al-Qurṭubī. They are of interest not only because of their extensive treatment of Samuel but also on account of Ibn Ḥazm's personal acquaintance with the subject of his remarks.[28]

Shortly after the collapse of the unified Islamic state in Spain (1013) during a period of profound social and political unrest Ibn Ḥazm and Ibn Naghrīlah were forced to flee Cordoba on account of the Berber riots that sacked the city. Ibn Ḥazm made his way to Almeria; Ibn Naghrīlah sought refuge in Malaga. As had been his practice in Cordoba Ibn Ḥazm consulted and often debated other religious scholars and literary intellectuals, including Jews and Christians. In this way he came into contact with Samuel in 1013, probably in Almeria. Although no mention of it is made in any Jewish source a report of their meeting and debate is preserved in Ibn Ḥazm's monumental heresiography *al-Fiṣal fil-milal wa-ahwāʼ wal-niḥal* (*Book of Opinions on Religions, Sects, and Heresies*) written between 1027 and 1030 but incorporating material from another, now lost work refuting Judaism and Christianity entitled *Iẓhār tabdīl al-yahūd*

[28] As noted above my primary interest lies in examining the figure of the Nagid represented in the texts—not in utilizing the sources for rehearsing details of Samuel's biography. Thus in addressing the early encounter between Ibn Ḥazm and Ibn Naghrīlah I am not specifically concerned with the specific views of Judaism set forth by Muslim heresiographers except insofar as their ideas are reflected in the literary construction of the Jew and might inform the attitude and behavior of Muslims toward Jews in eleventh-century al-Andalus. The subject of religious polemics between Muslims and Jews in including Ibn Ḥazm has now been capably and dispassionately studied by Steven M. Wasserstrom, *Species of Misbelief: A History of Muslim Heresiography of the Jews*, unpublished doctoral dissertation (University of Toronto, 1985), and Camilla Adang, *Muslim Writers on Judaism and the Hebrew Bible from Ibn Rabban to Ibn Hazm* (Leiden: E. J. Brill, 1996).

wal-naṣārā lil-tawrāt wal-injīl (*Exposure of Jewish and Christian Falsifications in the Torah and Gospels*).[29]

Al-Fiṣal introduces Ibn Naghrīlah as "the most knowledgeable and the most accomplished debater among the Jews."[30] It is scarcely surprising that Ibn Ḥazm would acknowledge Samuel's merits in the context of this report, if only because so excellent a disputant as 'Alī surely deserved to be matched against an intellectually worthy, although religiously misguided opponent. Ibn Naghrīlah's forensic talent aside *al-Fiṣal* expresses contempt for Judaism and antipathy towards its adherents.[31] The text's disdain for the Jews proceeds primarily from familiar Islamic theological objections with Judaism, chiefly the "unreliable transmission" (*tawātur*) of the corrupted Hebrew Bible (*taḥrīf*) and the counterfeit Jewish tradition of the rabbis. Nevertheless readers of *al-Fiṣal* have long been struck by the abrasive manner with which it transfers rejection of the belief onto the believers themselves:

> They, both the ancient and the contemporary, are altogether the worst liars. Though I have encountered many of them, I have never seen among them a truth seeker, except two men only.[32]

For a heresiographical text to take issue with doctrinal claims put forward by a rival monotheism and reject the validity of its tradition is perfectly understandable. That, after all, is the purpose of such a text. Yet to our rhetorical sensibility as readers only a degree of *al-Fiṣal*'s caustic argumentation against Judaism and the Jews can reasonably be attributed to the requirements of the genre and its style. Ibn Ḥazm's vitriolic treatment of Christianity and Christians in *al-Fiṣal* is in fact characterized

---

[29] On the incorporation of the earlier into the later work, see Perlmann, "Eleventh-Century Andalusian Authors," 270.

[30] *Al-Fiṣal fil-milal wal-ahwā' wal-niḥal,* 5 vols. in 2 (photocopy of Cairo ed. 1899–1903; Baghdad, 1964), 1:152.

[31] Perlmann, "Andalusian Authors," 271, refers to the sections in *al-Fiṣal* as "the only extensive work written by a Muslim author on the subject; it is the only work of anti-Jewish polemics written by one of the great minds of Islam."

[32] *Al-Fiṣal,* 1:156 (trans. Perlmann, "Andalusian Authors," 279) and elsewhere follows the Qur'anic prooftext (5:41-45) on the Jews' innately mendacious nature.

by similar rhetorical excesses. Many readers have also noted 'Alī's stylistic trademark—his tendency to engage various opponents, including Muslims not belonging to the Ẓāhirī *madhhab*, with hyperbolic and venomous language. Ibn Ḥazm's blanket condemnation of the national character of the Jews, while perhaps deeply felt and drawing upon the Qur'anic topos of the deceitfulness of the Jews, appears to be a function of the discursive style established by al-Jāḥiẓ (d. 869) in the ninth century.[33]

The text of *al-Fiṣal* (noted above) spares Samuel as the central target of its spirited barbs. But labeling all (but two) Jews, ancient and modern, mendacious in effect renders their written and spoken discourse undeserving of serious attention. It thus serves to dismiss and *silence them* and to marginalize Ibn Naghrīlah as unrepresentative of his religious and textual community. An even more blunt articulation of this polemical and rhetorical strategy is *Ifḥām al-yahūd* (*Silencing the Jews*), a tract by Samau'al al-Maghribī a twelfth-century Jewish convert to Islam residing in the Muslim East.[34] Moses Maimonides, a refugee from Almohad persecution in Spain and North Africa, further testifies to the diffusion of this topos and the apparent effectiveness of its message at some times and in some places in the famous "Epistle to Yemen" which characterizes the Jews as a people required "to bear its suffering [under Islam] *in silence*."[35]

---

[33] See J. Sadan, "Some Literary Concerning Judaism and Jewry in Medieval Arabic Sources," *Studies in Islamic History and Civilization in Honour of David Ayalon*, ed. M. Sharon (Jerusalem: Cana, 1986), 353ff., and Joshua Finkel, "A Risāla of al-Jāḥiẓ," *Journal of the American Oriental Society* 47 (1927): 311-34.

[34] Samau'al al-Maghribī, *Ifḥām al-yahūd*, ed. and trans. Moshe Perlmann, *Proceedings of the American Academy for Jewish Research* 32 (1964).

[35] *Iggeret teiman le-rabbenu moshe ben maimon*, ed. Abraham S. Halkin (New York: American Academy for Jewish Research, 1952), 96; trans. in Abraham Halkin, *Crisis and Leadership: Epistles of Maimonides* (Philadelphia: Jewish Publication Society, 1985), 127. As the historian S. D. Goitein observed, *A Mediterranean Society*, 2:284, "Worship of the non-Muslim denominations under Islam had to be inconspicuous ...." While strictly addressing Christians the so-called "Pact of 'Umar" also applied to the Jews. That document states, trans. Bernard Lewis, *Islam* [Volume II: Religion and Society] (New York: Oxford University Press, 1987), 218: "We shall not display our crosses or our books in the roads or markets of Muslims. We shall only use our

The political subtext as opposed to strictly religious text of *al-Fiṣal's* discourse emerges in one of the crucial points of engagement in Ibn Ḥazm's report of the debate with Ibn Naghrīlah, namely, the famous discussion regarding the historical significance of Genesis 49:10 ("The scepter shall not depart from Judah, nor the ruler's staff from between his feet till Shiloh (i.e., "tribute") come [to him]").[36] Ibn Ḥazm's account emphasizes the Jews' loss of sovereignty:

> This verse is untrue because the scepter departed from Judah and leaders from his offspring,[37] but the One sent, whom they await, did not come. The kingdom of Judah found its end in the time of Nebuchadnezzar more than one thousand five hundred years ago... I have repeated this passage to one of the Jews' most learned polemicists, namely Ishmū'āl b. Yūsuf al-Lāwī, the famous author known as Ibn al-Naghrāl, in the year 1013. And he said to me: "The Exilarchs are the offspring of David and from the sons of Judah and they have leadership and kingdom and authority in our days." But I told him: "This is a mistake, because the Exilarch cannot exert power on the Jews or on anybody else and it is therefore a title only, but no reality."[38]

For the Jews of al-Andalus as elsewhere belief in the uninterrupted continuity of the "House of David" was a necessary and certain article of faith. Seemingly relegated to the margins of a history dominated by Islam and Christendom, at least they could look to the figure of the Exilarch or

---

clappers in our churches very softly. We shall not raise our voices in our church services or in the presence of Muslims, not shall we raise our voices when following our dead."

[36] *Al-Fiṣal,* 1:152-53.

[37] Although this passage avers that leadership of the Jews ("leaders from his offspring") departed from the House of David, in *Jamharat ansāb al-'arab,* ed. 'Abd al-Salām Muḥammad Hārūn (Cairo: Dār al-Ma'ārif, 1982), 506, Ibn Ḥazm asserts that the leaders of the Jews down to his day do indeed descend from David.

[38] Trans. Hava Lazarus-Yafeh, *Intertwined Worlds: Medieval Islam and Bible Criticism* (Princeton: Princeton University Press, 1992), 98-99. Lazarus-Yafeh notes Samau'al al-Maghribī's contrasting treatment of the biblical passage in Perlmann (ed.), *Ifḥām al-yahūd,* text: 23; trans.: 41-42. Ironically, Samuel the Nagid seems to have been partly responsible for moving the Jews of Spain away from complete dependence upon (if not allegiance to) the Eastern rabbinical authorities.

"Head of the Exile" (Heb. *ro'sh ha-golah*; Aram. *re'sh galuta'*; Ar. *ra's jālūt*) for a sign of hope in the messianic promises of their eventual political restoration (recorded in the Hebrew Bible).[39] Consider, for example, Benjamin of Tudela's (twelfth-century) account of his visit to Baghdad. In this blend of realia and fantasy we find a vivid depiction of the dignity of the *ro'sh ha-golah*. The Muslims of Baghdad, for whom the biblical David is a prophet, pay tribute to the Exilarch referring to him as "*sayyidnā bin dāwūd*."[40] According to Benjamin's imaginative reconstruction the ceremonious recognition of the Exilarch as a genuine sovereign and equal at the Caliph's court represents the literal realization of the prophecy voided by Ibn Ḥazm. Here are his words of encouragement for the disempowered Jews of his age:

> And the Head of the Captivity is seated on his throne opposite the Caliph, in compliance with the command of Muhammad, to give effect to what is written in the Law—"The scepter shall not depart from Judah..."[41]

Benjamin of Tudela's message of comfort notwithstanding Ibn Ḥazm was correct in assessing the actual authority of the Exilarch during the eleventh century. As the historian S. D. Goitein has shown, the Exilarch's power, like the caliph's, had long since declined. The *ro'sh ha-golah* was reduced to little more than an ecumenical figurehead and limited to dispensing honorific titles.[42] Real communal authority rested in the hands

---

[39] On the history of this office during the High Middle Ages, see Avraham Grossman, *The Babylonian Exilarchate in the Gaonic Period* [Hebrew] (Jerusalem: Merkaz Zalman Shazar, 1984).

[40] Benjamin of Tudela, *Sefer massa'ot,* ed. and trans. Marcus Adler, *The Itinerary of Benjamin of Tudela,* (reprinted New York: Feldheim, 1960), ff. 61-63 [Engl. trans., 39-41].

[41] Benjamin of Tudela, *Sefer massa'ot*, f. 62; Adler, *The Itinerary,* 40. For a discussion of Benjamin's world and his message of consolation see the introduction by Michael A. Signer, *The Itinerary of Benjamin of Tudela* [*Travels in the Middle Ages*] (Malibu: Joseph Simon Pangloss Press, 1983), 13-33.

[42] S. D. Goitein, *A Mediterranean Society,* 2:17ff. On Muslim attitudes toward the Exilarch see Ignaz Goldziher, "Renseignements de source musulmane sur la dignité de *Resch-Galuta*," *Revue des Études Juifs* 8 (1884): 121-25, reprinted in *Gesammelte*

of the talmudic academies and their heads, the *g^e^onim.* Ibn Ḥazm's rejoinder to Samuel concerning the Exilarch goes further still, stripping the Jews of even the appearance of temporal power and wresting from them the semblance of hope for the future.[43] Perhaps the reader can sense in Ibn Ḥazm's rejection of the chain of symbolic Jewish political authority a sign of the Andalusi Muslim's dismay over the demise of the Umayyad caliphate in eleventh-century al-Andalus and his disgust at the succession of Umayyad pretenders to that dignified office.[44]

What of the second and chronologically later text in which Ibn Ḥazm mounts a frontal assault on Judaism, the Jews, and an unnamed opponent bearing a resemblance to Ismāʿīl ibn Naghrīlah? A comparison of the representation of Ibn Naghrīlah in *al-Fiṣal* and Ibn Ḥazm's literary adversary in the so-called *"Al-Radd ʿalā ibn al-naghrīlah al-yahūdī"* (*"The Refutation of Ibn Naghrīlah, the Jew"* = "The Refutation") is instructive, for the intellectually resourceful (although greatly mistaken) Ibn Naghrīlah in the former is replaced by a variously obtuse, base and diabolical figure in the later work. That figure has been identified with Ismāʿīl ibn Naghrīlah or alternately with his son and successor Yūsuf.[45] Embracing tradi-

Schriften, ed. Joseph Desomogyi (Hildesheim: Georg Olms Verlag, 1967–68), vol. 2: 132-36; Walter I. Fischel, "The *Resh Galuta* in Arabic Literature" [Hebrew], in *The Magnes Anniversary Book,* ed. F. I. Baer et al. (Jerusalem: Hebrew University Press, 1938), 181-87, and now on the specifically Shīʿī interest in this figure Wasserstrom, "'The Shīʿīs are the Jews of our Community'."

43 There are good reasons why Jewish messianism might appear seditious even if its prospects for realization were beyond reason. See Ross Brann, "Power in the Portrayal: Representations of Muslims and Jews in Judah al-Ḥarizi's *Taḥkemoni,*" *Princeton Papers in Near Eastern Studies* 1 (1992): 1-22.

44 On which see David J. Wasserstein, *The Caliphate in the West: An Islamic Political Institution in the Iberian Peninsula* (Oxford: Oxford University Press, 1993), 192-93.

45 In his introduction to *"Al-Radd," Rasāʾil ibn ḥazm,* 3:17, Iḥsān ʿAbbās reasons that the pamphlet's author was not Ismāʿīl but Yūsuf ibn Naghrīlah with whom such an impudent effort would supposedly have been more in character. ʿAbbās thus attempts to solve the problems associated with ascribing the work to the first Ibn Naghrīlah. Arabic historiography does indeed paint a more crass and insolent picture of the son than the father making Yūsuf a more likely candidate for authorship in ʿAbbās' thinking. Yet no mention is made of Yūsuf as the author in any other

tional elements from *tafsīr* and *ḥadīth* literature in its defense of Islam and polemic against Judaism, employing Qur'anic prooftexts cautioning Muslims to avoid fraternizing with *ahl al-dhimmah* (e.g., 3:118; 5:51-56), and incorporating arguments already employed in *Al-Fiṣal*, "The Refutation" is a piece of political propaganda as well as a religious polemic.[46] It nevertheless sets a new standard for vilification of a religious group.[47] As is well known Ibn Ḥazm supposedly undertook writing "The Refutation" when he learned a Jew had written a book exposing alleged inconsistencies and logical contradictions in the Qur'ān.[48] Unable to obtain a copy of the text Ibn Ḥazm reports that he had to rely upon the work of another Muslim scholar who had already come to the defense of Islam in refuting the arguments put forward by the Jew.[49] Without identifying the offending party Ibn Ḥazm signals his familiarity with him in the following cryptic remark:

> "By my life, the argument he makes demonstrates how limited is his knowledge and how narrow the extent of his understanding, *about which I already know something.*" [emphasis mine].[50]

Ibn Ḥazm's account and enigmatic comment notwithstanding there is much to suggest that "The Refutation" may have been undertaken as a politically motivated literary exercise rather than as a response to a contemporary anti-Qur'anic work.

---

source. See also Eliyahu Ashtor, *Qorot ha-yehudim bi-sfarad ha-muslimit*, 2 vols. (Jerusalem: Kiryat Sefer, 1960–66), 2:354 (note 116); Paul B. Fenton, "Jewish Attitudes to Islam: Israel Heeds Ishmael," *Jerusalem Quarterly* 29 (1983): 91, and the other sources cited by Stroumsa, "From Muslim Heresy to Jewish-Muslim Polemic," 770 [n. 28].

46 Wasserstein, *Rise and Fall*, 205.

47 See the comments of E. Garcia Gomez, "Polémica Religiosa entre Ibn Ḥazm e Ibn al-Naghrīla," *al-Andalus* 4 (1936): 3-5.

48 Ibn Ḥazm, "*Al-Radd*," 42.

49 "*Al-Radd*," 42. Following Stroumsa, Maribel Fierro, "Ibn Ḥazm et le *zindīq* juif," *Revue du monde musulman et de la Méditerranée* 63-64 (1992): 85, posits that al-Jubbā'ī served as Ibn Ḥazm's Muslim source for refuting the anti-Qur'anic arguments.

50 "*Al-Radd*," 43.

"The Refutation" may be outlined as follows: the Introduction assails the Jewish culprit and the party-kings who permit such and other offenses against Islam and Muslims (pp. 41-43); Part One in the form of eight chapters represents the body of the work as defined in the introduction (pp. 43-60). This is where the text undertakes a point-by-point defense of the problematic Qur'anic passage followed by a counterattack on passages in the Torah more objectionable than the one questioned in the Qur'ān. Part Two, an epilogue (pp. 60-67), mounts a full blown assault on the theological absurdities in the Hebrew Bible and rabbinic tradition. The conclusion (pp. 67-70) restates the reasons for which the treatise was composed and reiterates the shrill diatribe against the Jewish author, the Jews in general, and the party-kings who grant the Jews license. The puzzling structure of "The Refutation" thus appears to offer a means of grappling with the contradictions of the text and provides a key to its significance.[51]

Here is how Ibn Ḥazm acquaints the reader with his adversary and introduces the subject of the treatise:

> Now then, a man whose heart burns with enmity toward Islam and its adherents and whose liver is molten with hatred of the Messenger, may God bless him and grant him peace, [a man who subscribes] to the materialism of the heretics who hide among the lowest of religious communities and the most contemptible of religious doctrines, namely Judaism, the curse of God having fallen continuously upon its adherents, and His wrath—may He be exalted and magnified—having settled permanently on its followers. Arrogance has loosened this man's tongue and vanity has slackened his reins. The abundance of wealth in his possession has caused his disgraceful soul to become haughty, and the surfeit of gold and silver that he owns has inflated his despicable ambition, inducing him to write a treatise in which he expressly indicated his intention to expose (alleged) contradictions in the Word of God—may He be exalted and magnified—in the Qur'ān..., while disdainfully mocking both the men of religion and the political leadership.[52]

[51] Perlmann, "Andalusian Authors on the Jews of Granada," 281, already noted the difference between the tone of introduction and conclusion and the so-called "body" of the work. This difference is also noted by Stroumsa, Fierro and others.

[52] Ibn Ḥazm, "*Al-Radd*," 42-43. My thanks to my colleague David S. Powers for

The manifestly political discourse of the introduction is grounded entirely in the social and political scene of eleventh-century al-Andalus. It makes no pretense of contributing to the world of religious ideas but instead excoriates the depraved ruler in whose realm the Jew resides, assails the wealth and influence of the Jews, and decries the insolence, baseness and idiocy of the unnamed author. By contrast Part One deals with theological differences between Judaism and Islam such as those explored at length in *Al-Fiṣal* and in other heresiographical works such as al-Shāhrastānī (d. 1153) [*Al-Milal wal-niḥal*]. The conclusion of "The Refutation" returns to the universe of political discourse, issuing an ominous warning to the party kings and passing the sternest of judgments upon the responsible Jew:

> It is my firm hope that God will treat those who befriend the Jews and take them into their confidence as He treated the Jews themselves... For whosoever amongst Muslim princes has listened to all this and still continues to befriend the Jews, holding intercourse with them, well deserves to be overtaken by the same humiliation and to suffer in this world the same griefs meted out to the Jews...[53]

Anticipating the rhetorical strategy and political goal of Abū Isḥāq al-Ilbīrī's famous poetic diatribe against Yūsuf ibn Naghrīlah and the Jews of Granada[54] the text neither marginalizes nor robs the Jew of cultural otherness but demonizes him for violating the essential regulations of

---

making available to me his draft translation of the "The Refutation" on which this passage is partially based.

[53] Ibn Ḥazm, "*Al-Radd*," 67; trans. Perlmann, "Andalusian Authors on the Jews of Granada," 281-83. Ironically, Ibn Ḥazm, "*Al-Radd*," 68-69, envisions for the culpable Andalusian elite the wretched and accursed fate reserved for the Jews (i.e., Israelites) in the ultimate *biblical* prooftext (Deuteronomy 28). Ibn Ḥazm's critique of the authenticity of the Hebrew Bible to the contrary, Lazarus-Yafeh observes in *Intertwined Worlds*, 43-44 [n. 66], that Muslim writers sometimes found it useful to employ biblical prophetic passages rebuking the Israelites.

[54] Text in James T. Monroe, *Hispano-Arabic Poetry: A Student Anthology* (Berkeley: 1974), 206-13. For a detailed study of this poem in its historical context, see Bernard Lewis, "An Ode Against the Jews," in *Islam in History: Ideas, People and Events in the Middle East*, new edition, revised and expanded edition (Chicago and La Salle, Il.: Open Court, 1993), 167-74.

the social contract stipulated by Islam going back to the so-called "Pact of 'Umar":

> giving him the punishment mandated by law: the shedding of his blood, the confiscation of his property, and captivity of his women and children. [He deserves this punishment] because he promoted himself, cast off the mark of submission from his neck, and disavowed the contract of protection.[55]

Setting aside the social-psychological factors that are thought to have shaped Ibn Ḥazm's attitude toward the Jews in general and Ibn Naghrīlah in particular what historical factors (between the original encounter of 1013, the drafting of *Al-Fiṣal fil-milal* [1027–30], its incorporation of materials from the *Iẓhār*, and the appearance of "The Refutation" around 1056) might have contributed to a deepening of the anti-Jewish rhetoric in the later text?[56] From the standpoint of a pious and

---

[55] Ibn Ḥazm, "*Al-Radd*," 47, trans. Stroumsa, "From Muslim Heresy to Jewish-Muslim Polemics," 772. For the circumstances under which the protection guaranteed non-Muslims must be withdrawn, see Lewis, *The Jews of Islam*, 39-40.

[56] Although set aside for purposes of this paper an inter-personal dimension may well inform some of the anti-Jewish animus and rhetoric of "The Refutation." By 1027–1030, when the literary account of Ibn Ḥazm's encounter with Ibn Naghrīlah was drafted, the issue of the exercise of Jewish temporal power within the *Dār al-Islām* had unexpectedly become entangled in the *personal* histories of Samuel and 'Alī. Both lives were profoundly touched by social and political upheaval, but while Samuel's fortunes rose as a result of changes in the administration of al-Andalus and the opportunities presented to ambitious and talented Jews, Ibn Ḥazm's once promising prospects for following in his father's political footsteps were effectively scuttled. Ibn Naghrīlah was already entrenched in the fiscal bureaucracy of the Zirid regime, a position from which he would eventually enter the confidences of the next *amīr* Bādīs. He had also acquired the title and attained prestige as the Nagid of the Jews of al-Andalus (c. 1027). By contrast, Ibn Ḥazm's political fortunes precipitously declined. The privileged son of a once-influential *wazīr* of the Umayyad caliph was set to flight, repeatedly elevated (including a very brief stint as *wazīr* of the ill-fated Caliph al-Mustaẓhir [c. 1024]) and incarcerated (his imprisonment in Granada by Ḥabbūs [Bādīs' father] is related in Ibn Bassām, *Al-Dhakhīrah*, part 1 vol. 2:660), largely on account of his unswerving loyalty to the Umayyad cause and Umayyad claimants, and finally owing to his aggressive advocacy of the *Ẓāhiriyyah*. When attempts at reviving his political career at provincial centers failed, Ibn Ḥazm's ambition and boundless intellectual energy turned exclusively to research. Accordingly,

ideologically-minded Muslim intellectual the events of the eleventh century were altogether lamentable. Dispirited scholars such as Ibn Ḥazm were all too aware of the progressive social and political disintegration of al-Andalus and the resultant evaporation of its influence as a Mediterranean power.[57] Troublesome rumblings of revitalized Castile under Ferdinand I (1035–1065) certainly reached al-Andalus further contributing to an abiding sense of unease. Consider the following remarkable passage transmitted by the North African historian Ibn 'Idhārī (thirteenth to fourteenth centuries). It preserves remarks attributed to King Ferdinand I of Castile (1035–65) addressed to a delegation of Muslims from Toledo:

> We seek only our lands which you have conquered from us in times past at the beginning of your history. Now you have dwelled in them for the time allotted to you and we have become victorious over you as a result of your own wickedness. So go to your own side of the straits [of Gibraltar] and leave our lands to us, for no good will come to you from dwelling here with us after today. For we shall not hold back from you till God decides between us.[58]

This address captures a sense of the shifting political fortunes of Islam and Christendom in eleventh-century Iberia, ostensibly from the perspective of a Christian Spanish monarch. But the discourse must have struck a chord among Muslim scholars in the *maghrib* who preserved and transmitted it on account of its particular reading of the Andalusians' failure and collapse.

---

some students of Ibn Ḥazm have imagined an embittered and disillusioned 'Alī reflecting upon the ascent and position of Ibn Naghrīlah, the Jewish interlocutor of his youth. Ismā'īl's success supposedly reminded Ibn Ḥazm of his own failures as much as of the collapse of an orthodox Islamic polity in al-Andalus and its replacement by the party-kings. See Adang, *Muslim Writers on Judaism,* 43-44; Stroumsa, "From Muslim Heresy to Jewish-Muslim Polemics," 769.

[57] For Ibn Ḥazm's highly vocative comments on the state of Cordoba after the *fitnah,* see *Ṭawq al-hamāmah fil-ulfah wal-ullāf,* ed. Ṣalāḥ al-Dīn al-Qāsimī (Baghdad: Dār al-Shu'ūn al-Thaqāfiyyah al-'Āmmah, 1986), 182-83.

[58] Ibn 'Idhārī, *Al-Bayān al-mughrib,* 3:282, translated by Wasserstein, *Rise and Fall of the Party Kings,* 250.

Besides the disintegration of the unified state and the resultant civil strife over conflicting claims to political authority, a visible sign of internal weakness directly related to the proliferation of competing principalities in Muslim Spain was the elevation of Jewish (and to a lesser extent Christian) officials to positions of power by the *mulūk al-ṭawā'if.* This practice was naturally seen by resentful Muslim intellectuals as violating the Islamic character of al-Andalus and experienced by them as undermining the social and political conditions necessary for the perfect practice of Islam. Influential Jews could already be found at the Umayyad and 'Āmirid courts of the tenth century—a development which apparently did not go uncriticized in some quarters[59]—yet Muslim anxiety over Jewish empowerment surfaced more sharply and openly during the eleventh century as a direct consequence of the loss of unified Muslim authority. Heightened concern about the proper place of non-Muslims in Andalusi society articulated in the introduction and conclusion of "The Refutation" found an echo in an admonitory and programmatic document by Muḥammad ibn 'Abdūn (eleventh to twelfth century) prescribing among other things strict regulations on the behavior of Jews and Christians.[60] Indeed, in drawing a typology of the persecution of minorities in pre-modern Islam Bernard Lewis identifies *dhimmī* arrogance and high public rank as primary causes in moving Islam to strike an aggressively defensive posture vis-à-vis its "protected peoples."[61] As evidenced by Ibn Ḥazm's habit of conferring with Jewish scholars neither the presence of Jews in Andalusi Muslim society nor even their relative prosperity were cause for concern. Rather the Jews' visible trespass

---

[59] Although the evidence seems scant Stern, "Two New Data about Ḥasdai ibn Shapruṭ," 141-43, and Allony, "Songs of Zion," 212-15, contend that popular anti-Jewish sentiment emerged already in the tenth century. In their view, the vilification of Samuel and Yūsuf ibn Naghrīlah in the eleventh century was simply a continuation of a predominant anti-Jewish vein in Andalusi society.

[60] "Un document sur la vie urbane et le corps de la métiers a Seville au debut du xiie siècle: Le traité d'Ibn 'Abdūn," ed. E. Lévi Provençal, in *Journal Asiatique* 224 (1934): 238-48.

[61] Lewis, *Jews of Islam,* 53.

into the affairs of state seemed threatening, never more so than while Islam was in retreat.

Recent research on "The Refutation" has focused on source-critical exposition of Ibn Ḥazm's polemic and on determining the identity of his literary adversary.[62] For our purposes we may set aside a definitive solution to the problem of whether or not Samuel the Nagid actually composed a treatise against the Qur'ān.[63] Suffice it to say that Sarah Stroumsa argues that the "*al-Radd 'alā ibn al-naghrīlah al-yahūdī*" actually refutes a ninth century heterodox Muslim source rather than an eleventh-century Jewish polemical text. In her view Ibn Ḥazm hoped to pin a capital offense upon Ibn Naghrīlah by ascribing to him the anti-Qur'anic arguments.[64] Maribel Fierro, by contrast, identifies two free-thinking Jewish physicians living in Almeria with whom Ibn Ḥazm was acquainted and who could have written such a work in the intellectual and social climate of eleventh-century al-Andalus, perhaps by drawing upon existing heterodox Muslim texts such as Ibn al-Rāwandī's *Kitāb al-Dāmigh* discussed by Stroumsa.[65] Either Ibn Ḥazm found it useful to ascribe an offensive anti-Qur'anic tract to a highly conspicuous Jew such as Ibn Naghrīlah or he genuinely believed the author of the unavailable text to be a Jewish contemporary in Muslim Spain.

To read "The Refutation" as an artifact of Hispano-Arabic culture in a moment of crisis we need not feel obliged (in the absence of compelling textual evidence) to identify the particular Jew who meets all of the various conditions set forth in the text: a free-thinking member of the

[62] See Moshe Perlmann, "The Medieval Polemics between Islam and Judaism," in *Religion in a Religious Age,* ed. S. D. Goitein (New York: Ktav Publishing, 1974), 108ff.

[63] The rationale for and against the existence of such a pamphlet are carefully discussed by Wasserstein, *Rise and Fall,* 199-205. Ibn Bassām, *Al-Dhakhīrah,* part 1, vol. 2:766, claims that Ibn Naghrīlah composed a book in response to something Ibn Ḥazm had written, perhaps *Al-Fiṣal*'s critique of the Hebrew Bible.

[64] Stroumsa, "From Muslim Heresy to Jewish Muslim Polemics."

[65] The two men are Ismā'īl b. Yūnus al-A'war (also mentioned in *Ṭawq al-ḥamāmah,* 67) and Ismā'īl b. al-Qarrād. See Fierro, "Ibn Ḥazm et le *zindīq* juif," 82. Fierro notes Ibn Ḥazm's reference already in *Al-Fiṣal* to his acquaintance of two Jewish physicians who were adherents of the *dahriyyah* (materialists and agnostics).

dahriyya; a dignitary known to Ibn Ḥazm; a Jew of such substantial means and influence that he was unafraid to openly voice criticism of the Qur'ān and Islam in the form of a religious polemical text written in Arabic.[66] Since "The Refutation" itself is silent on the identity of the alleged Jewish polemicist we may wonder why the editors (or editor) responsible for supplying the title of the treatise and later literary historians such as Ibn Bassām al-Shantarīnī and Ibn Sa'īd al-Maghribī (d. 1286) all take it for granted that Ibn Naghrīlah was the object of the "The Refutation's" invective?[67] Other high ranking Jews could be found during the eleventh century in Saragossa (Abū al-Faḍl ibn Ḥasdai; Yequtiel ibn Ḥasan), Almeria, Seville (Abraham ibn Muhājir), and Toledo.[68] The answer I believe is that Samuel was the most visible and important member of this group and the only one to attain ecumenical status among the Jews of al-Andalus. Imagine what Muslim scholars might have thought had they access to the Nagid's Hebrew poetry produced for Jewish consumption or if a hint of the Jewish hubris he expresses in that verse was evident in his public demeanor.[69]

---

66 "Free-thinking materialism" could not reasonably be attributed to Samuel.

67 Ibn Bassām, *al-Dhakhīrah*, part 1, vol. 2:766; Ibn Sa'īd al-Maghribī, *Al-Mughrib fī ḥulā al-maghrib*, ed. Shawqi Ḍayf, 2 vols. (Cairo: Dār al-Ma'ārif bi-Miṣr, 1955), 2:114.

68 See Eliyahu Ashtor, *The Jews of Moslem Spain*, trans. Aaron Klein and Jenny Machlowitz Klein, 3 vols. (Philadelphia: Jewish Publication Society, 1973–84), 2:197; 217-21; 225, 238; 253-64; and Wasserstein, *Rise and Fall*, 190-222.

69 I am thinking specifically of the Nagid's preoccupation with his aristocratic (Levitic) lineage, his concerted effort to bring his public image into line with the typology of King David, and his pretensions to higher authority. See Ross Brann, *The Compunctious Poet: Cultural Ambiguity and Hebrew Poetry in Muslim Spain* (Baltimore: The Johns Hopkins University Press, 1991), 47-58. As Gerson Cohen noted, *The Book of Tradition*, 277: "the hope for the fulfillment of the messianic dream in Andalus, through the class of Jewish courtiers, was not a secret of the Jewish underground. The Jewish pride, which the Muslims construed as Hubris and defiance of Islam, drew its nourishment from the assumption that the age of the Bible was again come to life and that the exiles of Judea in Sefarad would soon assume their rightful station." Open, public defiance toward Islam is another matter even if the Nagid never uttered an Arabic word on the subject.

If Ismā'īl appears to his Muslim counterparts as the incarnation of Jewish empowerment and arrogance, the city-state of Granada under the administration of successive Ibn Naghrīlahs, sometimes referred to in Arabic texts as *gharnāṭat al-yahūd* ("Jewish Granada"),[70] is a perfect locus for various grievances against Jewish power and influence within the Islamic polity.[71] Indeed, Ibn 'Idhārī charges that Yūsuf ibn Naghrīlah sought to establish an independent Jewish kingdom (in Almeria), giving the impression that under successive Ibn Naghrīlahs the Jewish community appeared to function as a quasi-independent polity and aspired to complete independence.[72] With respect to the unusual powers of Ismā'īl and his son as well as in the number of ranking Jewish officials serving at the courts of other party-kings, the Andalusian situation did not exist elsewhere in Islam, including Fatimid Egypt where Jews (and Jewish converts) served in positions of government.

Ibn Ḥazm, subsequent Muslim literary intellectuals, or the medieval editor of "The Refutation" might have identified Ibn Naghrīlah as the source of the subversive discourse or thought it natural to cast him in this menacing role on account of his singularly conspicuous position, prominence, and political agency, all of which can be identified as contributing to *fitnah*.[73] Later sources such as Ibn 'Idhārī and Ibn al-Khaṭīb, it will be recalled, cite the Jews of eleventh-century Granada in general and the

---

[70] *The Tibyān*, 206-7, citing al-Ḥimyarī, *Kitāb al-Rawḍ al-Mi'ṭār*, ed. and trans. E. Lévi-Provençal (Leiden: E. J. Brill, 1938), 23.

[71] During the Zirid era the Jews of Granada represented a significant perhaps even predominant segment of the town's population. Appointment of two successive *dhimmīs* to high office appears to have been part of a system of checks and balances specific to Berber rule in eleventh-century Granada. See Andrew Handler, *The Zirids of Granada* (Coral Gables, Fla.: University of Miami Press, 1974), 26; 45. For an estimate of the Jewish population in al-Andalus, see Eliyahu Ashtor, "The Number of Jews in Moslem Spain" [Hebrew] *Zion* 28 (1963): 34-56.

[72] Ibn 'Idhārī, *Al-Bayān al-mughrib*, 3:266, and Ibn Bassām, *Al-Dhakhīrah*, part 1, vol. 2:766.

[73] According to the *Encyclopedia of Islam* [second edition], 2:930 (s.v. "Fitna," L. Gardet) the idea of *fitnah* came to be understood as "'revolt', 'disturbances', 'civil war', but a civil war that breeds schism and in which the believers' purity of faith is in grave danger."

Ibn Naghrīlahs in particular for their accumulation of wealth.[74] Yūsuf is further singled out for his partiality toward Jewish secretaries in filling lower level administrative and financial offices.[75] The episode involving Ibn Naghrīlah and Aḥmad ibn 'Abbās, *wazīr* of neighboring Almeria, is also indicative of Ismā'īl's notorious standing among some Andalusi Muslims (and instructive as a failed rehearsal of what eventually befell Yūsuf ibn Naghrīlah in 1066). Unremittingly hostile to the Zirid's Jewish *wazīr* Ibn 'Abbās is said to have circulated letters among influential Muslims of Granada and petitioned Ḥabbūs and Bādīs successively in a concerted effort to depose Samuel from office. For good measure he also enlisted Ibn Abī Mūsā, the Ḥammūdid prince of Malaga, and Zuhayr, the Slav prince of Almeria, in a plan to isolate Granada, intervene in its administration and bring down the Jew and his supporters.[76] Ibn Ḥazm himself must have been aware of the opposition to Ibn Naghrīlah because these events coincided with his term of service in Almeria's army as reported by Ibn 'Idhārī.[77]

In accordance with "The Refutation's" fuzzy testimony on the identity of the Jewish polemicist and the traditional identification of the treatise with Ibn Naghrīlah, it seems preferable to think of Ibn Ḥazm's alleged literary adversary as a composite Andalusian Jewish notable, courtier, and intellectual suggestive of Samuel—a construct of the social imagination of an eleventh-century Muslim intellectual. The Jew in the text, uniformly assumed by subsequent Islamic tradition to be Ibn Naghrīlah, is thus a *typological figure* comparable in function to Almanzor (i.e., al-Manṣūr) in Latin and Romance texts.[78] He embodies a spectrum of offensive beliefs, attitudes, and conduct considered dangerous to

---

[74] Ibn 'Idhārī, *Al-Bayan al-mughrib,* 3:264-65.

[75] Ibn 'Idhārī, *Al-Bayan al-mughrib,* 3:265.

[76] Ashtor, *Jews of Moslem Spain,* 2:71-79.

[77] Ibn 'Idhārī, *Al-Bayan al-mughrib,* 3:171.

[78] For example, see the Latin account (preserved as an appendix to the *Historia Turpini*) of al-Manṣūr's affliction with dysentary in Colin Smith [ed. and trans.], *Christians and Moors in Spain Volume I: AD 711–1150* (Warminster: Aris and Phillips, 1988), 76-79.

Islam and threatening to the well-being of Muslims in al-Andalus.[79] A typological approach to the cast of character presented in "The Refutation" explains why Ibn Bassām and Ibn Sa'īd al-Maghribī rely on Ibn Ḥazm but confuse and conflate Ismā'īl and Yūsuf ibn Naghrīlah, apparently unwittingly. Whatever Ibn Ḥazm's intention in drafting "The Refutation" (and whoever his target) the text took on a life of its own in subsequent Hispano-Arabic tradition.[80]

Hispano-Arabic discourse on Ismā'īl ibn Naghrīlah presents the reader with seemingly contradictory figures at whose poles are an intelligent, skilled, and noble Jew deserving of homage, and a vile, stupid, and fiendish enemy of God and Islam. Despite differences in tone and approach that can be attributed to genre (e.g., history of science; historical chronicle; heresiography; religious polemic), each of the textual representations of Ibn Naghrīlah discussed in this paper is directly or indirectly concerned with issues of sovereignty and the exercise of power and reflective of concerns and paradigms internal to Islam for which the Jew serves as a mirror. The discourse variously depicts Ibn Naghrīlah as a wise and skilled reader whose own texts are valid for him and his textual community (Ṣā'id al-Andalusī, *Ṭabaqāt al-umam*); strips Ismā'īl of his cultural

---

[79] Maribel Fierro, "Religious Beliefs and Practices in al-Andalus in the Third/ninth Century," *Rivista degli Studi Orientali* LXVI (1992): 21-22, cites an Andalusian anecdote related in *Kitāb al-'āqibah*, an unpublished treatise on eschatology by Ibn al-Kharrāṭ (d. 1186), in which a person is described as a Jew so as to disqualify him. Fierro writes: "It is worth noting that the anonymous person who liked to discuss God and the Qur'ān is described as a Jew by Abū Marwān...As he tried to introduce young Muḥammad to certain theological doctrines considered suspect, he resembled more a Jew than a Muslim, in the same way that his doctrines were not Islamic."

[80] John Dagenais's recent study *The Ethics of Reading in Manuscript Culture: Glossing the Libro de buen amor* (Princeton: Princeton University Press, 1994), argues that scholars frequently place too much emphasis on the establishment of a single authoritative text in order to recover the "author's intention." In so doing they commit themselves to a process that deprives us of the possible readings supplied by variant traditions, that is, the scribal notations found on the margins of the manuscripts. This instructive argument can be extended to the dialectical relationship between the author's text, in this case Ibn Ḥazm, and the place of the text within the broader literary and cultural tradition.

otherness by embracing him as (almost) one of its own (Ibn Ḥayyān; *Al-Iḥāṭah*); and depicts him as belonging to a community of liars, asserting the absolute discursive authority of the Muslim textual community over others and depriving the Jew of speech (Ibn Ḥazm; *Al-Fiṣal*). At its most extreme ("*Al-Radd*") the discourse indicts the Jew for violating the essential conditions of the contract between Islam and *ahl al-dhimmah* and consequently divests him of his property and his life in accordance with Islamic law.

In this study we have seen that divergent textual strategies for making sense of or objectifying the historical Ibn Naghrīlah signify an unstable construction of the Jew in eleventh-century al-Andalus. To re-read the conflicting literary representations of Ismā'īl ibn Naghrīlah in their textual environment further illuminates some of the subtleties of the paradoxical relations between Muslims and Jews in Islamic Spain in which extended periods of tolerance are punctuated by outbreaks of reaction and hostility.[81] Accordingly, the representations of the critical historical figure of Ibn Naghrīlah suggest that the Hispano-Arabic sources can be read as a textualization of the shifting, fluctuating, and ambivalent relations between the Muslims and Jews of al-Andalus at least on the level of elites.

[81] See Bernard Lewis, *The Jews of Islam*, 87.

THE ARABICIZATION AND ISLAMIZATION OF THE CHRISTIANS OF AL-ANDALUS: EVIDENCE OF THEIR SCRIPTURES

HANNA KASSIS *

IN THIS PAPER I propose to address the question of the acculturation of a community that may have been numerically sizeable but that became disempowered as the result of Muslim domination of the Iberian Peninsula. This disempowerment resulted not only in the loss of sovereignty to an alien invader, but in the marginalization of the religious ethos of a subjugated society notwithstanding its toleration by the conqueror. I will argue that regardless of the attempt of some of its members to resist, the community inevitably was transformed in language and culture as it adapted itself to those of the new masters, Arabic and Islamic, and that this came about without violation of its religious (Christian) orthodoxy. I will illustrate my argument by reference to the Scriptures of that community.

Faced with the reality of the Muslim conquest of their country in A.D. 711, the vanquished Christians of Spain (*Hispania* to the Romans, and *al-Andalus* to the Muslims) were confronted with the need to preserve their identity in spite of their disempowerment. Under Muslim rule, the rights of those Christians who chose to maintain their faith were protected, at least in principle, by the dictates of the Qur'ān and the practices of the Prophet as these were rendered by competent interpreters. Referred to as *ahl al-dhimmah* in the formulations of the jurists (*fuqahā'*), Christians living under Muslim rule were grouped under two categories in legal

* Research in the different archives was made possible with the assistance of the Social Sciences and Humanities Research Council of Canada.

documents pertaining to al-Andalus: *ahl ṣulḥ* ("people brought in by peace-treaty"), or *ahl 'unwah* ("people brought in by compulsion"). It seems, however, that such a distinction was brought to the fore only in litigation before a Muslim court and primarily in cases regarding disputed property involving Christians and members of either of the two other religious communities. Otherwise, it appears that unless there were mitigating circumstances, both groups of Christians were left to manage their own affairs and were generally treated by the Muslims in accordance with those terms of the treaty that defined the rights of *ahl ṣulḥ*.

The text of one such treaty, preserved by later Muslim historians, is purported to have been that of one concluded in A.D. 713 between Theodmir, the defeated Visigothic governor of the region of Murcia, and the victorious Muslim commander, 'Abd al-'Azīz ibn Mūsá ibn Nuṣayr. According to the extant text, "they [the Christians] shall not be taken into captivity nor would they be separated from their women or children. They shall not be killed; their churches shall not be burnt nor shall their cult objects be desecrated; they shall not be forcibly converted out of their religion."[1] These guarantees were given in return for loyalty to the new masters and the payment of tribute (*jizyah*).

There is little doubt that this treaty—be it authentic or fabricated—reflects the broad lines that governed the relationship of the Muslim rulers and their Christian subjects and echoes the tenor of the legal position of the Christians under Muslim rule in al-Andalus. Even if the authenticity of such a treaty or the accuracy of its text were to be called into question, the self-imposed perception in Muslim writings that a pact such as this existed and obligated the Muslims to abide by its terms, is sig-

[1] I refer to this treaty in my paper, "Arabic-speaking Christians in al-Andalus in an age of turmoil (fifth/eleventh century until A.H. 478/A.D. 1085)," *Al-Qanṭara,* 15 (1994): 401-22; see especially note 6 where I mention that "The earliest version of the text of this treaty is preserved by Aḥmad ibn 'Umar ibn Anas al-'Udhrī known as al-Dilā'ī (d. A.H. 478/A.D. 1085)," *Nuṣūṣ 'an al-Andalus* (*Fragmentos geográfico-históricos de al-Masālik ilá Jamī' al-Mamālik*), ed. 'Abd al-'Azīz al-Ahwānī (Madrid: Instituto de Estudios Islámicos en Madrid, 1965), 4-5; a translation is also included.

nificant. But, aside from leaving the Christians to manage their own internal affairs and to maintain their existing religious rites and edifices, the treaty is silent regarding the preservation of the identity of the Christians. If such identity were to be sustained, the responsibility of cultural self-preservation and nurture was left up to the Christians themselves to undertake. That responsibility must by necessity address matters of religion and language, the two elements that more than any other give a minority a foundation upon which to establish its exclusiveness. Such interplay of the search for identity, on the one hand, and an emphasis on the preservation of religion and language, on the other, is very much in evidence in al-Andalus.

While the treaty itself was written in Arabic, at least as far as the preserved text is concerned, the Muslims recognized the linguistic barrier that separated them from their vanquished subjects. Evidence for this must be derived from numismatics. During the first decade of their dominion in the Peninsula, the Muslim rulers accommodated their subjects by utilizing Latin on their coins. Thus, following the numismatic tradition that was started after the fall of Carthage in North Africa, and in spite of the fact that the reform of the minting policy had already taken place two decades earlier in the Near East, the earliest coins issued in the Peninsula by the Muslims, beginning with A.H. 94/A.D. 712, bear legends containing the fundamental statement of faith of Islam in Latin rather than Arabic. The legend on one of the earliest of these coins reads, *INNDINN D SNSDSSLSNDSA*, a condensed and abbreviated form of *IN Nomine DominI NoN Deus NiSi DeuS SoLuS Non DeuS Alius*, "In the Name of God; there is no deity other than God, alone, without compeer." However, less than a decade later, Arabic was to replace Latin and the new legends included the Arabic original of which the Latin text cited above was a translation, *bism Allāh lā ilāha illā Allāh waḥdaḥu lā sharīka lahu*, as well as the Qur'anic chapter, *Allāhu aḥad Allāh uṣ-ṣamad lam yalid wa-lam yūlad wa-lam yakun lahu kufu'an aḥad*, "He is God, He is Unique; God is the Eternal One; He did not beget, nor was He begotten; He has no compeer" (*Sūra* 112, *al-Tawḥīd*). There is no doubt in my mind that the primary intention of the legends on these coins—whether written in Latin or subsequently in Arabic—was to inform the subjugated Christians of the central content of the faith of the victors, rather than to engage in polemics. It is worthy of mention that the first authenticated piece of Islamic writing to be introduced in the conquered territory contained a chapter of the Muslim Scriptures, albeit on a coin. I am inclined to believe that this had a significant bearing on the nature of the relations between the conquering Muslims and the disempowered Christians, and the eventual desire of the Christians to present their own Scriptures in the language of the conqueror.[2]

The process of arabicization of al-Andalus was quick to evolve, and unless they chose to become increasingly marginalized, the Christians were under pressure to adopt the language of the conqueror as their own. Whether or not such pressure was overt is of little import as far as the results are concerned. More significant for our discussion is the question of the beginning of the process of arabicization (or auto-arabicization).[3] As the conquest became an irreversible reality, and in spite of the religious-legal definition and protection of their status, the Christians who came under Muslim rule had limited options for the preservation of their identity. Needless to say, some opted for conversion to Islam, a conversion which nonetheless did not override the desire among some of

---

[2] Citing one sacred Scripture in response to another is very well attested at a later time in the Peninsula. The classic example is that of the numismatic response of Alfonso VIII to the Qur'anic message that appeared on the coins of the Almoravids and their partisan successors. The Qur'anic legend in the circle on the obverse of the dinars of the Almoravids declared, *wa-man yabtaghi ghayr al-islāmi dīnan fa-lan yuqbala minhu wa-huwa fil-ākhirati min al-khāsirīn*, "Whoso seeks a religion other than *islām*, it shall not be accepted from him, and in the world to come he shall be among the losers." In turn, Alfonso VIII responded by inscribing the Christian invocation on the golden dinars that he had minted in Toledo, followed by a verse from the Gospels: *bism al-āb wal-ibn wal-rūḥ al-quddūs al-ilāh al-wāḥid man āmana wa-i'tamada yakun sāliman*, "In the Name of the Father and of the Son and of the Holy Spirit, the One God; whoso believes and is baptized shall be saved" (Mark 16:16).

[3] I use these terms to point out the difficulty that arises from the name *mozárabe* itself and the problem of whether it is derived from *musta'rib*, the active participle of the verb *ista'raba*, meaning "one who seeks to be arabicized" ("auto-arabicized"), or *musta'rab*, the passive participle of the same verb, meaning "one who is made to be arabicized (by someone else)."

them for the preservation of their ethnic-cultural identity. Ibn Ḥafṣūn, the religiously oscillating rebel who in the end repudiated Islam, and Ibn Gharsiyah, the *shu'ūbī* writer who was able to embrace with equal energy his Muslim faith and Iberian heritage, are but two well-known examples. A more serious situation engulfed those who chose to retain their Christian religious identity within the Muslim polity. Of those, some continued to identify with their deposed Latin heritage, according it an emphasis it could hardly have possessed under the Visigoths. Others held on to their Christian identity within an Arabic framework, acquiring a mastery of the language while retaining their religious orthodoxy. In both cases, the responsibility of defining the means by which the marginalized culture could be preserved was assumed by the clergy and the church. Not unexpectedly, without the presence of an intellectually and administratively gifted clergy, the community would be weakened. This is well demonstrated by Mohammed Ṭālbī, in the case of the demise of Christianity in North Africa,[4] and Mikel de Epalza, who examines its import in the case of al-Andalus.[5] It is not surprising, therefore, that the preponderance of literature created by the Christians of al-Andalus was religious in nature.

We know very little about the Christians living under Muslim rule during the first century of the Muslim conquest; the Muslim sources hardly touch on the details of their life. By leaving the Christians of al-Andalus alone, Muslim writers left them out of their records as well. From the Christian side, there are sufficient details surrounding some events of particular interest to the Christians themselves. Perhaps the

[4] See his "Le Christianisme maghrébin de la conquête à sa disparition: une tentative d'explication," in *Conversion and Continuity: Indigenous Christian Communities in Islamic Lands—Eighth to Eighteenth Centuries*, edited by Michael Gervers and Ramzi Jibran Bikhazi (Toronto: Pontifical Institute of Mediaeval Studies, 1990), 313-51.

[5] See his essay, "Falta de obispos y conversión al Islam de los cristianos del Al-Andalus," in *Al-Qanṭara*, 15 (1994): 385-400; see also his essay (translated into English) "Mozarabs: An emblematic Christian minority in Islamic al-Andalus" in *The Legacy of Muslim Spain*, edited by Salma Khadra Jayyusi (Leiden: Brill, 1992), 149-70.

one event that has attracted more of the attention of the Christian historian was the so-called "Martyr Movement" of the mid-ninth century.[6]

It is safe to assume that by the middle of the ninth century many Christians of al-Andalus had acquired the language, customs and other social practices of the Muslims and that the Muslims, in turn, had been similarly influenced by them. The extent of the impact of Islam on the Christians alarmed some of the leading members of the Christian community. Eulogius, who was to become one of the "Martyrs of Cordoba" abhorred the close association between Christians and Muslims. He lamented that "[the Cordoban Christians] consider it a delight to be subject to these people [the Muslims], and do not resist being led by the yoke of the infidels. They even make use of many of their sacrileges on a day to day basis and seek their company rather than trying to save themselves, like the Patriarch Lot, who departed Sodom for the mountains."[7] Paul Albar of Cordoba, his childhood friend and biographer, was concerned about the demise of Latin among his coreligionists who, he said, favoured the use of Arabic instead of Latin as their literary medium. "The Christians forgot their language," he bemoaned, "to the point that you would not find among a thousand of them one person who could write a letter to a friend in Latin which is free from error. As for writing Arabic, you will certainly find a large number who master that language, possessing an elegant style, writing poetry that at times surpasses in quality that which is composed by the Arabs themselves." At times, it is hard to determine whether Albar is lamenting or celebrating the achievement of his coreligionists.

But Albar's remarks against his coreligionists for forsaking Latin in favor of Arabic must not be seen as resulting only from the fear of ara-

[6] For a detailed study of the "Martyrs Movement," see Edward P. Colbert, *The Martyrs of Córdoba (850-859): A Study of the Sources* (Washington: Catholic University of America, 1962); Kenneth Wolf, *Christian Martyrs in Muslim Spain* (Cambridge, 1988); and recently, Jessica A. Coope, *The Martyrs of Córdoba: Community and Family Conflict in an Age of Mass Conversion* (University of Nebraska Press, 1995).

[7] Translation by Wolf, *Christian Martyrs,* 68. Interestingly enough, the very same concern was expressed by Muslim jurisconsults (the *fuqahā'*), who feared that consorting with the Christians could lead to the dilution of Islam.

bicization; Isaac, the Monk of Tábanos and the first of the so-called martyrs, was described by Eulogius in his *Materiale Sanctorum* as "a youthful monk, well-versed in Arabic learning."[8] He was able to employ Arabic as he addressed the *qāḍī* before whom he blasphemed the Prophet and the religion of Islam. It is very likely that Albar himself, an urban Cordoban, had a command of Arabic. It was, perhaps, the weakening of Latin as the sacral language of the Church under Muslim rule that alarmed Albar and his friends. Undoubtedly he and his friends were well acquainted with St. Isidore of Seville's (d. 636) praise of the Vulgate (of Jerome), declaring it to be "justly preferred to all others," and commending it for use in the liturgy. Albar's apprehension may rather have been the product of fear that the Christian faith itself was weakening among his co-religionists as a result of the growing appeal of the Arabic language and Islam. Arabicization could only hasten the impending danger, while linguistic isolation could be the sole remaining line of defense. Such fear of dilution of identity through assimilation, linguistic or otherwise, is not limited to the Christians of al-Andalus in the ninth century. For any minority community, the expiration of its language or dialect is but the beginning of its disintegration.

But, how widespread was the fear of the demise of Latin among the Christians of al-Andalus and to what extent did the Muslims actively and obtrusively contribute to the process of arabicization of their Christian subjects? Regrettably, we do not possess sufficient and conclusive information in this regard. What little information we have is fragmentary, and becomes fertile soil for hasty conclusions and generalizations. At the same time, information does exist that demonstrates that the adoption of the language of the conquerors was in fact balanced by the preservation of Latin. Juan Gil assembled sources that were written by some Mozarabs in Latin;[9] Angel Gonzalez Palencia, in turn, assembled docu-

[8] Translation by Colin Smith, *Christians and Moors in Spain*, vol. 1 (Warminster: Aris and Phillips, 1988), 45.

[9] See his *Corpus scriptorum muzarabicorum*, 2 vols. (Madrid, 1973).

ments written in Arabic by the Mozarabs of Toledo in the period following the return of that city to Latin-speaking Christian rule.[10]

As the Christians of al-Andalus became increasingly arabicized, the need for the translation of their Sacred Scriptures into Arabic ensued. How soon after the Muslim conquest this process began is subject to debate. There is a suggestion that the earliest translation of the Christian Bible into Arabic in al-Andalus took place within twelve years of the conquest. In the context of the discussion of the first five years of the reign of Don Pelayo, king of the Asturias (A.D. 718–737), the *Primera Crónica General* (which dates from the reign of Alfonso X, the Wise) refers to a translation of the Christian Bible into Arabic by a bishop named Juan of Seville, who is referred to by the Arabic name *Saʿīd al-maṭrān*, "Saʿīd the Bishop,"

> At this time, there was in Seville the saintly Bishop Juan, a man of great sanctity and a good and holy life, whom the Arabs called in Arabic *Çaeyt almatran*. He was very knowledgeable in the Arabic language and through him God performed many miracles. He translated the Holy Scriptures into Arabic and interpreted them in accordance with the Holy Scriptures ....[11]

How authentic is this report? This is not the place for a discussion or even a summary of the debate surrounding it.[12] This said, the account in the *Primera Crónica General* appears to be a variation on a slightly earlier statement by Rodrigo Ximenes (d. 1237), Archbishop of Toledo during the reign of Alfonso VIII and the primary instigator of the crusade that

---

[10] Angel González Palencia, *Los Mozárabes de Toledo en los Siglos XII y XIII* (Madrid, 1926–1930).

[11] *Primera Crónica General: Estoria de España que mandó componer Alfonso el Sabio y se continuaba bajo Sancho IV en 1289*, edited by Ramón Menéndez Pidal (Madrid, 1906), vol. I, see entry *El Rey Don Pelayo*, 326.

[12] The debate is best summarized by Eugène Cardinal Tisserant, "Une feuille Arabo-Latine de l'Épitre aux Galates," *Revue Biblique*, vol. 7, sér. 2 (1910), 321-43, esp. pp. 325-27. To this should be added P. Sj. van Koningsveld's discussion in his *The Latin-Arabic Glossary of the Leiden University Library* (Leiden, 1977), 51-52. Van Koningsveld reads *Sayyid*, apparently following Guidi.

led to the Battle of Las Navas de Tolosa in A.D. 1212. In his *De Rebus Hispaniae*, Rodrigo Ximenes refers to Juan, Bishop of Seville, as follows,

> *Et in isto medio fuit apud Hispalim gloriosus et sanctissimus Ioannes Episcopus, qui ab Arabibus Caeit (Zaeyt) almatran vocabatur, et magna scientia in lingua Arabica claruit, multis miraculorum operationibus gloriosus effulsit, qui etiam sacras Scripturas catholicis expositionibus declaravit, quas in formationem posterorum Arabice conscriptas reliquit.*[13]

A few centuries later, the claim that Bishop Juan of Seville did in fact translate the Sacred Scriptures into Arabic was echoed by Juan de Mariana (A.D. 1537–1624) in his *Historia General de España*,

> At the same time, there was Juan, prelate of Seville, who translated the Bible into the Arabic language with the intention of aiding the Christians and the Moors, because the Arabic language was widely and commonly used by all while ordinarily Latin was neither used nor known. There are several versions of this translation that are conserved until this day and may be found in various parts of Spain."[14]

There is no doubt that there were several translations of the Christian Bible in existence in various parts of Spain at about the time of de Mariana. There was mention of the existence in El Escorial of a work entitled *Liber Evangeliorum versus in linguam Arabicam à Joanne Episcopo Hispalensi qui ab Arabibus appellatur Said Almatrud tempore Regis Alphonsi Catholici.*[15] But this work is now regrettably lost and may have been destroyed by the fire that consumed a large portion of the Arabic collection of that library in 1671.[16] It is not clear if the title was given on the strength of the account in the *Primera Crónica General*. It is noteworthy

[13] Rodericus Ximenius de Rada, *Opera* (Valencia: *Textos Medievales, 22,* 1968; reprint of 1793 edition), Book IV, Chapter 3, 77; cited as well by Tisserant, *op. cit.*, 325.

[14] *Historia General de España,* VII, 3.

[15] Alonso del Castillo, *Índice de los libros Aráuigos que están en la libreria de San Lorencio el Real por órden del alphabeto aráuigo.* See Francisco Simonet, "Estudios históricos y filológicos sobre la literatura arábigo-mozárabe," *Revista de la Universidad de Madrid,* segunda época, 55.

[16] There is no mention of this work in Casiri's otherwise complete catalogue of its manuscripts.

that it was not known to biblical scholars in Spain and that an Arabic version of the Bible did not merit inclusion in either the Complutensian Polyglot, published in Spain in 1513–1517, or the Antwerp Polyglot, published in 1569–1572 and dedicated to Philip II of Spain.[17]

The dates of Bishop Joannes (or Juan), as presented in the text of Rodrigo Ximenes, are rather vague.[18] Generally speaking, he appears to be situated chronologically within very broad parameters, somewhere between the conquest in A.D. 711 and the arrival of the Almohads in the middle of the twelfth century. Simonet, followed by Tisserant, dates him to the ninth century,[19] and places him in the company of those prelates who attended the Council of Cordoba in A.D. 839. If this were the case, we should assume that he had died prior to the next Council of Córdoba in A.D. 852, which was presided over by Recafred, then Bishop of Seville.

But while we are not certain regarding the authenticity of the report in the *Primera Crónica General*, suffice it to say that during the age of Alfonso X it was not considered inconceivable to speak of the translation of the Sacred Scriptures into the language of the "infidel," and that by a man to whom sanctity is ascribed. It may be inconceivable to imagine a process of arabicization of the Christians of al-Andalus within only twelve years of the arrival of the Muslims. If Bishop Juan, *al-maṭrān Saʿīd*, did in fact exist during the first quarter of the eighth century as bishop of Seville and had translated the Scriptures into Arabic, he would most likely not have been indigenous to al-Andalus. One could envisage him as a migrant cleric tending the needs of a similarly migrant Arabic-speak-

---

[17] The Arabic text first appears in the Paris Polyglot of 1645, and again in the London Polyglot of 1654–1657.

[18] The vagueness arises from the uncertainty as to what exactly the expression *in isto medio* refers.

[19] Francisco Javier Simonet, *Historia de los Mozarabes de España* (Madrid, 1867, reissued by Ediciones Turner, 1984), vol. II, 320; Tisserant, *op. cit.*, 327-28. Van Koningsveld, *op. cit.*, 52, proposes a date for the debated bishop in the middle of the twelfth century. It is rather curious that he identifies *Çayet almatran* of the *Crónica General* or *De Rebus* ("a man of great sanctity through whom God has performed many miracles...") with the mid-twelfth century Bishop Juan of Seville who abjured his faith and was subjected to the harsh rebuke of Hugh of St. Victor.

ing Christian community which, unacquainted with the Latin of the West, had need for scriptures in a language it could comprehend. Arabic translations of the Scriptures existed in the Near East although the date of the earliest ones remains the subject of discussion.[20]

The collection of canon laws compiled in Arabic in the middle of the eleventh century by a priest named Vincentius for a Bishop named 'Abd al-Mālik and which I have discussed elsewhere,[21] includes a statement defining which writings constitute Scriptures for the Christian community of al-Andalus. In accordance with the established canons of the Christian church, these include all the books of the Old Testament as defined by the Septuagint and translated by Jerome, as well as the Books of the New Testament. But defining the corpus of the Scriptures posed no problem either for the church in al-Andalus or for its relations with the other churches beyond the realm of Islam. Instead, the pressing issue to be resolved by the church in al-Andalus seems to have been the language in which the Scriptures were to be recited or chanted within

[20] Perhaps the earliest translation is that of a fragment of the Book of Psalms (Psalm 77:20-31 and 51-61), found in the Umayyad Mosque in Damascus in 1901; see B. Violet *Ein Zweisprachiges Psalmfragment aus Damaskus* (Berlin, 1902). A more complete Arabic translation (Vatican ms. 13) is dated to the eighth century by I. Guidi, *Tradizioni degli evangeli in arabo e in etiopico* (Rome, 1902), and to the ninth century by G. Graf, *Geschichte der christlichen arabischen Literatur.* Recently, Harvey Staal edited the Mt. Sinai Arabic Codex (151), which contains the Pauline and Catholic Epistles, as well as the Book of Acts. The text is a translation from the Syriac by Bishr ibn Sirrī and was done in Damascus in Ramaḍān A.H. 253 (A.D. 867). In the colophon of one of the manuscripts used in the preparation of the London Polyglot, reference is made to Fathyūn ibn Ayyūb, a Syrian Christian scholar who lived in Baghdad in the middle of the ninth century, as a translator of the Bible from Syriac (Peshitta) into Arabic; see the brief study by J. A. Thompson, *The Major Arabic Bibles* (New York, 1956), 15. These translations predate the Arabic translation of the Hebrew Bible (Old Testament) by Saadia Gaon (died A.D. 942), so far considered the earliest extant biblical text in Arabic and employed, for the books of the Old Testament, in the Paris Polyglot.

[21] El Escorial, ms. 1623, which I am currently editing; I discuss this document in my paper, "Arabic-speaking Christians in al-Andalus in an age of turmoil (fifth/eleventh century until A.H. 478/A.D. 1085)"; see note 1.

the liturgy. For Paul Albar and his circle, the language of the Scriptures and the liturgy was Latin, the *lingua sacra* of the Western Church, praised by St. Gregory I and St. Isidore of Seville.

In the introduction to an Arabic translation of the Book of Psalms (Vatican, cod. arab. 5), the anonymous tenth-century translator presses a different point of view. He adopts a stance contrary to that taken by the Western Church and argues in favour of the use of the vernacular which may be commonly understood in prayers and lectionaries. He bolsters his reasoning by paraphrasing passages from one of the first of Paul's Epistles to the People of Corinth (I Corinthians 14) in a manner that makes Paul's teachings support his view. The case as he puts it warrants being cited, in translation, at length:

> The apostle said, "If a believer utters his prayers in his own tongue, he benefits himself with the spiritual gifts. Whosoever instructs the community (*al-jamā'āt*) and proclaims and interprets to them in his own tongue, realizes the spiritual benefits both for himself and the community." The Apostle further said, "I wish you all to speak in your own tongue. But more than that I want you to understand the interpretation of the prophecies."
>
> The Apostle further said, "Unless the inanimate cymbals and horns are sounded, how can listeners comprehend what they intone? For trumpets are sounded only when one is readied for battle. It is likewise with you my brethren if you do not understand your own speech and prayers; how would you comprehend what you utter and your supplications to God? If you do not understand what you say, you will only feel it within yourselves. There are many families of languages in the world and each has its own sound and intonation."
>
> The Apostle said, "If I, then, do not comprehend the meaning of a sound and its interpretation in that [specific] language, I shall be a barbarian to the one with whom I converse; similarly, the one who addresses me in a language I do not understand would appear to me to be barbarian. So it is with you if you do not understand your own prayer."
>
> After that the Apostle said, "What then do you do, brethren? When you gather together each of you has a hymn, a law, and a revelation, each has a language, eloquence and interpretation. Let everything you possess be for the edification, good and benefit of others."

> The Apostle informs us that the first to believe—the Greeks, the Jews, the foreigners [*al-'ajam*] and the Romans—declared their faith and prayed to their Lord in the language they each knew: the Greeks in Greek, the Syrians in Syriac, the foreigners [*'ajamīy*] in Latin, in order that each tongue may be strengthened in the faith in God. Similarly, the prayers of the Christians in the East and the West, whether they be bishops, kings, patriarchs, monks, or the masses of their laymen, be they Franks, Arabs or Syrians, those who believe in Christ, they all pray using the Psalms that are translated from Hebrew into many languages. These include Greek, Latin, Syriac, Indian (?), and Arabic. Understand this, may God prolong your life.

Thus, counter to the tradition that established Latin as the sacral language of the church, the use of Arabic by the Christians of al-Andalus as the language of the Scriptures and, most likely, the liturgy, was advocated and defended. So far we possess complete translations of only the Gospels and the Psalms. But in spite of the paucity of the evidence, we could safely assume that the entire Christian Bible was translated into Arabic by the Christians of al-Andalus.

In a colophon to Book VIII of the collection of canon laws mentioned earlier, the compiler Vincentius informs his patron bishop that he is going to send him the books of Jeremiah and Ezekiel which, we could assume, he was in the process of translating. We could also assume that the brief passages of the Old Testament that are cited by Vincentius in this compendium of canon law are his own translation. These infrequent references (there are altogether only 48 quotations by my reckoning) are derived mainly from *al-tawrāt*, without specific reference, or from the books of the Prophets, with a general reference such as *kamā qāla al-nabīy*, "As the Prophet said." The sources are occasionally mentioned by name and are limited to Isaiah, Jeremiah, or Ezekiel, as well as a single reference to each of Zechariah and Daniel. One reference is made to Job and several to *al-nabīy al-zabūrīy*, the "Prophet of the Psalms." Examples of these passages include, *iksir lil-muḥtāji min khubzika*, "Break some of your bread for the needy" (Isaiah 58:7), or *sakira sayfī fīl-samā'*, "My sword is satiated in the heavens" (Isaiah 34:5) or *man dhā yahabu li-rāsī mā'an am man yaftaḥu li-'aynayya yanbū'a al-dumū'ī ḥattá abkī 'alá hādhihi al-ummah laylan wa-nahāran*, "Who shall give water to my head or shall open for my eyes the fountain of tears that I might weep for this nation by night and by day" (a variation of Jeremiah 9:1).

Citations from the books of the Old Testament in Vincentius' work were, without exception, intended as a Scriptural verification of one or another specific position taken by the church. But that was not the sole purpose of possessing a complete text of the Christian Scriptures as these are defined by the canons of the Church. The liturgical requirements of the church accentuated the need for those parts of the Scriptures that were employed in the ordinary of the mass. Citing the Council of Laodecia (A.D. 365?), Vincentius lists these in the order in which they are to be read in church: the Prophets (*al-anbiyā'*) and Epistles (*al-ḥawārīn*), to be read by the *lectores* (*al-qurrā'*), and the Gospel (*al-injīl*), to be read by *al-diyāqun* ("deacon"). The Psalms were to be sung by *al-mizmārīn* ("psalmodists"). As these instructions, contained in the canons of the church, were written in Arabic, we should safely assume that the liturgy with which they deal must have been in Arabic as well.

While a desire for an Arabic text existed, it did not necessarily generate a single translation accepted by all. On the contrary, we appear to have several strands of translation: two, so far, for the Gospel (Munich vs. Madrid), and three for the Psalms (Vatican, London, Milan).[22]

In addition to two translations in prose (Vatican and London mss.), the Psalms were also rendered in verse (Milan ms.) by Ḥafṣ ibn Albar al-Qūṭī (the Goth) in A.D. 989. Ḥafṣ remarks that as the original of the Psalms which he used was written in poetry (Mozarabic Latin), he found it necessary to execute his own translation also in poetic form, choosing

[22] The main mss. of the translation of the Book of Psalms in prose are those in the Biblioteca Apostolica Vaticana (cod. arab. 5) and the British Library (Arab. Add. 9060). The translation in verse by Ḥafṣ ibn Albar al-Qūṭī has survived only in a copy (now in the Biblioteca Ambrosiana, in Milan) made by David Colville, probably in 1616, from the original in El Escorial which has since disappeared, probably consumed by the fire of 1671. The mss. of the Gospels are more numerous. The main ones are in the Bayerische Staatsbibliothek in Munich (cod. arab. 238), the Biblioteca Nacional, Madrid (Ms. aráb. 4971), and the Qarawiyīn Library in Fās, Morocco (al-'Ābid al-Fāsī, No. 730). Other mss., in the Archives of the Cathedral of León and the British Library, appear to be duplicates.

rajaz as his meter.[23] He alludes to an earlier Arabic translation in prose for which he reserves a rather harsh criticism, describing the translator as inexperienced, self-opinionated and ignorant of the laws of language:

> Since he wished to produce it in Arabic
> Word for word—the action of one inexperienced
> And self-opinionated—he ruined the meanings
> Through his ignorance of the laws of language.
> He saw himself obliged to transpose
> The words, till he spoiled the interpretation.[24]

Unfortunately, we do not know to which earlier translation he refers. Van Koningsveld suggests that "Ḥafṣ' severe criticism in fact refers to the version as preserved in MS.Vat.Ar.5."[25] Unfortunately, he offers no reasoning for this conclusion. Although this may have been the case, it would be rather difficult to identify the basis of Ḥafṣ' criticism of the translation contained in the Vatican manuscript. Was he critical because it was in prose and not in verse? The unknown translator of the text (Vatican 5) is not ill-disposed to the Psalms being sung. On the contrary, quoting Jerome, he emphasizes the significance of sung verse,

> The first to praise God by means of a hymn was Moses who sang to God with the poem (*qaṣīdah*) that is recorded in the Torah. He was followed by Deborah. Then Moses wrote another poem in the Book of Deuteronomy, and made it as a final testament to his people near the time of his death in order that they should know what calamities might befall

---

[23] He employs the meter of *al-rajaz al-mashṭūr*:

mustaf'alun mustaf'alun mustaf'alu,

as for example, Psalm 1:3a:

mithāluhu shajaratun qad ghurisat 'alá sawāqi l-mā'i ḥīna nuqilat

or Psalm 14:1 (or 53:1):

qāla l-jahūlu fī ḍamīri qalbihi an lā ilāha jāḥidun li-rabbihi.

A poem employing this meter is known by the name *urjūzah*.

[24] The translation here quoted is that of D. M. Dunlop, "Ḥafṣ b. Albar — the last of the Goths?," *Journal of the Royal Asiatic Society* (1954), 139-51, here *ll.* 30-33. There now is an edition and French translation of the *urjūzah* by Marie-Thérèse Urvoy, *Le Psautier mozarabe* (Toulouse: Presses universitaires du Mirail, 1994).

[25] *The Latin-Arabic Glossary*, 54.

> them if they abandon their Lord. Hannah, the mother of the Prophet Samuel, sang a poem to God. That was before David the Prophet whom God had chosen to sing the Psalms (*al-zabūr*)....

The fact is that judging by his lengthy introduction, Ḥafṣ appears to have taken great pains to complain. He would certainly have been justified in his complaint about other translators if he had taken the trouble to consult those knowledgeable of the Hebrew original. Was he himself not criticized by Moses ibn 'Ezra' for occasional carelessness?

Ḥafṣ explains that there are always difficulties in translating and that a single word in one language may require several in another to explain it clearly. He is aware that this difficulty is compounded when the translation is in verse. He tells us that he consulted trusted leaders of the community to verify the accuracy of his translation. However, his translation was not without bitter opposition, presumably by those who adhered to Latin as the sacral language:

> I well know that among the ignorant
> And among the obstinate and impossible,
> Of those whom I have omitted and neglected to consult,
> And those whom I was ignorant of and will not assist,
> Are people who will ridicule what I have done
> And will delight in blaming my work.
> And they at the same time know
> That they are hostile towards me,
> And that what I have done is a right thing,
> To which men's minds and hearts will assent,
> And that in it is instruction for them
> And understanding of what was previously not understood.[26]

In the Middle Ages the Book of Psalms was used as an educational tool.[27] Consequently, one wonders if Ḥafṣ' poetic rendition of Arabic

---

[26] Dunlop, *op. cit., ll.* 108-13.

[27] See the summary statement by Beryl Smalley, *The Study of the Bible in the Middle Ages* (Oxford: Blackwell's, 1952), xiv, "The little clerk learned his letters from the Psalter and the Bible would be used in teaching him the liberal arts," citing F. Falk, *Bibelhandschriften und Bibeldrucke in Mainz von achten Jahrhundert bis zur Gegenwart* (Mainz, 1901), where examples are given of the use of the Psalter in education.

Psalms may have been intended for a similar purpose. The meter lends itself to this end and an *urjūzah*[28] was used in the twelfth century to instruct Muslim youth in the fundamentals of their faith.[29]

Different translators are responsible for the two renditions of the Psalms in prose. This is evident even from a cursory glance at the text. Here in parallel columns are the first few verses of Psalm 1:

VATICAN	LONDON
ṭūbā lil-rajul alladhī lam yasluk	*ṭūbā li-rajul alladhī lam yasluk*
fī mū’āmarat al-munāfiqīn	*fī ra’y al-kāfir*
wa-fī ṭarīq al-khāṭi’īn lam yaqum	*wa-fī ṭarīq al-khuṭāt lam yaqif*
wa-‘alá majlis al-mufsidīn lam yajlis	*wa-fī majlis al-mufisidīn lam yajlis*
wa-lākin fī nāmūs al-rabb mashyatuhu	*wa-lākin fī nāmūs al-rabb hawāhu*
wa-fī nāmūsihi yadrus al-nahār wal-layl	*wa-fī sharī‘atihi yadrus nahāran wa-laylan*
wa-yaṣīr mithl al-‘ūd al-maghrūs	*fa-yushbih mithl al-‘ūd al-maghrūs*
‘alá majārī al-miyāh	*‘alá majārī al-miyāh*
alladhī yu‘ṭī thamaratahu fī ḥīnihā	*alladhī yu‘ṭī thamarahu fī waqtihi*

Judging by their respective calligraphy, the Vatican manuscript appears to be the older of the two texts before us. Each demonstrates in its own way the degree of Islamic influence on the translators. While the London manuscript begins with the typical Christian invocation, *bism al-āb wal-ibn wal-rūḥ al-quddūs ilāh wāḥid*, "In the Name of the Father, and of the Son, and of the Holy Spirit, One God," the Introduction ends with a clearly Islamic formula *wa-Allāh a‘lam wa-aḥkam waḥdahu lā sharīka lahu rabb al-‘arsh al-‘aẓīm*, "God alone is All-Knowledgeable, All Wise, having no associate, Lord of the Great Throne." The expression *waḥdahu lā*

[28] See note 23.

[29] There is a striking metric similarity between Ḥafṣ's *urjūzah* and a later one by Yaḥyá al-Qurṭubī (probably twelfth century) known as *al-muqaddimah al-qurṭubīyah* or *urjūzat al-wildān* ("the *urjūzah* of the youth"), which was intended to teach the fundamentals of the faith of Islam to the young; see R. Y. Ebied and M. J. L. Young, "The *urjūzat al-wildān* of Yaḥyā al-Qurṭubī (486-567/1093-1172)" in *Islamic Quarterly* 18 (1974): 15-32.

sharīka lahu is part of a phrase used widely in Islam, particularly on coinage, as we have pointed out earlier in our discussion. Similarly, *rabb al-'arsh al-'aẓīm* is a Qur'anic expression widely used in Muslim devotions.

Unlike its London counterpart, the introduction of the Vatican text begins with the Muslim invocation of the Divine Name, *bism Allāh al-raḥmān al-raḥīm 'awnaka yā rabb*, "In the Name of God, the Most Merciful, Compassionate; [I seek] Your help, O Lord." Similarly, the text of the Psalms proper begins with the Muslim *basmalah* followed by *wa-bihi asta'īn*, "His help I seek." The collection of the Psalms is referred to as *al-zabūr*, the Qur'anic term for the revelation to David, which, we are told in the introduction, contains 150 *sūrah*.

The two strands of the translation of the Gospel (Munich and Madrid) offer a different picture to that of the Psalms. To begin with, however, it should be mentioned that the Madrid text is not complete and is bound together with different parts of the Christian Scriptures from different periods. The writing styles are varied, as is the medium on which the text is written. The most recent portion of this collection—and the longest—is written on paper and dates from A.D. 1542. The earliest part, which includes the Gospels, is fragmentary, written on vellum, and not dated. Within this portion, there is certainly a difference in the writing style between the Gospel according to Matthew and the Gospel of John. Undoubtedly, the fragment containing the latter is the earliest and may be dated on stylistic grounds to the eleventh century. But, whatever the date, it represents a tradition of translation quite distinct from that of the Munich manuscript.

The Munich manuscript (cod. arab. 238) is dated. The introductory remarks to the Gospel according to Luke indicate that the translation was carried out by Isḥāq ibn Bilashku (Velázquez) of Cordoba in the year A.D. 946. The manuscript includes the four Gospels as well as introductory remarks to each.[30] In addition, the work concludes with a lectionary

---

[30] It is quite evident that Ibn Ḥazm had access to yet another, complete, text of the New Testament, which included (in the order presented by Ibn Ḥazm) the four Gospels, the Book of Acts, Revelation, seven Catholic (he refers to them as *al-*

(appointed readings from the Gospels) arranged according to the calendar of the feasts of the Church, as well as an excursus on the means of determining the dates of the beginning of Lent and of Easter.

While the opening page of the introduction to the Gospel of Matthew begins with the Christian invocation, the text of the Gospel itself begins with the Muslim *basmalah*, as do the remaining parts of the text, introductions and Gospels alike. Aside from this, Ibn Bilashku's translation contains some Islamic expressions and other interesting vocabulary. For example, he uses *Yaḥyá*, instead of *Yūḥannā*, for "John" (whether the Baptist or the disciple), but *Ḥannā* for the Ananias, the High Priest, in the passages pertaining to the trial of Jesus. Other terms employed are the Qur'anic term *ḥawārīy* for "disciple," *'arīf* for "centurion," *sukrujah* (a *muwallad* word) instead of *ṣiḥāf* ("plates"), and *arkhūn*, the arabicized Greek term αρχον (*archon*) to mean "principality" or "authority." He uses the term *al-baraqlīṭ*, the term cited by some Muslims as foretelling the prophethood of Muḥammad, but later renders it as *al-rūḥ al-ḥaqq*.

Like its Munich counterpart, the translation contained in the manuscript of Madrid employs the name *Yaḥyá* as the name of the Baptist as well as the writer of the fourth Gospel, but refers to the Son of Zebedee as *Yūḥannā* and to the High Priest as *Ḥannā*. It carelessly uses the term *qissīs* and *usquf* for the Jewish priest and high priest, respectively.

As they underscored their religious identity, the Christians of al-Andalus did not employ the translation of their Scriptures, particularly

---

qānūnīyah) Epistles, and 15 (sic.) Epistles of Paul; see his *Al-Fiṣal fil-milal wal-Ahwā' wal-Niḥal* (Cairo: Muḥammad 'Alī Ṣabīḥ, 1964), vol. 2: 20. The information he gives about the authorship of the Gospels differs from that given by Ibn Bilashku, which prompts me to conclude that the text examined by Ibn Ḥazm is different from that in either the Munich or Madrid manuscripts. This conclusion is confirmed by a comparison of the texts. For example, compare the text of Matthew 5:17 (common numbering) in the Munich manuscript with that of Ibn Ḥazm, *loc. cit.*, p. 34:

Munich: *lā taḥsibū annī ataytu li-naqḍ al-kitāb wal-anbiyā' lam āti li-naqḍihā illā li-itmāmihā*

Ibn Ḥazm: *lā taḥsibū annī ji'tu li-naqḍ al-tawrāt wa-kutub al-anbiyā' innamā ataytu li-itmāmihā*

In this instance, the Madrid and Munich texts are in agreement.

the introductory remarks, to disparage their Muslim overlords or their religion. This, unfortunately, cannot be said of their attitude toward the Jews. After an eloquent statement regarding the ultimate substance of the Psalms, the translator (Vatican manuscript) has a negative comment to make about the Jews,

> [The Psalms indicate] that God is One, idolatry is evil, faith is required, disbelief is to be abandoned. [They affirm] that justice is indispensable and oppression is forbidden, that mercy is laudable and the truth is to be sought, that steadfastness is a gift and lies are reprehensible, that humility is praiseworthy and necessary, that aggression is forbidden, that purity and meekness are praiseworthy, that vanity is ignoble and repentance is ordained, that peace-making is decreed and hope in God is commendable. But more than all of this, [the Psalms] contain the mainstay of the faith of Christianity in its entirety, in the east and the west, and the banner of their religion.

Then, totally unaware of the contradiction, he concludes:

> For they [the Psalms] contain the birth of Christ, God's wrath toward the Jews, and the entry of the gentiles into the faith.

The contrast between the two strands of translation of the Gospel is quite marked. The translation by Ibn Bilashku portrays a society very much at home in its Muslim environment, fully arabicized and not uncomfortable with being islamicized. On the other hand, the Madrid manuscript portrays an Arabic-speaking Christian community that appears to have defined its arabicization to exclude or minimize its islamicization. Fully arabicized, each of the two strands represents a certain stance adopted by the Christian community of al-Andalus vis-à-vis Islam and islamicization. Judging by the contents of their Scriptures, neither compromised its faith; in varying degrees, each comfortably took the cultural and linguistic mantle of Islam as its own.

AMBIVALENCE IN MEDIEVAL RELIGIOUS POLEMIC:

THE INFLUENCE OF MULTICULTURALISM ON THE *DIALOGUES* OF PETRUS ALPHONSI

BARBARA HURWITZ GRANT

THE PREFACE to Peter Abelard's *Dialogue of a Philosopher with a Jew and a Christian* cites the following comment by St. Augustine: "There is no teaching so false that there is not some true teaching mixed in."[1] This maxim also could apply well to Petrus Alphonsi's view of the Muslim and Jew as reflected in his *Dialogues*. This work provides a critique of their religious traditions, and yet shows admiration for them as well. Alphonsi's apparent ambivalence might lead the reader to question either his logical coherence or the sincerity of his conversion from Judaism to Christianity. Yet perhaps it can be traced more easily to the dual purpose of the *Dialogues*. The work is certainly a religious debate, but Alphonsi also uses it as a vehicle to transmit Greco-Arabic science and philosophy as well as more accurate knowledge of Jewish and Muslim religious tradition to the Western Christian world.

This second goal is rare in the polemical tradition, but more common in medieval Christian philosophy and apologetics. Consider the efforts of Clement of Alexandria in the *Protrepticus* or Augustine in *The City of God* to defend Christianity in light of classical Platonism.[2] Perhaps

---

[1] Augustine *Libri duo quaestionum evangeliorum* 2.40, cited in Abelard, *Dialogue of a Philosopher with a Jew and a Christian*, trans. Pierre J. Payer (Toronto, 1979), 23.

[2] Clement of Alexandria, *Protrepticus*, in *Ante-Nicene Fathers*, vol. 2 (Grand Rapids, Mich., 1979), 191-92; Augustine, *The City of God*, trans. Henry S. Bettenson (Harmondsworth, England, 1972), 304-15.

it is more accurate to characterize the *Dialogues* of Alphonsi as apologetic than as polemic; indeed, this is precisely how he describes his own work. Alphonsi explains that after his conversion, some members of his former (Jewish) community accused him of pride, in rejecting God and the law, or ignorance, in misunderstanding the truth of the law; others felt he converted for personal gain, since the Christians now ruled their land. Therefore, in order to explain that his conversion was based on the rational examination of the merits of Christianity, he composed this interior dialogue with his former Jewish self.[3]

Alphonsi's ability to see both positive and negative aspects of Jewish and Muslim culture stems as well from his Spanish milieu. Prior to his conversion, Alphonsi acquired knowledge of medicine, geography, astronomy and Arabic literature, as well as some philosophy and both Jewish and Muslim theology. One might call him an *adīb* in the tradition of the Judaeo-Arabic culture of al-Andalus. Alphonsi records that he was baptized in 1106 in the city of Huesca,[4] which had only been reconquered from the Muslims by Pedro I in 1096. If Huesca was Alphonsi's home, he was raised in a strong Muslim and Jewish environment. And, as court physician to Alphonso I of Aragon and Henry I of England, Alphonsi had ample opportunity to transmit his knowledge of Jewish and Arabic culture to the Christian West. Moreover, his origins in the Jewish community and immersion in Muslim culture bred a deeper understanding. His *Dialogues* could not discuss these traditions superficially. Indeed, to characterize his views of Jews and Muslims accurately, one must distinguish among his attitudes toward (1) their religious beliefs, (2) their personal character, and (3) their cultural achievements. From this, not only can one come to understand Alphonsi's complex view of religious culture, but also begin to re-evaluate the nature of inter-religious debate itself.

---

[3] Petrus Alphonsi, *Dialogi* (Migne *PL*) 157.538.

[4] *Dialogi*, 537.

Religious Belief

The question of religious beliefs and practices as reflected in the law and scripture of Islam and Judaism is central to polemic, and forms an important part of Alphonsi's *Dialogues.* Alphonsi's view of Jewish scripture is generally quite positive. In fact, the two disputants agree to base their debate on the *hebraica veritas.*[5] The Christian speaker infrequently accuses the Jews of textual corruption or debates the meaning of the Hebrew text. This is especially odd since Alphonsi was a convert, and could have used his knowledge of Hebrew and Latin to question Jewish interpretations. As we shall see, he did use his knowledge of Jewish and Muslim traditional literature for this purpose elsewhere in the debate. Alphonsi even permits the Jewish speaker to accuse the Christian of misreading the Hebrew scripture.

Rather than criticizing the Jewish text of the Bible, Alphonsi employs it to prove the truth of the Trinity based on the use of the plural form in the Hebrew names for God. Because God is called *eloha* and *adon* in scripture as well as *elohim* and *adonai,* Alphonsi argues, He is both one and many. Alphonsi adds that, in fact, both plural and singular verb forms are also used of God in the Hebrew text.[6]

Alphonsi's treatment of rabbinic material is innovative within Christian polemic and rather ambivalent. On the one hand, he argues that Jewish post-biblical literature is blasphemous of both the Christian and Jewish concepts of God; on the other hand, as we shall see below, he also uses this literature to prove Christian truths.

Many rabbinic statements which Alphonsi claims to be blasphemous to Judaism are also blasphemous to Christianity, as they concern concepts of God that Jews and Christians hold in common. However, these must be distinguished from statements against Christ and Mary which are blasphemous to Christianity alone. Earlier Christian polemicists who mention post-biblical material tend to stress blasphemies against Christ

---

[5] *Dialogi,* 539.

[6] *Dialogi,* 608-10.

and Mary. Origen, in particular, relates many tales of the promiscuity of Mary and Christ's sorcery and immorality found in the *Toledot Yeshu* and the Talmud.[7] Alphonsi mentions no blasphemies against Mary and only the accusation of sorcery against Christ.[8]

He is much more concerned, however, with blasphemies against God in rabbinic material which are not only heretical to Christianity, but even to Judaism itself. These blasphemies *in Deum* are more numerous in Alphonsi's debate than in the earlier Christian polemics which consider Jewish post-biblical literature.[9] Alphonsi argues primarily that Talmud and midrash contain statements unfitting of God. Anthropomorphism in references to God's tefillin, prayer, dwelling place and emotions degrade God by denying his unity and incorporeality.[10] Similarly, the legend, found in *Ketubot* 77b, that Joshua b. Levi entered Paradise alive by tricking the angel of death degrades God by implying that God was not powerful enough to expel a man from Paradise. As the legend progresses, Alphonsi argues, God also appears to lack omniscience, as he must ask the angel to consult the book of life to see if Joshua had ever sworn falsely.[11] In Alphonsi's opinion, some Jewish post-biblical literature directly contradicts Scripture as well. In particular, he cites biblical authority to prove that talmudic anthropomorphisms are blasphemous.[12]

Alphonsi seems to distinguish between a critique of the Talmud and criticism of Judaism as a whole. It should be noted that a major source for his Talmudic critique is Karaite polemic, and thus reflects debate

---

[7] Origen, *Contra Celsum*, trans. Henry Chadwick (Cambridge, 1965), 1.32, bks. 1 and 2 passim; Marc Lods, "Étude sur les sources juives de la polémique de Celse contre les chrétiens," *Revue d'histoire et de philosophie religieuse* 21 (1941): 9-10.

[8] *Dialogi*, 647.

[9] Cf. Agobard of Lyons, *De judaicis superstitionibus* (Migne *PL*) 104.87-88; Amolo, *Liber contra judaeos* (Migne *PL*) 116.167-69.

[10] *Dialogi*, 543, 549-51. For the tradition of God's tefillin and prayer, cf. *Berakhot* 6a-7a; for God's dwelling place, cf. *Baba Batra* 25a and *Sanhedrin* 91b; for God's emotions, cf. *Berakhot* 7a, 59a, 3a.

[11] *Dialogi*, 567.

[12] *Dialogi*, 553-54.

within Judaism itself about the authority of post-biblical tradition. Primarily, Alphonsi adopts standard Karaite polemical arguments against the authority of the Talmud. His criticism of the anthropomorphism of God in *Berakhot* 3a and 7a (God's tears, prayers and tefillin) appears to be drawn from Karaite polemicists such as Kirkisānī.[13] One could possibly add to the list of Karaite elements in Alphonsi's polemic the general accusation that the truth of Jewish post-biblical literature cannot be trusted because of its human authorship and transmission. Kirkisānī notes that its falsehood is demonstrated by the variety of contradictory rabbinic opinions on many matters.[14]

Alphonsi also offers the general view that talmudic literature is contrary to reason and nature (as reflected in science). There is some evidence that Alphonsi may have drawn upon the *Kitāb al-fiṣal* of Ibn Ḥazm for his arguments from reason,[15] but given the generally rationalist tone of Alphonsi's entire dialogue, he may well have developed these arguments himself. His application of science to this topic appears completely original. Talmudic anthropomorphisms, Alphonsi argues, are both irrational and unnatural. For example, traditions concerning God's anger and tears are contrary to reason because they contradict God's incorporeality. They are unnatural, because medicine proves that anger and tears are caused by the humors, which are material. Since God is incorporeal, He cannot have these emotions.[16]

Although Alphonsi argues that rabbinic literature is blasphemous to both Christianity and Judaism, he sees no contradiction in also claiming that this material can be used to prove Christian truths. He asserts that

---

[13] *Dialogi*, 541-43, 550-51; Leon Nemoy, "Al-Qirqisānī's Account of the Jewish Sects and Christianity," *Hebrew Union College Annual* 7 (1930): 351; Wilhelm Bacher, "Qirqisānī, the Qaraite, and his Work on Jewish Sects," in *Karaite Studies*, ed. Philip Birnbaum (New York, 1971), 270.

[14] *Dialogi*, 542-43; Bacher, "Qirqisānī," 268.

[15] *Dialogi*, 564-67; Ibn Ḥazm, *Kitāb al-fiṣal*, in *Abenházam de Córdoba*, trans. Miguel Asín Palacios, vol. 2 (Madrid, 1928), 379-91.

[16] *Dialogi*, 549-50.

the rabbis themselves knew that Christ was the Messiah, and that the second captivity was a punishment for the crucifixion.

As rabbinic evidence that Christ was the Messiah, Alphonsi alludes to the talmudic legend, found in *Sanhedrin* 98a, of Joshua b. Levi and the Messiah at the gates of Rome, implying that he recognized that the Messiah had already come. Alphonsi comments:

> When asked when the son of David would come, [Joshua b. Levi] said, "today, if you would believe his words." He meant by this that the son of God would come to whomever, at any hour, was obedient and believed Christ's mandates.[17]

Rabbi Gamaliel I is also said to have recognized that Christ was the Messiah. Alphonsi argues that he changed the Jewish calendar so that Passover did not fall on Monday, Wednesday or Friday, for he did not wish the Jews to rejoice on the days when Christ was tried, convicted and executed. However, Gamaliel kept his reasons for the change a secret from the Jewish people.[18]

To prove that the rabbis also knew that the crucifixion was the true cause of the second captivity, Alphonsi cites a talmudic tradition, found in *Yoma* 39b, concerning portents of the second destruction of the Temple. He notes that forty years before the Temple's destruction, the candelabra facing west were extinguished before the accustomed time, and the doors of the Temple opened loudly and spontaneously. When Johanan b. Zakkai saw this, he declared that the Temple would be burned a second time, citing Zechariah 11.1, which states: "Open thy doors, O Lebanon, that the fire may devour thy cedars." Alphonsi argues that since these portents coincide with Christ's death, Johanan b. Zakkai and the other rabbis knew that the cause of the destruction was the crucifixion, but they were silent and attributed it to other causes.[19]

---

[17] *Dialogi*, 581. All translations from Alphonsi's *Dialogi* are my own.

[18] *Dialogi*, 665.

[19] *Dialogi*, 573-74.

Later debates, such as the thirteenth-century disputations at Barcelona and Paris, would take a position either in opposition to the Talmud or in support of it. At Paris, Nicholas Donin accused the Talmud of blasphemies against God and Jesus, as well as foolishness, and he questioned the authority of the Talmud and rabbis.[20] As a result of this disputation, the Talmud was condemned and burned in Paris. On the other hand, Pablo Christiani attempted to show at Barcelona that the Talmud proved the truth of Christianity. Like Alphonsi, he used the story of Joshua b. Levi and the Messiah at the gates of Rome, but more directly and effectively. Christiani stressed the implications in this legend that the Messiah had already come since Joshua speaks to him. He also notes that the Messiah's presence in Rome binding the lepers bears great resemblance to the life of Christ.[21]

As we have seen, Alphonsi presents the Talmud both positively and negatively. It is possible that he had not noted the inherent contradiction in this, or perhaps he simply wished to provide his Christian audience with all possible uses of rabbinic literature in polemic. Yet, it should be noted that it is in the Spanish disputation, not the French, that the Christian disputant chooses the less destructive use of Talmud for Christian polemical purposes. Similarly, Alphonsi may be influenced by the multicultural atmosphere of Spain to argue, as Augustine does, that even false doctrine can have some truth intermixed.

We now turn to Alphonsi's view of Muslim religious belief. His critique of Islam generally seems more harsh than his views on Judaism; yet upon closer examination, even this discussion becomes more subtle than it first appears. Alphonsi begins by allowing his Jewish disputant to enumerate at length the virtues of Islam over Christianity. Islam is depicted as a religion of divine love and reason, distinguished by monotheism, daily prayer, cleanliness, fasting and moderation. The Jew praises Mus-

---

[20] Judah M. Rosenthal, "The Talmud on Trial: The Disputation at Paris in the Year 1240," *Jewish Quarterly Review* n.s. 47 (1956): 76.

[21] Naḥmanides, *Disputation at Barcelona*, in *Writings and Discourses*, trans. Charles B. Chavel (New York, 1978), 2:658-60, 667-71.

lim laws of purity regarding food and drink, and a legal system that protects women and the innocent. He also notes without criticism other practices, such as the Meccan cult, sensual Paradise and *jihād*, which a Jew would certainly view less positively.[22] This leads the reader to suspect that Alphonsi is in fact setting up strawmen to be demolished later by the Christian disputant. Nonetheless, the length and tone of this description indicate that Alphonsi not only wished to prepare the groundwork for his critique, but also desired to provide a relatively complete and accurate description of Islamic beliefs and customs to a Christian West that had little direct knowledge of the Muslim. Norman Daniel notes that the *Dialogues* were, in fact, one of the earliest sources of sound information about Islam to the West.[23]

Alphonsi's assertion of Islamic monotheism alone is a positive step, as it appears that there was a popular assumption in Western literature that Islam was a polytheistic religion. Consider the following lines from the *Song of Roland*:

> The Emir calls upon Apollo,
> Tervagant and also Mohammed:
>
> "My lord gods, I have served you very long,
> I shall make all your graven images pure gold."[24]

This "trinity" of Muḥammad, Apollo and Tervagant is found throughout the chansons de geste, and chronicles of the First Crusade also speak of Islamic "gods." The idea, present in the romances, that Muslims worshipped an image of Muḥammad may be derived from legends about the Black Stone of the Ka'ba.[25] Although Alphonsi also describes the

---

[22] *Dialogi*, 597-99. For a discussion of Jewish criticism of the Meccan cult, see Bernard Septimus, "Petrus Alphonsi and the Cult at Mecca," *Speculum* 56 (1981): 517-33.

[23] Norman A. Daniel, *Islam and the West: The Making of an Image* (Edinburgh, 1960), 234.

[24] Gerard J. Brault, ed. and trans., *The Song of Roland* (Oxford Text) (University Park-London, 1978), laisse 253, lines 3490-93.

[25] Dorothée Metlitzki, *The Matter of Araby in Medieval England* (New Haven, 1977), 209-10.

stones of the Ka'ba, he clearly and accurately considers them a vestige of pre-Islamic paganism, rather than evidence of Muslim idolatry.

The refutation of Islam in the *Dialogues* is rooted in a critique of Muḥammad and the early Arabs. The weakness of the origins of Islam is meant to undercut its system of belief and custom. Alphonsi begins with an attack on Muḥammad's status as prophet. He depicts an early life of poverty and idolatry, and attributes Muḥammad's wealth to his marriage with the widow Khadīja. Alphonsi claims that Muḥammad fashioned himself a prophet in order to use his eloquence to rise to power among the Arabs, since he was not of noble birth.[26]

Subsequently, he argues that even the miracles attributed to Muḥammad were not legitimate when compared with those of the Old Testament prophets.[27] The Jewish disputant then notes several miracles credited to Muḥammad, and found in various accounts of the life of the prophet. These include the sheep that gave milk when touched by the prophet, the fig tree that came when he called, and the leg of mutton that warned the prophet that it was poisoned. Alphonsi dismisses such stories as frivolities not attested by the Qur'ān. In fact, he notes that Muḥammad himself records that Allah did not permit him to work miracles lest he be refuted by miracles like other prophets.[28]

There are numerous parallels between Alphonsi's critique of Islam and the Arabic *Risālah* attributed to a certain Christian named al-Kindī (not to be confused with the ninth-century Muslim philosopher). The authorship and date of this work are disputed,[29] but it appears to date

[26] *Dialogi*, 599-600.

[27] *Dialogi*, 600.

[28] *Dialogi*, 600-1. For the miracles attributed to Muḥammad, cf. Ibn Hishām, *Al-sīrah al-nabawiyyah* (Cairo, 1955), 1:391, 1:487, 2:337-38; Ibn Ḥazm, *Jawāmi' al-sīrah* (Cairo, n.d.), 11-13, cited in Georges Tartar, trans., *Dialogue islamo-chrétien sous le calife al-Ma'mūn (813–834)* (Paris, 1985), 162-63 (hereafter cited as al-Kindī, *Risālah*).

[29] For a more detailed discussion of the scholarly debate on these points, see *The Encyclopedia of Islam*, new ed., *s.v.* "Al-Kindī, 'Abd al-Masīḥ b. Isḥāk," which notes that al-Birūnī alone refers to the author as "'Abd al-Masīḥ b. Isḥāq al-Kindī," while the headings of certain manuscripts give the name "Ya'qūb b. Isḥāq al-Kindī," perhaps

from before the eleventh century, and is of Spanish origin. The *Risālah* was another major source of information about Islam to the Christian West. Translated by Peter of Toledo as part of the Cluniac corpus, excerpts were included in the thirteenth-century *Speculum Historiale* of Vincent of Beauvais. The *Risālah* also appears to have had considerable influence on Alphonsi's polemic.[30] This work mentions the same miracles attributed to the prophet[31] and asserts that they are based on false texts outside the Qur'ān. Like Alphonsi, the author of the *Risālah* notes the Qur'ānic statement that Allah did not permit Muḥammad to work miracles lest he be refuted like earlier prophets.[32]

Alphonsi states that the prophet's personal character and pragmatic goals, not divine inspiration, were at the root of many Muslim customs. For example, the prohibition of pork was a pragmatic decision to distinguish Islam from Christianity.[33] The laws permitting multiple wives were instituted out of Muḥammad's own excessive lust. Alphonsi notes the story in which Muḥammad tells his adopted son Zayd b. Ḥāritha that Allāh commanded that Zayd divorce his wife Zaynab bint Jaḥsh. When this was done, Muḥammad immediately took her as his own wife. This tale is also recorded in the *Risālah*; its source is to be found in Qur'ān 33.37.[34] Alphonsi notes further that when Muḥammad's wife 'Ā'isha was caught in adultery, he asserted that by the authority of Gabriel and the testimony of others, she was not an adultress. Muḥammad did this, Alphonsi argues, because he desired her and did not wish to lose her as

---

confusing him with the philosopher. See also Daniel, *Islam and the West*, 6.

[30] This view is shared by Guy Monnot, "Les citations coraniques dans le 'Dialogus' de Pierre Alphonse," *Cahiers de Fanjeaux* 18 (1983): 270-72, and by J. H. L. Reuter, "Petrus Alphonsi: An Examination of his Works, their Scientific Content, and their Background" (Dissertation, Oxford University, 1975), 68-90, 238-39, cited in John Tolan, *Petrus Alphonsi and his Medieval Readers* (Gainsville, Fla., 1993), 219 n. 54.

[31] Al-Kindī, *Risālah*, 161-63.

[32] Al-Kindī, *Risālah*, 159, citing Qur'ān 17.61(59).

[33] *Dialogi*, 604.

[34] *Dialogi*, 601; al-Kindī, *Risālah*, 149.

his wife. Again, this story, based on Qur'ān 24.11ff., and repeated by Ibn Isḥāq, is also found in the *Risālah*.[35] Alphonsi mentions twice the tradition that Muḥammad possessed forty times the lust of normal men, and that Allah praised that lust, and congratulated him that the beauty of women pleased him so greatly. This tradition, traceable to al-Bukhārī, is again found in the *Risālah*.[36] These three stories, among others, became quite popular in later Latin literature in which Alphonsi's implication that Muḥammad invented revelations to fulfill his lust was repeated. However, Alphonsi's comment that Muḥammad "loved women greatly" was moderate in comparison to the judgments of later Christian writers, who reviled Muḥammad as "stinking with the sin of lust" and "mad with desire for women."[37]

To undermine Muḥammad's prophetic status naturally sheds doubt upon the legitimacy of his revelation. To this end, Alphonsi argues that the Qur'ān was heavily influenced by Jewish and Christian heresy, rather than divine truth:

> There was, in that time, in the region of Antioch, a certain archdeacon who was a friend of Muḥammad. And this Jacobite was called to a council and condemned. Grieved by the shame of condemnation, he fled the region and came to Muḥammad...There were also among the Arabs two Jews, whom we call heretics, named Abdias and Cahbalahabar, and they joined with Muḥammad...And these three tempered the law of Muḥammad according to their heresy, and advised him to say on the part of God those things that the Jewish and Christian heretics who were in Arabia believed to be true.[38]

The reference to a Jacobite archdeacon appears to be a version of the legend of the Nestorian monk Sergius, who fled to Arabia after his condemnation by the Church and proceeded to corrupt Islam by influenc-

---

[35] *Dialogi*, 601; Ibn Isḥāq, *The Life of Muḥammad*, trans. Alfred Guillaume (Oxford, 1955), 731ff.; al-Kindī, *Risālah*, 150-51.

[36] *Dialogi*, 604-5; Daniel, *Islam and the West*, 96-97, citing al-Bukhārī 6.xii; al-Kindī, *Risālah*, 149.

[37] Daniel, *Islam and the West*, 102.

[38] *Dialogi*, 600.

ing Muḥammad with his heresy. This story, present in the *Risālah* as well,[39] is again found in numerous later Latin works. The confusion of Jacobite (Monophysite) and Nestorian is understandable for someone such as Alphonsi, who, living in Spain, may never have encountered either. The Nestorian doctrine, of course, was more in harmony with Islam than the Jacobite. The names Abdias and Cahbalahabar are apparently Latin corruptions of ʻAbd Allāh b. Salām and Kaʻb al-Aḥbār, two Jews also mentioned in the *Risālah* as an influence on Muḥammad.[40]

Alphonsi asserts that the establishment of the Qur'ānic text after the prophet's death led to rational contradictions within it. Noting conflicting passages in the Qur'ān concerning conversion by force versus persuasion, he states that Muḥammad's version was revised by his followers after his death so that it is impossible to distinguish between the words of the prophet and those of his associates. This argument is made in even greater detail in the *Risālah*.[41]

The second part of Alphonsi's critique of Islam centers on certain aspects of Muslim law. But here too personal character is linked to the development of belief and custom. As Bernard Septimus has shown, Alphonsi draws upon Hispano-Jewish sources to argue that the Meccan cult of the Kaʻba was an adaptation of a pagan, polytheistic custom to Islam. In particular, Septimus notes that like Hispano-Jewish tradition, Alphonsi does not view the Meccan cult as evidence of Muslim polytheism. Rather, he, like the Jewish sources, affirms Islam's monotheism while condemning its retention of this pagan practice.[42] Alphonsi claims that Muḥammad kept this ritual in order to encourage conversion among the Arabs.[43] In much the same way, one could argue, the early Christian Church kept customs of Roman and Germanic paganism in order to facilitate conversion.

---

[39] Al-Kindī, *Risālah*, 180-81.

[40] Al-Kindī, *Risālah*, 181.

[41] *Dialogi*, 603-4; al-Kindī, *Risālah*, 182-92

[42] Septimus, "Cult at Mecca," 517-33.

[43] *Dialogi*, 603.

Alphonsi attributes the permission of several wives and limited fasts in Islam to the natural lust and gluttony of the early Arabs. He notes, with a certain elitism, that the first converts to Islam were of the lower classes. Alphonsi's view of early Arab character is best summarized by his own words:

> [M]en in the time of Muḥammad—without law, without scripture, ignorant of all good except the army and farm, lustful and given to gluttony—could easily be preached to according to their desires. For if he [Muḥammad] had done otherwise, he would not have attracted them to his law.[44]

Personal Character

To this point, Alphonsi has hardly presented an attractive picture of Arab character, and one must ask whether he speaks only of the Arabs of the seventh century, or also of the more sophisticated Muslims he knew in twelfth-century Spain. When discussing Jewish character, Alphonsi specifically mentions both Jews of the Old Testament and the time of Christ, as well as his contemporaries. Yet here he never refers to Arabs of his own age, and is careful to note that those he describes so disparagingly are "men in the time of Muḥammad." Indeed, there was a tradition within Islam itself to characterize the pre-Islamic period in Arabia as *jāhiliyyah*, variously translated as "time of ignorance" or "time of barbarism."[45] So contemporary Muslims might not have considered this characterization as a criticism of themselves, nor may Alphonsi have meant it as such. Furthermore, in the *Disciplina Clericalis*, Alphonsi depicts many Arabs as intelligent or noble,[46] so it is possible that his view of Arab character is more complex than it first appears. His critique clearly centers on

---

[44] *Dialogi*, 605.

[45] My thanks to Suzanne Stetkevych for bringing this tradition to my attention. Cf. Qur'ān 33.33; *Encyclopedia of Islam*, new ed., *s.v.* "djāhiliyya;" F. E. Peters, *Allah's Commonwealth* (New York, 1973), 45, 251.

[46] Petrus Alphonsi, *Disciplina Clericalis*, ed. and trans. Eberhard Hermes and P. R. Quarrie (Berkeley-Los Angeles, 1977), 112-14, 156-58.

early rather than contemporary Islam. It is unlikely that Alphonsi is attempting to protect himself personally or politically, since he wrote the *Dialogues* after his region of Spain came under Christian control. It is more likely that he had personal respect for his Muslim contemporaries and did not wish to insult them directly or present them unfavorably to his Christian audience.

It is also essential to note that Alphonsi's picture of the Arab may be harsh, but it is decidedly more realistic than the popular Western Christian view of the evil, bestial or monstrous Saracen that one finds in the contemporary *Song of Roland*.[47] As Benjamin Kedar has remarked, Alphonsi's *Dialogues* "undemonize" the Arab.[48] Clearly, the humanizing of the Muslim is an enormous step within the context of Western Christian perception.

Alphonsi's view of Jewish character is less harsh than his view of the Arab. This is no doubt due to his origins in the Jewish community. Alphonsi repeats the traditional accusations that the Jews willfully opposed God by killing Christ, just as they had killed or persecuted their prophets in the Old Testament.[49] He complains of the obstinacy of the Jews in not accepting Christianity; but while he shows occasional frustration with his Jewish opponent, he prefers to argue rationally that Jewish beliefs and practices contradict religious truth. In comparison, consider the twelfth-century Christian polemicist Peter the Venerable, abbot of Cluny, who argues rationally as well, yet uses reason to attack Jewish character. As Amos Funkenstein notes, Peter argues the following syllogism: Since man is a rational animal, and the Jews will not listen to reason, therefore the Jews are not men, but beasts.[50] Clearly, this sort of personal invective against the Jew surpasses even Alphonsi's view of early Arab character.

---

[47] *Song of Roland*, laisses 232-36.

[48] Benjamin Z. Kedar, *Crusade and Mission: European Approaches toward the Muslims* (Princeton, 1984), 92.

[49] *Dialogi*, 567-81.

[50] Amos Funkenstein, "Basic Types of Christian Anti-Jewish Polemics in the Later Middle Ages," *Viator* 2 (1971): 378.

As we have seen, Alphonsi employs his knowledge of Jewish and Muslim traditional literature to critique these two religions. We will see that he even draws upon Jewish and Muslim philosophy and science for this purpose, and so one must also discuss Alphonsi's view of Judaeo-Arabic culture in relation to belief and character.

Cultural Achievement

Petrus Alphonsi is best known for his contributions to Western Christian knowledge of Greco-Arabic science. As court physician to Henry I of England at the beginning of the twelfth century, it has been recognized that he taught astronomy to Walcher of Malvern and others. Alphonsi's astronomical tables, based on al-Khwārizmī, were also used by Adelard of Bath in 1126. Although primarily a theological treatise, the *Dialogues* also provide a medium for the transmission of science.

Alphonsi's knowledge of science, as well as philosophy, was drawn from Arab culture directly and through the filter of Jewish society. It is often difficult to determine whether his source was Jewish or Muslim because many of his arguments are based on rather generic principles. For example, he explains the transformation of man from immortality to mortality after the fall of Adam in terms of a change in the balance of humors within the body. Alphonsi argues that when Adam was created, the balance of humors which he possessed also kept his temperament even. But as soon as he considered disobedience, the humors lost equilibrium, and he became proud and so defied God.[51] The theory of humors is a principle of medicine found in Aristotle and Galen, and adopted generally in both Jewish and Muslim medicine.[52] It is not possible to pinpoint Alphonsi's source; yet he is unique in applying this theory to theology.

---

[51] *Dialogi*, 642.

[52] Galen, *On the Natural Faculties*, trans. Arthur J. Brock (London-New York, 1928), 173; Aristotle *De generatione et corruptione* (trans. McKeon) 2.1.

In the realm of philosophy, his discussion of the Trinity is informed by the arguments concerning God's unity and the question of divine attributes found in Muslim *kalām*. As H. A. Wolfson notes, orthodox Islam stated that these attributes were real and eternal, a view influenced by Christian trinitarian doctrine during the early contact between Christianity and Islam. Orthodox Muslims denied, however, that these attributes were gods themselves, asserting that they were merely properties of God. In the first half of the eighth century, an anti-attributist position arose, held mainly by the Mu'tazilites, which denied the reality and eternity of attributes, based on the argument that eternity implies divinity, and that the unity of God excludes internal plurality.[53] The Jewish Mutakallimūn, such as Saadia Gaon, drew upon this Muslim critique of attributes to argue that the reality of attributes compromised God's unity, simplicity and incorporeality.[54]

This Judaeo-Arabic philosophical tradition is evident in Alphonsi's attributist discussion of the Trinity. He argues that the Creator must have wisdom and will. So that He knows what He could create, He first has wisdom. But since He does not create what He does not desire to create, He must also have will.[55] Following Christian doctrine and the concerns of anti-attributists, Alphonsi proceeds to prove that the attributes of wisdom and will are eternally with God. He argues that these attributes cannot be separated from God after He has them, for if they were, then God would be unknowing after He was knowing, or without will after He had will. This would imply that God possessed accidence, which is impossible.[56]

Alphonsi's argument presents a peculiar twist on the view of Saadia and other Jewish Mutakallimūn that divine attributes are with God eter-

---

[53] Harry Austryn Wolfson, *The Philosophy of the Kalam* (Cambridge, Mass., 1976), 132-33, 313-14.

[54] Daniel J. Lasker, *Jewish Philosophical Polemics against Christianity in the Middle Ages* (New York, 1977), 57-60, 63.

[55] *Dialogi*, 606-7.

[56] *Dialogi*, 607.

nally, while human attributes can be acquired or lost. They argue that therefore, only man's attributes have real distinct existence apart from man. God's attributes have no such ontological status, and therefore, one cannot equate them with the Trinity.[57] Alphonsi takes this proof of the eternity of attributes and uses it to prove trinitarian doctrine. On the whole, Alphonsi is particularly creative in his use of Jewish philosophical arguments to counter the Jewish position, and it has been noted that Alphonsi makes extensive use of Jewish philosophy in his debate.[58]

Alphonsi's statement concerning accidence is also an ironic twist on a Muslim anti-attributist argument. The Muslim philosopher al-Kindī argues, in Yaḥyā b. 'Adī's *Defense of the Doctrine of the Trinity*, that if the hypostases of the Trinity are accidents, then they are composite and therefore physical, which is unfitting of God.[59] Here, Alphonsi argues that only by accepting the Trinity can one avoid attributing accidence to God's nature.

The influence of Islamic astronomy and geography is also extensive, particularly in the first chapter of the *Dialogues*. During a critique of the attribution of place to God in Jewish tradition, Alphonsi demonstrates the ease with which he will leave his polemical point for a scientific discussion. Having mentioned the fact that the sun rises and sets at different times depending on the longitude of a city, he proceeds to explain the Muslim method of determining longitude by astronomical calculation. The example he gives is of the distance between a city called Aren and a neighboring city. (Aren was an ideal city located by Muslim geographers at the center of the world.) Alphonsi explains the determination of longitude, as Muslim geography does, by reference to the difference in the time of a solar eclipse and the position of the constellations in each city.[60]

---

[57] Lasker, *Philosophical Polemics*, 54, 56; Saadia Gaon, *The Book of Beliefs and Opinions*, trans. Samuel Rosenblatt (New Haven, 1948), 2.5.

[58] Funkenstein, "Basic Types," 379.

[59] Wolfson, *Kalam*, 323-24, citing *Defense*, 6-10.

[60] *Dialogi*, 546; G. H. T. Kimble, *Geography in the Middle Ages* (London, 1938), 65.

The purpose of this digression is unclear, unless Alphonsi is merely clarifying the previous point about longitude. However, he is also indirectly providing practical information for his Latin readers. The astronomical determination of longitude was used by Muslim geographers to determine distances between cities. This, in turn, was useful for commerce, travel and diplomacy. It was through translators such as Alphonsi that this information came from the Muslims to the Latin West. In a letter addressed to the peripatetics of France, and found in an English manuscript as a preface to Alphonsi's astronomical treatise, he criticizes Latin scholars for their reliance on old authorities such as Macrobius. He urges them to rely instead on their own observation and experiments, and to learn from him the superior astronomical knowledge of the Arabs.[61] Since Alphonsi indicates in this letter his strong desire to teach Arabic astronomy to Latins, and to correct Latin misconceptions based on old authorities, it is likely that this was also his motivation for the astronomical digressions in the *Dialogues.*

Later in the same chapter, he digresses again for more than the purposes of clarification or useful knowledge. In this case, Alphonsi wishes to correct a Western Christian view according to Muslim science. Alphonsi's Christian disputant notes that Aren is located in the first climate, which leads the Jew to ask him to describe this climatic system. The Jew notes that many books divide the earth into five zones: the middle zone (equator), uninhabitable because of heat, two polar zones, uninhabitable due to cold, and the two zones between the equator and the poles, which are temperate, and therefore habitable.[62] This tradition is found in Pliny, and was accepted by early medieval writers such as Macrobius, Isidore of Seville and Bede.[63] It was not, however, the view of Ptolemy and the Arab geographers, nor of Alphonsi. His Christian disputant rejects the stan-

---

Muslim geographers more commonly used the lunar eclipse.

[61] MS BM Arundel 270, fols. 40v-44v, cited by Metlitzki, *Matter of Araby*, 22-23 and n.

[62] *Dialogi*, 546.

[63] Kimble, *Geography*, 41-42, citing Bede *De natura rerum* 9; Macrobius *Commentarius* 2.5.

dard Latin Christian view, asserting that the equator is part of a temperate zone stretching northward, which is divided into seven climates. The north pole is uninhabitable due to extreme cold, and the land south of the equator is uninhabitable because of extreme heat. There is no part of the seven climates that is uninhabitable, except for portions that are too dry or mountainous.[64] This was the standard theory of Greco-Arabic and Jewish geographers, although there was some debate over the inhabitability of the equator.[65]

Alphonsi appears to be addressing the conflict between the Plinean and Ptolemaic theories. It is also possible that he was aware of the conflict over the habitability of the equator, and was expressing his own opinion. Clearly, Alphonsi considered the disagreement between Latin Christian and Judaeo-Arabic science significant enough to warrant his digression from the polemical point.

In another case, Alphonsi takes a rather large risk in following Muslim learning. During a discussion of the Creation, he raises the question of the eternity of time and space, noting that Christians deny their eternity while ancient philosophers affirm it. This is partially true. Orthodox Christians, Jews and Muslims denied the eternity of time and space because this would imply that things exist outside of God which are coeternal with Him, and therefore uncreated. The ancient philosophers were divided on the issue; Aristotle denied their eternity, while Plato affirmed it.[66]

Alphonsi not only refutes the Christian position, but he draws on the free-thinking Muslim philosopher, al-Rāzī, to do so.[67] Aristotle argued

---

[64] *Dialogi*, 546; Kimble, *Geography*, 50-51, citing Ibn Khurdādhbih, *Kitāb al-masālik wal-mamālik*, trans. M. J. de Goeje, vol. 6, *Bibliotheca geographorum arabicorum* (Leiden, 1889), 2-3.

[65] *Encyclopedia Judaica*, Jerusalem ed., *s.v.* "geography."

[66] Aristotle *Physica* (trans. McKeon) 4; Plato *Timaeus* (trans. Jowett) 37c-d, 52b.

[67] Reuter ("Petrus Alphonsi," 110-14) notes as well that Alphonsi borrows al-Rāzī's concept of five eternal essences, which include God, soul, matter, time and space (see Tolan, *Medieval Readers*, 222 n. 19).

that space is defined only by a body occupying it. Alphonsi uses al-Rāzī's distinction between universal and particular space to argue that only particular space is defined this way. Universal space—the void—is caused by itself and is eternal. Denying Aristotle again, Alphonsi implements al-Rāzī's argument that time is independent of motion to prove that time is also uncaused. Motion does not produce, but only reveals time. To use the example of Alphonsi, the motion of water in a water clock does not cause time, but is only a sign of time's passing.[68]

Al-Rāzī was one of the leading medical authorities of his time, a philosopher, and like Alphonsi, generally well trained in the Greco-Arabic sciences. Although al-Rāzī was more radical than Alphonsi in asserting the superiority of philosophy to prophetic revelation,[69] both men in this case chose philosophy over religious doctrine. This is remarkable in both theology and polemic. Although the *Dialogues* became a major source for later Christian polemical literature, and the text was copied throughout the High and Late Middle Ages, the attention of Church authorities apparently was never drawn to these questionable arguments. In the later Middle Ages, the text of the *Dialogues* is found in excerpted form, but this appears to have been for the purpose of making his material on Islam and the Talmud more accessible, rather than censorship.

One question remains. Does Alphonsi consider the science and philosophy he cites in the *Dialogues* to be a Greek achievement rather than the product of Judaeo-Arabic culture? He never names his Jewish or Muslim sources; but, on the other hand, the only philosophical or scientific sources identified in the entire work are Plato (cited once), and "the ancient philosophers" noted above.[70] Alphonsi occasionally refers to "philosophers" in general, but he does not distinguish ancient from contemporary Arab or Jewish philosophers. It is typical of medieval authors

---

[68] *Dialogi*, 560-61; Majid Fakhry, *A History of Islamic Philosophy*, 2nd ed. (New York-London, 1983), 103-4, citing al-Rāzī, *Opera philosophica*, ed. Paul Kraus (Cairo, 1939), 258f.

[69] *Encyclopedia of Islam*, new ed., *s.v.* "al-Rāzī, Abū Bakr Muḥammad b. Zakariyyā'."

[70] *Dialogi*, 560.

not to cite all of their sources, so Alphonsi may not be attempting a deliberate deception here. In any case, what reader, even in the Christian West, would be unaware that the source of Alphonsi's knowledge was the Judaeo-Arabic society of Spain? In drawing so heavily on this culture, Alphonsi again reveals his second purpose—the transmission of Judaeo-Arabic learning to the Christian West—and appears to express the view that even false religious traditions can possess some truth.

Conclusions

What conclusions can be drawn from this complex of attitudes present in the *Dialogues*? First, Alphonsi appears more harsh in his critique of Islam than of Judaism, although this may be counterbalanced by the fact that he devotes five chapters to the refutation of Judaism and only one to Islam. Furthermore, his criticism of both Judaism and Islam is directed at their law rather than Jews and Muslims themselves. Although Alphonsi's view of the early Arabs is derogatory, his purpose is to undermine the origins of their law, and he does not extend this to contemporary Islam. He offers to the West in particular a more human Arab, and his depiction of the Jew is more tolerant than certain other twelfth-century rationalists. Even Alphonsi's criticism of Jewish and Muslim law is not unmitigated. He argues that the Talmud is a source of Christian truth, and asserts Islamic monotheism. The separation of Arab from Islam and Jew from Judaism is particularly apparent in his view of Judaeo-Arabic culture. As we have seen, Alphonsi draws upon Judaeo-Arabic science and philosophy freely (and in some cases extensively) to elucidate his religious arguments as well as to contradict misconceptions of Western Christian science.

This ambivalent view of Jew and Muslim is not due to the insincerity of his conversion, but rather to the power of Judaeo-Arabic culture in shaping Alphonsi's personal views and interests through his experience of living in Islamic Spain. Familiarity also bred in Alphonsi a multidimensional understanding of Jews and Muslims not available to Northern Europe. He is very much akin to the author of the contemporary *Poem of the Cid*, who presents the Muslim as a human being who acts as honorably as Christians, and occasionally even surpasses the Christian in nobility.[71] The many levels of Alphonsi's *Dialogues* lead the reader to realize that this work considers more than just religious doctrine. Integrally related are the issues of ethnic character and intellectual culture. Alphonsi may be unusual in terms of his use of science in religious debate, yet polemic before and certainly after him also operated on levels beyond doctrine. A study of Alphonsi's work merely underscores the social and intellectual, as well as theological, dimensions of religious debate literature.

[71] Consider, for example, the Moor Abengalbón, who escorts the Cid's family to Valencia, and who later correctly mistrusts the intentions of the Heirs of Carrión toward the Cid's daughters; (W. S. Merwin, trans., *Poem of the Cid* [New York, 1975], 147-51, 227-33).

LONGING, BELONGING, AND PILGRIMAGE IN IBN 'ARABĪ'S *INTERPRETER OF DESIRES (Tarjumān al-Ashwāq)*

MICHAEL A. SELLS

SUZANNE STETKEVYCH began the discussion of discourses of power in Andalusia by demonstrating the relationship of the formal *madīḥ-qaṣīdah* to the legitimization of power within the Andalusian state, particularly within the context of rivalry between Andalusian and Baghdadian imperial claims. She showed how the *madīḥ-qaṣīdah* brings into the orbit of the Caliph the various realms—military, economic, and cultural—of the Andalusian world.

The paper I offer here examines Ibn 'Arabī's collection of poems, the *Interpreter of Desires* (*Tarjumān al-Ashwāq*). In these poems, power is dispersed, rather than centralized. Authority and meaning are in a continual state of movement, just beyond the reach of the implied poet and the reader.

Muḥyiddīn Ibn al-'Arabī was born near Murcia in 1165 of a noble family that traced its roots back to Arabia. His father was an official in the court of Ibn Mardanish, whose rebellion, centered at Murcia, was finally crushed by the Almohads in 567 H. His father then took on positions within the Almohad court at Seville. Leading the life of a highly educated son of a noble, Ibn 'Arabī looked forward to a career within the Almohad court. He chose a very different future: the world of *siyāḥah* or wandering. After adopting the Sufi life, Ibn 'Arabī began a lifelong journey that would lead, through and in Andalusia, between Andalusia and Morocco, between Fez and Tunis, to Cairo, Mecca and then throughout the Arab *Sharq* (Damascus, Alepp , Baghdad, Mosul, the Jezira) to Konya, until he finally settled in Damascus in his old age. He died in Damascus in 638/1240 where his tomb became an important Sufi shrine.

According to Ibn 'Arabī's own recollections, the last difficulty in the way of a life of wandering was the death of his father, which left Ibn 'Arabī with the responsibility of finding marriages for his sisters.[1] The Almohads urged him to marry the sisters within the Almohad ruling class. With obvious difficulty and with the need for tact, Ibn 'Arabī managed to marry his sisters outside the world of political transaction, and after that time, cut his connection to the Almohads for good. In doing so, Ibn 'Arabī was to replace the centralized, centripetal hierarchy of the urban court, described so eloquently in Suzanne Stetkevych's paper, for a new hierarchy—a Sufi hierarchy of pole (*quṭb*) and tent pegs (*awtād*) and substitutes (*abdāl*), not to mention such figures as the seal of Muḥammadiyyan saintship. The historical development of such a hierarchy of saints and Ibn 'Arabī's place has received important new attention.[2] The development of an internationalized, non-centralized Sufi hierarchy and its mode of operation will no doubt continue to generate further important work. The focus of this study is on Ibn 'Arabī's famous collection of poems, *Tarjumān al-Ashwāq* (*The Interpreter of Desires* or *The Translation of Desires*) and upon the counter-hierarchical dispersal of power which is key to Ibn 'Arabī's poetics.

The *Tarjumān* exists with a number of different prefaces by the author. In one, he dedicates all the love poems to Niẓām, the daughter of a Meccan Shaykh, whose beauty, Ibn 'Arabī tells us, is too overpowering to be described directly. In a second, he suggests that the poems are also depictions of his experiences on the *ḥajj*, the pilgrimage to the Ka'ba at Mecca, and indeed, many of the stations of journey (*manāzil*) depicted in the poems (such as the stoning-place at Minā) are part of the *ḥajj* pilgrimage. Most of the stations, however, are far more linked to the

---

[1] The above short summary is based upon the recent biography of Ibn 'Arabī by Claude Addas, *The Search for the Red Sulfur: The Life of Ibn 'Arabī* (Oxford: Islamic Texts Society, 1993), published originally in French, *Ibn 'Arabī ou La quête du Soufre Rouge* (Paris: Edition Gallimard, 1989).

[2] See Michel Chodkiewicz, *Le Sceau des aints: prophétie et sainteté dans la doctrine d'Ibn 'Arabī* (Paris: Gallimard, 1986).

idealized topography of the classical Arabic love-poetry tradition: *Dhāt al-Ghaḍā* (tamarisk grove), a central site of remembrance of the beloved within the Majnūn Laylā tradition; *Ḥājir* (the Nabataean ruins of *Madā'in Ṣāliḥ* that served as reminders to the bedouin poet of what fate does to all civilizations, and all loves); the *ḍāl* tree (a species of lote tree) that was for the poets the locus of elegiac vision, enveloped with memories of the *locus amoenus*, the place of union with the beloved, just as the *sidr* (another species of lote tree) is enveloped with a prophetic light in vision of Muḥammad.[3]

This elegiac topography, particularly the emphasis upon the stations of the beloved's journey, is grounded in the pre-Islamic poetic tradition of the *ẓa'n* theme, the remembrance of the beloved's departure, along with a recounting of the stations of her journey. The *Interpreter of Desires* is a hermeneutic poetics, simultaneous adding creative new movements to the classical lyric and retrieving ancient and partially buried meanings from within the tradition. Representative of this hermeneutic is the following poem (number 24 from the *Tarjumān*):

Ibn 'Arabī's "Stay now at the ruins in La'la'i"
(*qif bi ṭ-ṭulūli d-dārisāti bi la'la'ī*)

[3] For this elegiac topography, see Jaroslav Stetkevych, *Zephyrs of Najd: The Poetics of Nostalgia in the Classical Arabic Nasīb.* Although I disagree with Stetkevych's evaluation of Ibn 'Arabī as a poet and critic, I find his treatment of the elegiac tradition in *Zephyrs* a rich resource for understanding the allusions of sacred topography within *The Interpreter of Desire.* For the Majnūn Laylā poems, centered around poetically sacred places such Ḥājir, Dhāt al-Ghaḍā, Dhāt al-Azjra'i, La'la', and 'Udhayb, see *Diwān Majnūn Laylā*, ed. 'Abd al-Sattār Aḥmad Farāj (Cairo: Maktabat Miṣr, 1973). See, for example, the poem (pp. 251-52) given in appendix no. 2: *ayā jabalay na'manin bi llāhi* (O twin peaks of Na'mān, by God!). For Ibn al-Fāriḍ, the essential mediator between the Majnūn Laylā tradition and Ibn al-'Arabī, see *Dīwān Ibn al-Fāriḍ* (Beirut: Dār Ṣādir, 1982). For an important recent study of Ibn al-Fāriḍ, see Th. Emil Homerin: *From Arab Poet to Muslim Saint: Ibn al-Fāriḍ, his Verse, and his Shrine* (Columbia: University of South Carolina Press, 1994). Particularly important for the argument of this paper is the proof of Ibn al-Fāriḍ's sanctity given by his biographers (Homerin, p. 25): his going into *wajd* (mystical ecstasy or trance) are hearing verses that are pure *nasīb*, with no explicit mystical connections.

Stay now at the ruins
in Lá'la'i, fading,
and in that wasteland, grieve,
for those we loved.

At the campsite, now abandoned,
stay and call her name,
as your heart is softly
torn away,

For the time of one like me
spent near her moringa's gossamer flowering,
plucking at fruits, in measure,
and at the petals of a rose, red, ripening.

Everyone who wanted you—
you showered with graces.
Only to me did your lightning flash,
unfaithful.

Yes, she said,
there we used to come together,
in the shade of my branches,
in that luxuriant land.

My lightning
was the flash of smiles,
Now it is the blaze
of barren stone.

So blame that time
we had no way of warding off.
What fault is it
of La'la'i?

I forgave her
as I heard her speak,
grieving as I grieved
with a wounded heart.

I asked her—
when I saw her meadows
now fields of the four
scouring, twisting winds—

Did they tell you
where they'd take their noonday rest?
Yes, she said,
at Sandrock,

Where the white tents gleam
with what they hold—
from all those rising suns—
of splendor.[4]

At the heart of this poem, the station is La'la'. The short love-elegy, continually re-visits the station of La'la', exploring its etymological and symbolic reservoirs of meaning, taking the root-meanings of flash and glare and working them into the associations of lightning (promise, ephemerality, blinding brightness, possible disappointment) within the Arabic poetic tradition. Finally, the station of La'la' is partially personified as the beloved speaks to the poet through it, or as it.

The classical associations of lightning upon which Ibn 'Arabī is drawing can be seen in the following verses of the ancient poet Al-A'shā:

Have you seen it blocking the horizon?
I passed the night in watch,
lightning kindled along its edges,
flickering,

[4] For the Arabic text see Ibn 'Arabī, *Tarjumān al-Ashwāq* (Beirut: Dār Ṣādir, 1966), 101-3 and for the commentary, see Ibn 'Arabī, *Dhakhā'ir al-A'lāq: Sharḥ Tarjumān al-Ashwāq*, ed. M. al-Kurdī, 136-40. For Nicholson's versions see Ibn 'Arabī, *The Tarjumān al-Ashwāq: A Collection of Mystical Odes*, trans. and ed. Reynold Nicholson (London: Royal Asiatic Society, 1911), 26-27, 96-97.

With a dark trail behind it,
    its middle full and moving,
girded and held together
    by buckets of rain.

        No play diverts me
    from foretelling the rain's direction,
        no pleasure from a cup of wine,
    no languor.

I told them at Dúrna,
    the drinkers already sodden:
Foretell! But how
    can a wine-faced drinker heed?

        Lightning lit up the slopes
    where the rain would fall,
        in Khabíyya, a blackening cloud
    against the horizon.

They said let it pour
    on Leopard Streak and Camel Belly,
on Horse Trappings, Tired Man,
    and Legland,

        Flowing over the Edgelands,
    then Boar with its tracts
        of rock and sand,
    until the hills and mountains burst,

Until the grouse meadows
    and the tree-hedged
soft-curved dunes
    take all they can bear,

A gushing, quenching draught
for abodes long since desolate,
off the track,
shunned by horse and camel mare.[5]

In these verses by Al-A'shā, the lightning promises—and ultimately delivers—a nourishing downpour. The poet first tries to foretell the direction of the storm by following the path of the lightning. Then, with the flickering, the poetic voice announces the passage of the storm as it passes from station to station, just as the pre-Islamic poet would sometimes follow the beloved and her companions (the *ẓa'n*), as they passed through the various stations of their journey away from him.

The station of La'la' was known to the later Arabic elegiac tradition. It was mentioned by the Ibn al-Fāriḍ in his poem on Laylā's fire, a poem that draws deeply on the Majnūn Laylā tradition.

Did lightning flash from far-off vale
Or did veils lift from Láyla's face?

Was the tamarisk aflame, with Sálma in its grove,
Or was this light the gleam of tear-filled yes?

The scent of lavender, perhaps
Or Hájir's balm,
Or in the Mother of Cities
'Azzah's languid redolence?

Would that I knew! Does Suláyma tarry still
in the valley of Híma,
Where one lovelorn roams?

Did rolling thunder rend the sky at Lá'la',
And did the generous cloud let down its load?[6]

---

[5] See Michael Sells, *Desert Tracings: Six Classic Arabian Odes by 'Alqama, Shánfara, Labíd, 'Antara, Al-A'sha, and Dhu al-Rúmma* (Middletown, Conn.: Wesleyan University Press, 1989), 62-63.

[6] Stetkevych, *Zephyrs of Najd*, 82, 212-13.

This elegiac topography of Arabia was also claimed by the poet of Valencia, Ibn Sa'd al-Khayr (d. 571/1175):

> O you, who ask the riders,
> did dew fall over Lá'la'
> As once its evenings were dew-laden, mild?
>
> Did they arrive and halt
> at al-'Udháyb's sweet waters
> that exhale redolence
> when greeted by soft breeze's palm?[7]

In the classical *nasīb* tradition, the stations of the departing beloved can be listed in sequence—as in the *ẓa'n* theme, when the poet remembers or imagines the stations the departing beloved and her companions pass through—or a single station can become the *aṭlāl*, the ruins of the beloved's campsite over which the poet meditates. Thus the poems oscillate between a fixed meditation upon one station, one enclosed space of remembrance and meaning, and a movement or sequence of stations.

Ibn 'Arabī's La'la' poem begins with the poet addressing himself: "Stay now" (*qif*) in the ruins. The self address continues through the third verse, in which the desolation of the present is compared to the time spent near the moringa (*bān*) that Arabian desert tree, with the exquisite foliage and delicate flowers that had become the quintessential symbol of the beloved and the time spent with her. The luxuriously sensual imagery (plucking a fruits, a rose, red, ripening), yields suddenly to a change in voice. Now the one addressed as "you" is the beloved, whose lightning, unlike that depicted in the poem of Al-A'shā, does not follow through with its promise.

In verse five the beloved responds, but seems to respond as something more than the beloved as well, referring to the love-union beneath the shade of "my branches," evoking the tree that symbolizes the locus amoenus, the *ghaḍā* or the *ḍāl* (lote), the poetic analogue of the Qur'anic

---

[7] Ibid, pp. 86, and 21, and note 70, p. 266.

lote (*as-sidr*) as the locus of vision. The lightning that was the flash of smiles then turns to the flash of barren stone, the kind of sudden inversion of value within the same image that the classical *nasīb* frequently entertains. The voice suggests that the agent to blame is time or fate (*dahr*), not the station of La'la'. With this statement, the exquisite partial personification is achieved; the voice is not simply that of the beloved, but also that of the station of La'la' itself, or herself. This personification leads to the emotive turning point in the poem: "I forgave her as I heard her speak, grieving as I grieved, with a wounded heart." Insofar as the station of La'la' is personified as the beloved, we have an intimation of the classic *khayāl* or *ṭayf*, the shade or phantom of the beloved that appears to the poet.[8] Here the beloved, following the more dialogical style emphasized in the Arabic *ghazal* tradition, converses with the poet, heightening and drawing out the paradoxical combination of presence and absence represented by the shade of the beloved.

Insofar as the beloved is symbolized by the station of La'la', then all the aspects of the station of La'la' can be referred to as hers; the branches of the tree that represent the remembered site of union, and the meadows that have become fields for the "four twisting, scouring winds." The poetic voice has now switched again, from second person to the third person, with a reference to "her meadows."

At the end of the poem, the voice of the poet's interlocutor fades back into the univocal voice of the station of La'la'. The poet asks where they (the beloved and her company, the *ẓa'n*) might take their noon rest. The voice answers (clearly differentiating itself in so doing from the beloved): at Sandrock (*dhāt al-ajra'i*), where the white tents gleam "with what they hold/of splendor." The last verse suggests something veiled, something that cannot be fully revealed, even as the poem ends with a question about the attainability of that splendor.

---

[8] See John Seybold, "The Earliest Demon Lover: *The Ṭayf al-Khayāl* in the *Mufaḍḍaliyāt*," in S. Stetkevych, editor, *Reorientations: Arabic and Persian Poetry* (Bloomington: Indiana University Press, 1994), 180-89.

This poem is one of several within the *Tarjumān* that exhibit a newly intensified version of a process at the heart of the pre-Islamic *nasīb*: the creation—as a parallel to the officially sacred topography of stations, sacred enclosures, spirits, and sacred times—of a poetic world of the sacred, which is neither pilgrimage nor non-pilgrimage and which inhabits a permanently ambiguous place between the sacred and the profane.[9]

This is not the only mode of bringing the religious and the poetic into an ambiguous zone between the two: Ibn Zaydūn would take an almost opposite approach, focusing on the urban world of Andalusian civilization, making the ruins of the Caliphal Palace at Zahrā' his *aṭlāl*; evoking images of cultivated gardens rather than the spring-meadow pasturing grounds as analogues for union with the beloved; integrating into the *nasīb* direct references to the Qur'ān, and using Qur'anic cadences in his poems.[10] The tradition represented here by Ibn 'Arabī, grounded in reconfigurations of the bedouin *nasīb*, traces a different trajectory through the Arabic tradition, from pre-Islamic poets such as Al-A'shā and Labīd, to the poems attributed to Majnūn Laylā, through Ibn al-Fāriḍ and Ibn 'Arabī.

At the same time, Ibn 'Arabī's poems open onto a more mystical horizon, in which the constant transformations and movements of the beloved are tied to Ibn 'Arabī's notion of ultimate reality as constantly eluding intellectual, dogmatic, and doctrinal grasp. According to this view, ultimate reality cannot be encapsulated in any particular image, its

---

[9] M. Sells, "Profanation and Consecration in the Early Arabic *Nasīb*," American Oriental Society, Cambridge, Mass., April 1992. I have made a similar argument for the *fakhr-madīḥ* sections of the *qaṣīdah*: "The Naqa Sacrifice and the Pre-Islamic Qasida," Middle East Literature Colloquium, University of Pennsylvania, May 1992. These essays are part of a book-in-progress of the pre-Islamic *qaṣīdah*. I discuss the implications of such a position on the interpretation of Islamic mysticism in M. Sells, "Bewildered Tongue: The Semantics of Mystical Union in Islam" in Bernard McGinn and Moshe Idel, ed., *Mystical Union and Monotheistic Religions: An Ecumenical Dialogue*, New York: MacMillan, 1989, 87-124.

[10] I will present a more extended comparison between Ibn Zaydūn and Ibn 'Arabī in regard to their respective notions of "the religion of love" in the *The Cambridge History of Arabic Literature, al-Andalus* (in preparation).

manifestations are constantly changing. The notion that one can possess it or possess its image leads to "Gods of belief," an intellectual idolatry. The constantly moving caravan of the beloved, always just behind the poet, in memory, or just ahead of him, in the states of her journey offers a lyrical understanding consonant with this mystical philosophy. The beloved is never possessed. The images of her (pluralized through the convention of the *ẓa'n*) are constantly changing. Union with her is ephemeral, separation from her recurring. In both poetics and mystical philosophy, power and meaning cannot be concentrated in any single place, but are constantly dispersed in every new loci. In the famous verse "My heart can take on every form," Ibn 'Arabī relates the constant transformation of the heart (*taqallub*) to the demand to give up the image of the beloved in each moment, to receive a new image of the beloved in the next.

The association between the poetics of wandering, the notion of a life of continued pilgrimage (*siyāḥah*), and the mystical philosophy of a never ending transformation (*taqallub*) toward reality are brought together in Ibn 'Arabī's famous poem announcing his confession of the "religion of love." This poem, number eleven in the *Tarjumān,* contains four intertwining themes: (1) The remembrance of the beloved (*nasīb*) motifs of the classical Arabic *qaṣīdah,* especially the theme of the *ẓa'n,* the journey of the beloved and her female companions away from the poet; (2) The Sufi state of *fanā',* the passing away or annihilation of the self of the Sufi in union with the divine beloved; (3) The pilgrimage of the *ḥajj,* the stations of the pilgrimage, and the circumambulation of the Ka'ba; and (4) The Sufi claim that the greatest Ka'ba is the heart of the divine lover at the moment of *fanā'.*

> Gentle now,
> doves of the thornberry and moringa thicket,
> don't add to my heartache
> your sighs.
>
> Gentle now,
> or your sad cooing
> will reveal the love I hide
> the sorrow I hide away.

I echo back, in the evening,
in the morning, echo,
the longing of a love-sick lover,
the moaning of the lost.

In a grove of *ghaḍā*
spirits wrestled,
bending the limbs down over me,
passing me away.

They brought yearning,
breaking of the heart,
and other new twists of pain,
putting me through it.

Who is there for me in Jám‘,
and the Stoning-Place at Mína,
who for me at Tamarisk Grove,
or at the way-station of Na‘mán?

Hour by hour
they circle my heart
in rapture, in love-ache,
and touch my pillars with a kiss.

As the best of creation
circled the Ka‘ba,
which reason with its proofs
called unworthy,

And kissed the stones there—
and he was the Natiq!
And what is the house of stone
compared to a man or a woman?

They swore, and how often!
they'd never change—piling up vows.
She who dyes herself red with henna
is faithless.

A white-blazed gazelle
is an amazing sight,
red-dye signaling,
eyelids hinting,

Pasture between breastbones
and innards.
Marvel,
a garden among the flames!

My heart can take on
any form:
a meadow for gazelles,
a cloister for monks,

For the idols, sacred ground,
Ka'ba for the circling pilgrim,
the tables of the Toráh,
the scrolls of the Qur'án.

I profess the religion of love;
wherever its caravan turns along the way,
that is the belief,
the faith I keep.

Like Bishr,
Hind and her sister,
love-mad Qays and the his lost Láyla,
Máyya and her lover Ghaylán.[11]

---

[11] "Gentle Now Doves of the Thornberry and Moringa Thicket" *(alā yā ḥamāmāti l-arākati wa-l-bāni),* poem number 11 from the *Tarjumān.* For the Arabic text, see Ibn 'Arabī, *Tarjumān al-Ashwāq* (Beirut: Dār Ṣādir, 1966), 41-44. For Nicholson's Arabic and English texts, see Ibn 'Arabī, *The Tarjumān al-Ashwāq: A Collection of Mystical Odes,* trans. and ed. Reynold Nicholson (London: Royal Asiatic Society, 1911), 19, 66-70. The translation I give here first appeared in the *The Journal of the Muhyiddin Ibn 'Arabi Society* 10 (1991): 9-11.

In the classical *qaṣīdah,* the dove—and particularly the cooing of the dove—is the sad sign of parting, rather than a sign of the joy of lovers united. The cooing of the dove either heralds the imminent separation of lover and beloved, or recalls that separation.[12] The *arāk* plant (translated as "thornberry") is a thorny, aromatic shrub with light purplish berries, the twigs of which the bedouin used for tooth picks. The *arāk* tooth twig is most often associated with the beloved; mention of it in a poem often leads to an extended simile in which the *arāk* twig leads to a recollection of the beloved's wet mouth and white teeth. The *bān* (*moringa peregrinis*) is a large shrub with elegant clusters of leaves and delicate white and soft-purple flowers, often used to evoke the beloved's hair or her stature. Its appearance in poem 11 foreshadows the reference to the moringa in poem 24 (translated above).

The themes from the classical Arabic *nasīb* and the Majnūn Laylā tradition continue on into verse 3 of "Gentle now doves," with the evocation of the love-sick lover. In verse 4, these themes are combined with the Sufi concept of *fanā'* in the kind of homonymic pun common in the later, *badī'* style of poetry.[13] While I could not replicate the pun in English, I tried to bring across its sense of surprise by using the expression "passing me away," in which the normally intransitive term "pass away" is used in the active, transitive sense. This passing away occurs in the grove of tamarisks in which spirits were wrestling, bending down the limbs over the poet.[14] This moment of passing away in the tamarisk grove

---

[12] Here the reference to the doves is accompanied by the untranslatable interjection *alā* which is used for the most tragic moments involving the loss of the beloved.

[13] The pun is one example of the extensive use of the play upon homonyms and verbal metathesis (*jinās*) to be found in the *Interpreter of Desires.* Here the word play based upon two meanings of *afnānī*: "various kinds" (i.e., of branches bent down by the winds, allegorically perhaps, of trials along the mystical path of love); and "causing me to pass away" (the causative, fourth form of *faniya,* to fade or pass away, and the first person object pronoun suffix).

[14] The word here for spirits (*arwāḥ*) is a central term in Ibn 'Arabī's writings, commonly referring to those bewildered spirits that encircle the divine throne (itself envisaged as a kind celestial Ka'ba). The word for winds or breezes (*riyāḥ*) is closely related to *arwāḥ,* and the poem is playing upon both meanings.

becomes a central moment of transformation for the poetic voice, which shifts from the voice of poet and lover, to the voice of the mystical Ka'ba. The tamarisk grove (*ghaḍā*) in which the passing away occurs puts the tree of vision or sacred tree into a central place in the poem, just as it was in the La'la' poem where the tree was partially personified and partially identified with the beloved.

In verse 6, there is presented a list of pilgrimage stations. The stations also have another meaning as well. The ancient litany of pilgrimage stations and stopping places (*maqamāt, manāzil, maḥallāt*) can be illustrated from the famous opening verse of the *Mu'allaqa* of Labīd:

> *'afat ad-diyāru maḥalluhā fa muqāmuhā bi minan*
> *ta'bbada ghawluhā fa rijāmuhā*:

> The tent marks in Mínan are worn away,
> where she encamped,
> and where she alighted.
> Ghawl and Rijám are left to the wild.

Later in the same poem the *ẓa'n* movement culminates with a listing of stations:

> But why recall Nawár?
> She's gone.
> Her ties and bonds to you
> are broken.
>
> The Múrrite lady
> has lodged in Fayd,
> then joined up with the Hijázi clans.
> Who are you to aspire to reach her?
>
> On the Eastern slopes
> of Twin Mountains or Muhájjar?
> Lonebutte has taken her in
> then Marblehead

Then Tinderlands if
  she makes toward Yemen—
I imagine her there—or at Thrall Mountain
  or in the valley of Tilkhám.

Ibn ʿArabī has combined stations of the *ḥajj,* such as the "stoning place of Minā," with stations from the ancient *nasīb,* such as Naʿmān, famous from the poetry of Majnūn Laylā. The litany of stations, echoing all the way back to the *Muʿallaqa* of Labīd, is a central element of Ibn ʿArabī's hermeneutic poetics. Such poetics reach back to retrieve old or lost meanings, such as the sacrality of the stations of the beloved, even as create new poetic forms and topoi. The new topics here include the deliberate intermixture of *ḥajj* and *nasīb* stations (an intermixture which is itself a powerful interpretation of the original *nasīb* stations), and the transformation affected by the "passing away" under the tamarisk.[15]

In the next verse the transformation that occurred with the passing away in the grove of tamarisk becomes apparent: "Hour by hour / they circle *my* heart." The poetic voice is now the center of the circumambulation, speaking from out of the divine abode or house (*bayt*), the Kaʿba,[16] reinterpreted in Sufism as the heart of the mystic lover who is annihilated in love for the divine beloved. The next two verses, depicting Muḥammad (*khayr al-bariyyah,* "the best of creation,") circumambulating the Kaʿba offer an argument on behalf of this mystical understanding of the Kaʿba.

The poem then shifts back to the images of the classical love-lyric: the henna-dyed lover (the henna commonly symbolic of the lover's blood),[17]

---

[15] Ibn ʿArabī makes this theme more explicit in his commentary, but to those immersed in the poetics of the *nasīb* (a large part of Ibn ʿArabī's audience), it would have been apparent even without the commentary.

[16] For the multivalent symbolism of the term *bayt* in Arabic culture, see the first part of Juan Campo's *The Other Sides of Paradixe: Explorations into the Religious Meanings of Domestic Space in Islam* (Columbia: University of South Carolina Press, 1991); and J. Stetkevych, *Zephyrs,* chapter 2.

[17] This topos of henna as the blood of the lover became truly internationalized,

gazelle, and meadow evoked through dissembling similes and serving as the poetic analogue of the lost beloved. The fickleness of the beloved is closely tied to the perishing (*halāk*) of the lover, which at this point in the poem is related to the mystical passing away of the self in *fanā'*.

There follows the famous verses concerning the heart that can take on every form (*qābil li kulli ṣūrah*). Here the forms are listed in a manner reminiscent of the listing of the pilgrimage stops earlier: the meadow for the gazelles, the sacred home of the idols, the Ka'ba, the Torah, the Qur'ān, followed with the famous profession of the creed of love: "I profess the religion of love" (*adīnu bi dīni l-ḥubb*). At this point, rhythm of the poem has changed, becoming as measured as that of the pilgrim moving through the stations of the pilgrimage. The rhythm contains a tension, a paradoxical combination of calm measure and increasingly fevered intensity. The poem ends with a tribute to the great lovers and beloveds.[18]

The commentary makes the mystical implications of the poem at this point most explicit.[19] The heart that can take on every form (*qābil li qulli ṣūratin*) is the heart that has achieved *taqallub*:

---

and can be found not only in the Arabic love lyric, but the Andalusian Hebrew, the Persian, the Ottoman, and the Urdu.

[18] The last lover mentioned, Ghaylān, was the great poet of the Umayyad period, Dhū al-Rūmma (d. *circa* 735 CE), who was also known as the "seal of the [classical] poets" (*khātam al-shu'arā'*).

[19] The exact date of the composition of the *Tarjumān* is a matter of controversy. After being criticized for writing love-poetry, Ibn 'Arabī later appended a mystical commentary to the *Tarjumān*. He admitted that the commentary was written in haste. At times it makes a clear and powerful connection between the love-lyricism of the poetry and the mystical philosophy. Thus, in the famous verses "My heart can take on every form," Ibn 'Arabī relates such a heart to the mystical understanding of *taqallub*, the constant change of the heart, in each new moment, to receive a new image of the divine beloved—a change that also demands a giving up of the old image.

At other times, the commentary is more indirect, even ironic. Thus, Ibn 'Arabī takes the explicitly erotic verse 4, which ends with the sexual imagery of the rose, red, ripening, and states that the redness of the rose symbolizes the station of *hayā'* or shame, although the love-lyric itself is completely lacking in any sense of shame. Just as al-Ma'arrī had used a criticism by a local Shaykh as the pretext for writing his

> "My heart can take on every form." Someone has said that the heart [*qalb*] takes its name from its own perpetual transformation [*taqallub*]. It changes with the influences that come upon it, which change with its conditions, which change with the divine manifestations to its heart-secret [*sirr*]. Tradition [*shar'*] calls this "alternation and substitution in forms" [*al-taḥawwul wa-al-tabaddul fī al-ṣuwar*].[20]

Concerning the list of famous lovers in the last verse of the poem, Ibn 'Arabī comments that "Allāh dazed them with love [*hayyamahum*] for their fellow human beings as a rebuttal to those who claim to love him, but are not similarly dazed with love." He then expands on the motif of the love-dazed lover in language that brings the erotic and mystical together: "Love deprived these [unrequited lovers] of their wits. It made them pass away from themselves at the sight in their imagination of the beloved."[21]

The reference to lovers being driven out of their wits (*'uqūlihim*, pl. of *'aql*) is an allusion to Ibn 'Arabī's critique of intellectual binding (*taqyīd*). The basic function of the intellect (*'aql*) is, as its etymology suggests, to "bind." For Ibn 'Arabī, we grasp reality by binding it into word-symbols, religious doctrines, theological systems, and cosmologies. This binding is a necessary and valued part of human intellectual endeavor. However, when binding is applied to the real (*al-ḥaqq*), a primal human error occurs. The infinite is delimited and bound within a particular image. That image becomes the locus for a concentration of power and the object of worship. Such idolatry is a persistent aspect of human life. The alternative is to realize that the real is infinite and cannot be bound into any single image. It is continually transforming itself in its manifestations. The heart that can take on every form must continually transform itself to each of the forms of the real. In each instant the mystic and

---

bitingly brilliant satire *The Epistle of Forgiveness (Risālat al-Ghufrān)*, so, perhaps, it is the critic who finds love-lyric objectionable and who demands a clear separation of divine and human love for whom the comment is made; such a critic, both prudish and prurient, can only read a verse like verse 4 with a sense of shame.

[20] Ibn 'Arabī, *Dhakhā'ir al-A'lāq* (n. 4, above), 49.

[21] Ibn 'Arabī, *Dhakhā'ir al-A'lāq*, 50.

lover passes away from his or her ego-self and is driven out of his wits (out of his binding intellect) into love-madness and mystic bewilderment within the constant changed facets of reality.

The passing-away of the ego-self and intellectual binding results in a mystical union (with deity becoming the hearing with which the lover hears, the seeing with which he sees, the feet with which he walks, and the hands with which he touches). But that union is ephemeral. The lover must give up the image of the beloved, to receive the new image.[22]

Ibn ʻArabī evokes the mournful cooing of the doves, and the *ẓaʻn*, the movement of the beloved and her companions *away* from the poem. Herein lies the elegiac lyricism of Ibn ʻArabī's understanding of mystical union. The heart that is receptive of every form must be willing to give up each image, each form, each beloved, in order to be receptive for the next form. This mysticism of perpetual transformation, *taqallub* (a play on the word heart, *qalb*), is tied in to a complex and sophisticated mystical dialectic that can be found in the commentary to the poem, and throughout Ibn ʻAṛabī's other works.

At the end of poem 11, the perpetually changing manifestations of the real are figured as the changing moods and states of the beloved (her *aḥwāl*), and as the continual moving around and past the poet of the beloveds, figured as the pre-Islamic *ẓaʻn*. The poet's heart has become receptive of every form, and the forms are now the stations of loci of the beloved: the meadow of the gazelle, the monastery, the Torah, the Qur'ān. In this elegiac vision, power is never concentrating in any single locus or station. Indeed, each station is only a trace of the beloved. Longing is perpetual, and the goal of the pilgrimage, belonging (in both the sense of possession and the sense of home), is deferred.

[22] For a more extended and detail development of Ibn ʻArabī's mystical philosophy in relationship to the theory of the "heart that can take on every form," see M. Sells, *Mystical Languages of Unsaying* (Chicago: University of Chicago Press, 1994), chapter 4.

PRACTICAL INTELLIGENCE: DON JUAN MANUEL

CIRIACO MORÓN ARROYO

IN A SYMPOSIUM titled "The Languages of Power in Islamic Spain," the inclusion of the Christian nobleman Don Juan Manuel is justified on account of the two parts of the title. With regard to Islamic Spain, he occupied a place at the frontier, and with regard to the languages of power, his position is central for an original intellectual discourse that is unique in his time, at least in Christian Spain. Born in 1282 to the Infante Don Manuel, the youngest son of King Ferdinand III of Castile (1217–1252), Don Juan Manuel was since his childhood *adelantado* of the kingdom of Murcia, a title he held almost all his life with some interruptions due to the political instability in Castile. *Adelantado* was the supreme ruler of a Christian kingdom bordering on a Muslim one.[1] In this capacity, Don Juan Manuel had the opportunity to interact with the Muslims in matters of war and peace. But, of course, the diplomatic relations of the Castilian nobleman with Islamic Spain were not guided by the principle of mutual recognition. For Don Juan Manuel, the Muslims had unjustly occupied Spain in 711, and no matter how long they stayed in the country, they never acquired the right to it. Peace with the Muslims could only be temporary truces: "There will be war between us and

[1] "Los adelantados et merynos an a fazer iustiçia et defender la tierra et parar se a las guerras et oyr las alçadas et librar todos los pleytos que ante ellos vinieren" (Don Juan Manuel, *Libro de los estados*, first part, ch. 93. Ed. José Manuel Blecua, Madrid: Gredos, I, 398). All quotations from Don Juan Manuel's works will refer to this edition.

the Muslims for as long as they occupy Christian lands."[2] "Christian lands" included the entire Iberian peninsula, North Africa, and the Holy Land, that is, the regions that had been Christian before the Muslim invasions. At some points in his life Don Juan Manuel sought help from the king of Granada against the king of Castile; he knew well some cultural practices of his neighbors and showed respect for the Islamic nobility and royalty.[3] But personal relations could not prevail over his felt obligation as a Christian knight to expel the Muslims from the Christian land. Obviously, the social obligation, which is never contradicted, may become blurred in expressions of gratitude and admiration for some Muslim individuals. In this case, the texts show an appearance of ambiguity, which probably reflects the ambivalence that existed in Don Juan Manuel's spirit: the principle of political enmity based on religion may coexist with personal friendship and sincere admiration for some friends in the ranks of the enemy—the perpetual "What's in a name" (Shakespeare).

This ambivalence is most explicit with regard to the Jews. In this case, since the Jews did not occupy land, the enmity was exclusively religious, not political. Theologians have always seen Judaism as one stage in the history of salvation, which comprised three ages: the Age of Nature (Paganism), the Age of the Law (Judaism), and the Age of Grace (Christianity). As a link in this chain, the Synagogue could be viewed in a positive light as the entrance hall to the Church, or in a negative one as a closed wall against the Church. The negative view has been almost exclusive till the twentieth century, and Don Juan Manuel is no exception. But in this case, his texts reveal a real contradiction between his attitude toward Judaism as religion and his personal admiration, gratitude, friendship, and respect towards a particular Jew and his family: Don Salamón, his physician. In the *Libro Enfenido*, Don Juan Manuel advises his son

---

[2] *Libro de los estados*, part I, ch. xxx. Ed. cit., I, 248.

[3] Maria Rosa Lida de Malkiel, "Tres notas sobre Don Juan Manuel," in *Romance Philology* 4 (1950–51): 160. Cf. also p. 174.

Fernando the following: "I enjoin and advise you that as soon as you are in the position to have a physician, he should be of the family of Don Çag, who was physician to my father and to me. For I say unto you truly that to this day I have never found physicians more competent and loyal with respect to medicine and all other business; and be sure that they will be all the same to you and your lineage."[4] The relationship with Don Salamón was so exceptional that the Christian nobleman highlights it in an exceptional document, his last will, with three mentions: in the first he appoints Don Salamón to take an inventory of the money stored in his treasury. In the third mention, Don Juan Manuel intimates his son to seek the advice of his sister and others for any important decision, and after naming the Christian relatives, he adds:

> Et sennalada mente de Don Salamón, ca yo sé que esto es más su servicio que otra cosa, e pues yo que so su padre e lo amo más que a mí esto le mando, non deue creer que él ha mejor nin más su pro que esto.[5]
>
> And above all /he should seek the advice of/ D. Salamón, for I know this is the best for him, and if I who am his father and love him more than myself enjoin this unto him, he should never believe that there is anything more to his advantage than this.

The anxiety of being forced to choose between the general principle and the particular attachment becomes clear in the following clause of the testament:

> Et como quier que don Salamón, mio físico, es judío et non puede nin deue seer cabeçalero, nin yo no lo fago mio cabeçalero. Pero por quelo fallé siempre tan leal que abés se podría dezir nin creer, por ende rruego a mis fijos quel quieran para su serviçio et lo crean en sus faziendas et so çierto que se fallarán bien dello. Et si cristiano fuesse, yo sé lo que yo en él dexaría. Et eso mismo ruego a mis cabe-

[4] *Libro enfenido,* cap. ii. I, 155.

[5] Andrés Giménez Soler, *Don Juan Manuel. Biografía y estudio crítico* (Zaragoza, 1932), 702.

> çaleros, ca çierto so que commo me fue leal al cuerpo, que así lo farrá a la mi alma.[6]
>
> And though D. S. my physician is a Jew and as such cannot and should not be my estate executor, I will not appoint him to such post. However, since I always found him loyal to a degree that it is hardly possible to say or believe, for this reason I request that my children keep him in their service and trust him in their business, and they will find themselves all the better for it. And if he were a Christian, I only know what I would leave to him. And the same I ask my estate executors, for I am sure that as he was loyal to me in my body so he will to my soul.

These words go beyond any normal testimony of friendship. The deep confidence of the Christian magnate in the Jew's loyalty indicates that the physician had showed such loyalty in some exceptional ways or situations.[7] One may suspect that in some of Don Juan's quarrels with the kings and other noblemen attempts may have been made to bribe the physician, or maybe the nobleman owed the Jew some inspiration that became the cornerstone of his life. Since Don Salamón seems to be the son of Don Çag, may the latter have been a basic influence in Don Juan's education? May Don Salamón have inspired the writings of Don Juan Manuel through their discussions of the subjects or through a direct intervention in the texts themselves? There is no positive proof for a conclusion. On the contrary, Don Juan Manuel speaks always with a high degree of involvement in his own writings. At the same time, the insistence

---

[6] Andrés Giménez Soler, *Don Juan Manuel,* 699. For the impossibility of salvation outside of Christianity, *Libro de la caza,* prologue, I, 519-20. A condemnation of Islam as religion, in *Estados,* p. I, ch. xxx, I, 248-49.

[7] Giménez Soler, 699. The loyalty to both body and soul, which deserves boundless gratitude, is referred to by Don Juan Manuel in ch. xxvi of the book: "La quarta manera de amor verdadero es quando algun omne por debdo sennalado o por buen talante, ama a otro et lo a provado en grandes fechos et peligros et fallo en él siempre verdad et ayuda et buen consejo...Digo vos que fasta aqui, maguer que he pasado çinquenta años, abés vos podría dezir que fallé de tales amigos más de uno, et non lo quiero nonbrar por non me perder con los otros...E aun fio por Dios que yo vos dire quien es, porque fagades vos eso mismo por él et por los que dél binieren" (*Libro enfenido,* cap. xxvi, I, 185).

on the necessity of following the Jew's advice demonstrates that Don Juan Manuel recognized his superior wisdom. If Don Salamón did not write the texts, he at least must have approved them. At the end of each story in *El Conde Lucanor* [1335], reference is made to some type of teamwork in the composition of the book: "And as Don Juan appreciated that this was a good story, he had it included in this book."[8] Don Juan presents himself only as the exclusive author of the couplets in verse at the end of the stories, while the dialogical discourse seems to recognize the collaboration of others in the examples.

My hypothesis of the collaboration of the Jewish physician in the works of the Castilian nobleman is ultimately based on the uniqueness of these works in comparison with the Christian literature of the epoch. The texts of Don Juan Manuel are pragmatic, psychological, secular, empirical, and vernacular. All these aspects have been recognized by scholars over the years, but I think not with sufficient precision. By comparing Don Juan Manuel with the prevailing types of discourse of his time, I hope to do justice to his immense originality. Indeed he was so original as to be anachronistic; Machiavelli, Bacon, and Montaigne will eventually rediscover the path that the Castilian nobleman had envisioned.

If Don Juan Manuel's discourse is pragmatic, psychological, secular, empirical, and vernacular, the knowledge imparted at the universities in his time was theoretical, moralistic, theological, speculative, and Latin. These contrastive characterizations of "systems" or "trends of thought" tend to be too encompassing, and it may be possible to adduce examples that counter the general statements. For this reason, it is imperative to circumscribe our terms. The sciences studied at the university were Theology, Canon Law, Civil Law, and Medicine. Theology was the "speculative," i.e., the theoretical science par excellence, since it used only the mind in order to think about immaterial realities. Canon and Civil law were "practical" knowledge in the sense that they also considered partic-

---

8 *El conde Lucanor.* Transl. by John England (Warminster: Aris and Phillips Ltd, 1987), 43. For writing as a collaborative effort, see *Libro de la caza,* prologue (I, 520).

ulars, but were "speculative" or theoretical in their principles, as derived from theology. Medicine began and ended in the individual, and the most universal propositions it could reach were based on the similarity between individual cases: "there are no illnesses but ill individuals" was a popular aphorism in medicine. Because the object of medicine was the individual, medicine was an art, not science. And the "liberal arts" also belonged to a mental level inferior to contemplative, universal knowledge. The disciplines that belonged in the curriculum of the university were always codified in systems and schools. When Don Juan Manuel, therefore, repeats that he does not know any science, he is not making disclaimers of false modesty, but confessing his lack of formal education and establishing a conscious distinction between the scholastic discourse and his own.[9] Far from being modest, he is proposing a new type of thinking, a research into the structure of the individual's and society's behavior in itself without inserting it into theological or moral categories. Since he cannot resort to the consecrated terminology of the schools, he delves into his native language and makes the first attempt to convert Spanish into a vehicle for philosophical expression.

The first characteristic of Don Juan Manuel's texts is pragmatism. He deals only with subjects that concern us everyday: how to fulfil our obligations according to our position in society, how to succeed in all our endeavors, and how to deal with the people who may help or stand in the way of our goals. A key term in his vocabulary is *aprouechar* (to profit) in the double meaning of profiting ourselves and benefiting others. He wrote his books "with the intention that the people who are not very learned and erudite may *profit* from what he would have to say" (II, 23-24). Intellect and will were, according to the philosophers, the two superior powers of the soul. In its most proper use, the intellect was theoretical; practical intelligence or *prudence* was the application of the intellect to particular situations that required decision. Don Juan Manuel concen-

[9] This point was well made by Ermanno Caldera. See "Retorica, narrativa e didattica nel *Conde Lucanor,*" in *Miscellanea di Studi Spanici,* Pisa, 14 (1966–67): 5-120. See *Estados,* p. I, ch. xcviii, I, 410.

trates on these situations and distances himself from the scholastic world by using the popular term *seso* instead of *prudencia*, which is the scholastic term. *Seso* is popular and practical common sense, while *prudence* is scholastic and moralistic.[10]

If *seso* is the intellect in its practical meaning as common sense, *cordura* and *juicio* are the sort of properties that constitute *seso*. It is the fusion of mental lucidity and strength to act: "Some people think that wisdom and strength (*el seso et el esfuerço*) are dissimilar, when they are one and the same thing."[11] This practical intelligence decides about the feasibility of each action on the basis of the advantage or harm that may derive from it. *Pro* (advantage) and *danno* (harm) are among the most frequent terms in Don Juan Manuel's lexicon. And at the end of each chapter in *Conde Lucanor* and of the *Libro enfenido* the success of an episode is measured in accordance with the *pro* or *danno* that resulted from the action.

Don Juan Manuel is usually described as a didactic writer; didactic is surreptitiously made synonymous of moralist, and by remembering the passages in which he claims a unique status in society, he is portrayed as an aristocrat who upholds the "medieval" hierarchical ideas about society. I, of course, write "medieval" with quotation marks, because I refer to a commonplace which I do not share and which is not based on Don Juan Manuel's texts. True, he is a didactic writer and, to the extent that he intends to teach a right behavior, he is a moralist. But, if we compare the use of the example in his texts to the use made by the author of *Calila y Dimna* and by his contemporary Juan Ruiz in the *Libro de buen amor*, the difference becomes clear. While the latter use the example in order to judge about the good or evil of actions, Don Juan Manuel uses it for psy-

---

[10] In the glossary of Blecua's edition the word *prudencia* is not entered. Huerta Tejadas includes one instance, in which *prudencia* translates the scholastic term for the cardinal virtue of prudence. Félix Huerta Tejadas, *Vocabulario de las obras de Don Juan Manuel* (Madrid, 1956), 143.

[11] *Proverbios*, in *El conde Lucanor*, ed. cit., II, 446. "El seso et la mesura et la raçon departen e judgan las cosas" (ibid., 449). In example 36 of *Conde Lucanor*, a man buys *sesos*, i.e., sentences of practical wisdom.

chological observation. Example seven in *El Conde Lucanor* narrates the tale of the milk maid. The moral approach laughs at the dreams of the maid as ambitious; Don Juan, on the other hand, studies the story as a case of confusion between reality and illusion. The moral of the story is not to condemn aspiration but to intimate that it be realistic. Experiences of complacency, timidity, procrastination, the right measure of confidence and caution in regard to other men, the experience of our own weaknesses as a reason for not trusting any human being absolutely, these examples of modern psychological observation define Don Juan Manuel's didactism.[12]

Pragmatism and psychological savvy convey a secular thrust to Don Juan Manuel's texts. To be sure, he frequently proclaims his faith in the Christian revelation and the doctrine and practice of the Church, and there is no basis for suspecting his sincerity. The goal of all human beings, in whatever state they are, is to save their souls, and Christianity is the only way of salvation. I have already referred to his respect for the Jew Don Salamón, but the religious allegiance ultimately opens an abyss between the two. Yet it is precisely on the basis of this religious background that Don Juan Manuel's insistence on success in this world becomes more striking. Consistent with his lack of theological knowledge, he devotes himself to the wisdom of this world. The nobleman must be educated for war and for the management of his estate and status. The defence of faith is the supreme value, but the theme of Don Juan Manuel's writings is the art of preserving the body, of increasing one's possessions, and of leaving a good name. In contrast to the ascetic idea of renunciation of this world propounded by the clergy as the official teachers of the way of salvation, Don Juan Manuel propounds a secular idea of salvation upholding the values of this world.

[12] For the parallel texts and a formal study of the differences between those texts and Don Juan Manuel's, see Reynaldo Ayerbe Chaux, *El Conde Lucanor. Materia tradicional y originalidad creadora.* Madrid: Porrúa Turanzas, 1975. See also *Estados*, p. I, ch. xviii, I, 229.

He recognizes that the clerical stand is superior—more perfect, more conducive to salvation—to the stand of chivalry. But the value of the stand in abstract terms does not condition the salvation of the individual. The nobleman is called to salvation through war against the Moors and through good government, and the idea of entering a religious order is a sign of cowardice. Example three of *El Conde Lucanor* tells the story of Richard the Lionhearted who made up for all the sins of his life by dying in the crusade against the Muslims. Don Juan Manuel accepts the idea of the crusade: anyone who dies in the war against the Moors goes immediately to heaven. Even the superiority of the clerical stand over the defenders has a secular twist to it. The cleric is superior because of his ministry of consecrating the body of Christ. For St. Thomas Aquinas and St. Bonaventure, on the other hand, the consecration of the body of Christ was not the criterion of the state of perfection, it was the three religious vows: poverty, chastity, and obedience. The secular priest was not in the state of perfection, according to those theologians. Don Juan Manuel's discourse is as far as it can be from the Dominicans and the Franciscans.[13]

The features mentioned harmonize with the empirical character of Don Juan Manuel's discourse. The *Livro del cavallero et del escudero* (1330) is a dialogue in which a young knight asks an old master questions that range from theology to astronomy and to the desirable behavior of the

[13] María Rosa Lida emphasized the coincidence between Don Juan Manuel and St. Thomas Aquinas. Up to a point, that coincidence is both natural and undeniable; a layman in contact with the Dominicans would hardly disagree on theological matters with the thinker who had defined the theological discourse for the Dominicans and had gained extraordinary authority in the Church. But Don Juan Manuel's discourse is so different and independent from the scholastic framework of St. Thomas, that the stress on the similarities may lead to confusion. See M. R. Lida, "Tres notas sobre Don Juan Manuel," in *Romance Philology* 4 (1950/51): 155-94. I feel compelled to side with Ermanno Caldera (op. cit., note 9) For a summary of other opinions see Alfonso I. Sotelo, ed., *El Conde Lucanor* (Madrid: Cátedra, 1976), 22 and 41. Lida's statement: "Su despego de la antigüedad no es sino reflejo de su laicismo" (op. cit., p. 177) is equally applicable to Don Juan Manuel's *despego* of scholasticism.

knight. In all the chapters the master occupies about two thirds of the space, reminding the disciple that those questions belong to codified sciences never learned by the old man. At the end of these warnings, nonetheless, he answers according to his *entendimiento*: natural understanding and experience.

The codified sciences are scholastic philosophy and theology. In contrast, his genres will be *fabliella, exemplo,* and *proverbio*—the means to put a body of knowledge which is both useful and illuminating side by side with the traditional disciplines of the university. This new empirical discourse differs completely from the scholastic "first degree of abstraction," which determined the object of natural philosophy. This degree was already universal and "speculative." Don Juan Manuel, on the other hand, remains on the level of the singular, and makes inferences from singular to singular. He reaches universal conclusions on the basis of personal introspection and observation of other individuals' behavior.

The empirical character manifests itself in at least these four aspects:

A) Both *El Conde Lucanor* and *Livro del cavallero et del escudero* raise practical questions of everyday life; the answer is given by means of an example related to a similar case.

B) The *Libro enfenido* (1332) consists of twenty-six chapters of advice to his son D. Fernando. It was conceived as an "unfinished book" because Don Juan Manuel wrote down the experiences of his life up to the moment of writing and left the book open for future notations. This open-ended book takes as the premise for all conclusions experience: "las pruebas que yo se que son verdat e probé para pro o danno del alma son estas" (ch. 1, I, 150) [These are the proofs that I know are true and I myself experienced for the good or harm of the soul]. All the chapters of the book end with another proof that is repeated like a refrain: "And the proof for this is that all those who behaved this way benefited from it, and the opposite" (Ch. 36, I, 189).

C) The principle of knowledge is not deduction or induction—from the universal to the particular or vice versa—but analogy: inference from the particular to the particular. Regardless of the content, the *exemplum* is first and foremost the type of discourse that concludes from particular premises. This level of knowledge was called by Aristotle *empeiria*, experience, and was respected by the scholastics only in reference to the "art" [not science] of medicine. No wonder Don Juan Manuel had such admiration for his physician.

D) Ramon Llull's *Book of Christian Chivalry* has been considered the inspiring "source" of the *Livro del cavallero et del escudero.* Don Juan Manuel could also be aware of the romances of chivalry, and especially of *Libro del cavallero Zifar* (ca. 1300). A collation of Don Juan Manuel's book with both Llull and the stereotype of the knight as described by Chaucer is the best way to highlight Don Juan's originality. Llull institutes from the beginning a scholastic, allegorical discourse founded on the symbolic meaning of the number seven: "In correspondence to the seven planets, which are celestial movements and govern and order the terrestrial movements, we divide this book, *Order of Chivalry*, in seven parts, in order to demonstrate that knights have honor and dominion over the people for its government and defence."[14] The structure of the book is inspired by the cosmology of the celestial bodies, which influences the movements of the terrestrial ones and indirectly influences the movements of the human spirit. Instead of looking at chivalry itself, Llull approaches it from a ready-made framework and converts chivalry into an allegory of virtues.

[14] "In significança de les set planetes, qui son corsos celestials e governen e ordonen los corsos terrenals, departim auqest *Libre de cavalleria* en set parts, a demostrar que los cavallers han honor e snyoria sobre lo poble a ordonar e a defendre" (Ramon Llull, *Livre de cavalleria.* ed. Pere Bohigas, in R. Llull, *Obres essenciels.* Ed. Miquel Batllori et al. Barcelona: Editorial Selecta, 1957, I, 527). Caxton's translation follows the French, which divides the books into eight sections instead of seven. Obviously this was a distortion of Lull's text. See William Caxton, *The Book of the Order of Chivalry.* Ed. Alfred T. P. Byles, London, 1926.

At the opposite end, the knight of the romances, as summarized by Chaucer, is a traveler in search of adventure and prowess:

> At Alisaundre he was whan it was wonne.
> Ful ofte tyme he hadde the bord bigonne
> Aboven alle nacions in Pruce;
> In lettow hadde he reysed and in Ruce,
> No Christen man so ofte of his degree.
> In Grenade at the seege eek hadde he be
> Of Algezir, and riden in Belmarye.[15]

In contrast to the scholastic framework of Llull and to the dispersion of the medieval knight, as pictured by Chaucer, chivalry is for Don Juan Manuel a humanism, a level of learning and conduct.[16] His knight is a young man eager to learn about theological and philosophical subjects, God, the angels, the devil, heaven, the stars, etc. The answers of the old knight will not come from learned sciences but from *experience.* The following passage is a beautiful example of the type of discourse developed in the book:

> Since I am very old and had a long experience concerning chivalry, I think I can speak about it with truth, and better than on sciences *that require great knowledge and study and must be learned from good teachers.* And with regard to the heavens, there are many things that should be asked from the teachers...but, since this knowledge *does not belong to the stand of chivalry,* in regards to what we must learn from others I can tell you nothing. But what I know about this science is because I learned it walking many a night at night, and getting up early, sometimes due to war, sometimes to hunting, and watching some stars when they appear and when they disappear; and how the sun and the moon and the other five stars surge in the East, and how

[15] Chaucer, *The Canterbury Tales,* Prologue. Ed. F. N. Robinson (Cambridge, Mass.: The Riverside Press, 1957), 17.

[16] The same conclusion is valid in a comparison of *El libro de los estados* with *Barlaam et Josaphat.* Once again, a free running empirical discourse contrasts with a symmetrical, allegorical and clerical text. R. B. Tate and I. R. MacPherson have noted similarities and differences between both texts but have not pinpointed the criteria that explain the noticeable differences. See their edition of *Estados,* Oxford: Clarendon Press, 1974.

> they set in the West, like the other stars. And seeing the sun and the moon and the other five stars that turn by themselves from West to East and that they cross each other, this lets me understand that there are eight heavens, and that each star moves in each of the seven heavens, and that one is higher than the other.[17]

This empiricism could, of course, remain on the level of the anecdotal. Not for Don Juan Manuel, who is perfectly aware that valid universal conclusions can be drawn from experience: "And it would be amazing if an individual to whom something happens would not find in this book something similar that happened to another one" (*Lucanor*, Prologue).

Finally, Don Juan Manuel's discourse differs from the official learning of his time for the fact the he uses Castilian, not Latin. He generally ignores the scholastic words in favor of the vernacular ones both in lexical (*seso* vs. *prudencia*) and semantic terms. The supreme faculty of the soul in St. Thomas Aquinas is the intellect. Don Juan Manuel uses frequently the word *entendimiento*, but for him the intellect is not the empty faculty of the soul, it is the practical ability of making the most beneficial decision, that is, the faculty in its right use. In this sense he speaks of the *entendimiento* of the ants (*Lucanor*, 23, II, 177), and a "subtle" intellect (one given to excessive thinking) can be detrimental. The capacity for discourse was the scholastic *ratio*. In Don Juan Manuel this sense is sometimes upheld but more frequently *razón* means the content of the discourse: *dezir una raçon*. Man is guided by his *manera e costunbre*. These two terms bear a certain resemblance with the scholastic *habitus et dispositio*, but differ in their meaning. *Voluntad* is for the scholastics the spiritual power that makes decisions according to the dictate of reason. Don Juan Manuel uses the term a few times with that meaning, but most often with the popular meaning of desire, and occasionally in the also popular sense of irrational sexual gratification. *To know oneself* meant for the scholastics basically to recognize one's sinfulness; for the Castilian nobleman it means to know one's worth.

---

[17] *Livro del cavallero et el escudero*, ch. xxxv, I, 69.

The effort at expression moved Don Juan Manuel to reflect about orality and writing. He experienced the potential for improvement involved in the arts of expression. For this reason, he defended writing as an honorable activity (I, 182) and took care that his texts would be well preserved. The originality of his discourse derives from the mental power of a seminal thinker who looked at human behavior and made a first effort at systematization. His *fabliella* would end in the modern social sciences by way of the humanistic dialogue and Montaigne's essay. He not only used language as a man in power; rather, he had an original perception of the power of language and of language as power: "Los mas de los fechos todos se fazen bien o el contrario por el oyr o por el fablar" (*Cavallero*, xxxvi, I, 72-73) ["Most of the facts turn out good or bad due to hearing or talking"].

INDEX

— A —

'Abbād ibn Sulaymān 57
'Abbādids of Seville 110
'Abbāsid 18, 24, 28, 31-32, 37
Abbey of Leyre 91
Abbot Hugh of Cluny 95
'Abd Allāh b. Buluggīn 116
'Abd Allāh b. Salām 167
'Abd al-Mālik 146
'Abd al-Manāf 24
'Abd al-Raḥmān I 83
'Abd al-Raḥmān III 42, 50, 52, 83, 90
'Abd al-Raḥmān Sanchuelo 42
'Abd al-Shams ibn 'Abd al-Manāf 37
Abdias 167
Abraham Abulafia 58, 60
Abraham ibn 'Ezra' 51, 58, 64, 66, 70, 73
Abraham ibn Muhājir 131
Abū al-'Atāhiyah 28-29, 31-32, 34
Abū al-Faḍl ibn Ḥasdai 109, 131
Abū al-Ḥasan al-Ash'arī 57
Abū Hāshim 37, 57
Abū Isḥāq al-Ilbīrī (Abū Isḥāq of Elvira) 109, 126
Abulafia 61, 67
Abū Marwān Ibn Ḥayyān al-Qurṭubī, see Ibn Ḥayyān
Abū Tammām 29, 32-34, 38-39, 46, 48
academies of Kufa and Basra 69
Acts, Book of 153
adab literature 109
Adelard of Bath 170
adīb 157
adoptionism 83
Age of
Grace 198
Nature 198
the Law 198
Aharon ben Asher 51, 71
Aḥmad ibn 'Abbās 133
'Ā'isha 165
al-'Abbās 37
al-Afshīn 34
al-Andalus 22, 28, 47, 49-50, 52, 54-55, 57, 62-63, 65, 71-74, 77-78, 80, 83-84, 88-91, 93, 106-8, 110-13, 115, 121, 123, 126-31, 134-35, 137-46,

148, 154-55, 157
Al-A'shā 182, 184-85, 187
al-Baṣrah 21
Albar, see Ḥafṣ ibn Albar
Al-Bayān al-mughrib 115
al-Bukhārī 166
Alcazar 103
Al-Dhakhīrah 43
Aleppo 39, 178
al-faṣāḥah 71
Al-Fiṣal 118-24, 126-27, 135, 160
Alfonso I of Aragon 157
Alfonso II 96
Alfonso VI 92-95
Alfonso VIII 139, 143
Alfonso X 145
al-Ḥakam II 15, 23
Alhambra 103-4
al-Ḥarizi, Judah 64, 68, 123
al-Ḥasan ibn al-Qāsim Gannūn 19
'Alid Muḥammad ibn al-Ḥanafiyyah 37
'Alids 24
Al-Iḥāṭah 117, 135
'Alī ibn Abī Ṭālib 19, 37
'Alī ibn Ḥazm, see Ibn Ḥazm
al-Jāḥiẓ 120
al-Jubbā'ī 124
al-Khwārazmī 170
al-Kindī 172
al-Mahdī 28-29, 31, 42-46
al-Ma'mūn 113
al-Manṣūr (Almanzor) 117, 133
Almeria 105, 131-33
Almohads 101, 120, 145, 178-79
al-Muhannad 3, 24, 28-29, 32
al-mulḥid 20
al-Munfatil 109
Al-Muqtabis 2, 17, 20
al-Mustanṣir 2, 17-19, 21, 23, 25-26, 32, 36, 39, 41-42
al-Mutanabbī 22, 34, 47, 48
al-Mu'taṣim 32, 34
al-Nā'ūrah palace 87
al-Qāhirah 18, 39
al-Rāzī 15, 174-75
al-raḥmān al-raḥīm 23
Al-Radd 113, 123, 130, 135
al-Shāhrastānī 126
al-Zahrā' 87-88, 187
Amalfi 88
'Āmirids 44, 129
'Ammūriyah 32-33
Amorium 32
analogy 72
Ananias, High Priest 154
annihilation of the self 188
anthropomorphism 159-60
anti-attributists 171-72
antithesis 38
Antwerp Polyglot 145
Apocalypse 83
Apollo 163
arabicization 142, 155
'arabiyyah 54-55, 69
Aragon 78, 81, 96-98, 102
Aramaic 62, 74
Archbishop Elipandus 83
Aren 172-73
Aristotle 170, 174, 207
Ashja' al-Sulamī 29
astronomy 170, 172-73
Asturians 78, 83, 94
Asturias 78, 90

— B —

Babylon 87, 89
Babylonian New Year Festival 17
Bacon 201
badī' 38, 191
Bādīs 116, 127, 133
Baghdad 18, 28, 112, 122, 178
Baltassar's Feast 87, 89
Banū Hāshim 18
Banū Isrā'īl 112
Banū Umayyah 18, 44
Banū Zīrī 110
Barcelona 88, 162
Bashshār ibn Burd 29
Basques 78
Basra 69, 72
Battle of Las Navas de Tolosa 105, 144
battle-description 26
bay'ah 44
Beatus 81-83, 87, 89-92, 106
Beatus of Liébana 81, 83
Bede 173
benediction 25, 33, 40
Benjamin of Tudela 122
Berbers 42, 78, 107
Bible 49-51, 68, 70-74, 119, 122, 125-26, 143-46, 148
Bible of San Isidoro 89
biblical purism 72
Birth of Maria de' Medici, The 27
Book of
  Ceremonies 19
  Christian Chivalry 207
  Opinions on Religions, Sects, and Heresies 118
  the Reconquest 90
Braga 91, 93
Burgos 94, 103
Byzantium 19

— C —

Cahbalahabar 167
Cairo 18, 50, 89, 178
Cairo Genizah 107
calendar 23, 35, 40-41, 45
Calila y Dimna 203
Carthage 138
Castile 93-94, 128, 197-98
Catalans 78
Cathedral of
  Braga 91
  Girona 91
  Leon 102-3
  Reims 103
  Santiago de Compostela 93
  Santa Maria del Mediavilla 99
Chaucer 207-8
Church of
  El Salvador 99
  San Martín in Oviedo 90
  San Miguel de Escalada 84
  San Pedro 99, 102
Clement of Alexandria 156
Cluny 92-93, 103, 169
Cluny III 93
Complutensian Polyglot 145
Compostela 93-94
Constantine VII 19
construction of social meaning 108
Cordoba 1-2, 11, 15, 17-19, 22, 28-29, 34, 37, 39-40, 42-43, 45-48, 50, 53, 83-84, 87, 90, 101, 153

Cordoba Mosque 87
Corinthians, Book of 147
Council of
  Cordoba 145
  Laodecia 149

— D —

dīwān 11, 110, 116
Damascus 178
Daniel, Book of 87, 148
David 153
  House of 121
David ben Abraham al-Fāsī 71
Day of Judgment 103
De Ceremoniis 19
De Rebus Hispaniae 144
Deborah 150
defeat-submission-mercy 26
Defense of the Doctrine of the Trinity, The 172
Destruction of Babylon, The 84
Deuteronomy, Book of 150
dhimmī 113, 117, 129
Dialogue of a Philosopher with a Jew and a Christian 156
Disciplina Clericalis 168
Dominicans 205
Don Juan Manuel 197
Don Pelayo, king of the Asturias 143
Don Salamón 198
Dunash ben Labraṭ 51, 75

— E —

Easter 154
Education of the Princess, The 27
'Egron 71
Egypt 114, 132
El Conde Lucanor 201, 204, 206
elegiac tradition 184
Elipandus, Archbishop 83
Epistles to the People of Corinth 147
Epistle to Yemen 120
equator 174
erotic verse 31
'Eruvin 63
ethical will 117
Eulogius 142
exigencies of meter 75
Exilarch 121-23
Ezekiel, Book of 148

— F —

fanā' 188, 191, 194
Fāṭimid 18-20, 24, 28, 37-39, 114, 132
Ferdinand I 92, 128
Ferdinand III of Castile 197
Fernando I 93, 95
Festival of
  Babylonian New Year 17
  Breaking the Fast 2
  the Sacrifice 2
Fez 178
First Crusade 163
flying buttresses 103
Franciscans 205
French Gothic 103
Fueros de Teruel 96
Fusṭāṭ 39

— G —

Gabriel 165
Galen 170
Genesis, Book of 56, 59, 61, 121
Geonim 67
Ghālib 19, 21
Ghāzī ibn al-Wāsiṭī 114
ghazal tradition 186
Giralda 101
Girona 91
Golden Age 75
Gospels 148, 153
Granada 103, 105, 110, 112, 114-16, 126-27, 132-33, 198
 "Jewish Granada" (*gharnāṭat al-yahūd*) 132
Gregory VII, Pope 94

— H —

Hāshim ibn 'Abd al-Manāf 37
Hāshimite 36-37
Head of the Exile 122
hebraica veritas 158
Hebrew, language
 Biblical 51-52, 69, 71-74
 neo-Biblical 5
 Rabbinic 69, 72, 74
Henri IV 27
Henry I of England 157, 170
heresiography 118, 134
hermeneutics 193
hieros gamos 31
Hishām II 42-43
Historia General de España 144
historiography 109
holy language 65, 71
Huesca 88, 157

— Ḥ —

Ḥabbūs 127, 133
ḥadīth 24, 124
Ḥafṣ ibn Albar al-Qūṭī 142, 149-51
Ḥajar al-Nasr 21
ḥajj 179, 188, 193
Ḥammūdid 133
Ḥasan ibn Qannūn 19-33, 36-38
Ḥasanid insurrection 40
Ḥasdai ibn Shapruṭ 50, 53, 109, 113
Ḥayyūj 51, 69-71

— I —

Ibn 'Abbās 133
Ibn 'Abd Rabbih 44
Ibn Abī Mūsā 133
Ibn al-Fāriḍ 180, 184, 187
Ibn al-Kharrāṭ 134
Ibn al-Khaṭīb 114-15, 132
Ibn al-Rāwandī 130
Ibn 'Arabī 178-96
Ibn Bassām (al-Shantarīnī) 43, 127, 131, 134
Ibn Bilashku, Isḥāq 154-55
Ibn Darrāj 10-11, 43-44, 47-48
Ibn Gharsiyah 140
Ibn Ḥafṣūn 140
Ibn Ḥanbal 24
Ibn Ḥayyān (al-Qurṭubī) 2, 15, 17, 19, 21-23, 29, 32-33, 36, 38, 41, 43, 48, 114-18, 134-35
Ibn Ḥazm 57, 62, 109, 113, 118-35, 153-54, 160

Ibn ʻIdhārī (al-Marrākushī) 115-16, 128, 132-33
Ibn Isḥāq 166
Ibn Janāḥ, Jonah 51, 58, 63, 72
Ibn Mardanish 178
Ibn Naghrīlah, Ismāʻīl (see also Samuel the Nagid) 107-35
Ibn Naghrīlah, Yūsuf 123, 126, 129, 132-34
Ibn Rushd 113
Ibn Saʻd al-Khayr 185
Ibn Saʻīd al-Maghribī 131, 134
Ibn Shukhayṣ 33-34, 37, 39, 41
Ibn Tibbon, Judah 67, 117
Ibn Zaydūn 187
ʻĪd 16, 22-23, 25-26, 35-36, 40, 43-44, 47
ʻĪd al-Aḍḥā 2, 11, 16, 43, 47
ʻĪd al-Fiṭr 2, 15-17; 21, 26, 32, 38, 40-41, 45
Idrīsids 3, 19-21, 37
Ifḥām al-yahūd 120
imamate 18, 23
Isaac ibn Shapruṭ 51
Isaac, monk of Tábanos 142
Isaiah, Book of 148
Isḥāq ibn Bilashku, see Ibn Bilashku
Isidore of Seville 94, 173
Iẓhār 127

— J —

Jacobite 166-67
jāhiliyyah 168
Jawhar 19
Jeremiah, Book of 148
Jerusalem 87
Jesus 154
Jezira 178
jihād 45, 163
jinās 38, 44, 47
Job, Book of 148
Johanan b. Zakkai 161
John, Book of 153-54
Joseph ibn Gikatilla 61
Joseph ibn Kaspi 65
Joshua b. Levi 159, 161-62
Jove 27
Juan de Mariana, bishop of Seville 143-44
Juan Ruiz 203
Judah ha-Levi 59, 63
Juno 27

— K —

Kaʻb al-Aḥbār 167
Kaʻba 163, 167, 179, 188, 191-94
kalām 171
Kallir 73
Karaite 55-56, 58, 71, 159-60
anti-Karaite 55
Ketubot 159
Khadīja 164
Khazars 51, 63-64
Kirkis 160
Kitāb al-Aghānī 29
Kitāb al-Dāmigh 130
Konya 178
Kufa 69
Kuzari 59, 63

— L —

Labīd 187, 192-93
language of Creation 62
laws of purity 163
Lent 154
Leon 78, 91-95, 102-3
letra fransisca 95
Libro de buen amor 203
Libro del cavallero Zifar 207
Libro Enfenido 198
Livro del cavallero et del escudero 205
Louis XIII 27

— M —

Machiavelli 201
Macrobius 173
Madīnat al-Zahrā' 87-88, 187
Maghrib 19
Maimonides 59, 61, 65, 72, 120
Maius 82
Majnūn Laylā 180, 184, 187, 191, 193
Malaga 133
mamdūḥ 34, 42, 47-48
Marduk 17
Maria de' Medici 27
Marrakesh minaret 101
Marriage Consummated in Lyons, The 27
Martyr Movement 90, 141
Martyrs of Cordoba 141
Marwānid 2, 42, 44-45, 47
Mary 27, 158-59
Materiale Sanctorum 142
Matthew, Book of 153-54
Mecca 178-79
medicine 170, 201-2
Menaḥem ben Saruq 50-52, 56, 58, 63, 66, 71-72, 75
Merida 83
messiah 161-62
midrash 51, 159
Minā 179
Mishnah 73
Mishnaic Hebrew 72
Mishneh Torah 72
monastery
  at Leyre 91
  of San Miguel de Escalada 82
  of Santo Domingo at Silos 91
  at Tábara 82
Monophysite 167
monotheism 162, 176
Montaigne 201, 210
Moors 205
Morocco 178
Moses 150
Moses ben Ḥanokh 53
Moses ibn 'Ezra' 54, 66, 70, 72, 151
Moses ibn Gikatilla 67
Mosque of Ḥasan 101
Mosque of Seville 101
Mosul 178
"mother of all languages" 60
Mozarabic 78, 80, 94-95, 107
Mu'allaqa 192-93
mu'āraḍah 28-29, 32
mudejar 80-81, 96-97, 99-104, 106
Muḥammad 18, 24, 37, 115, 134, 154, 163-68, 179-80, 193
Muḥammad ibn 'Abdūn 129
Muḥammad ibn Shukhayṣ 5, 32

multiculturalism 157, 162
mulūk al-ṭawā'if 129
Murcia 105, 178, 197
Musnad of Ibn Ḥanbal 24
Mutakallimūn 171
Mu'tazilites 58, 171

— N —

Naḥmanides 60, 65
nasīb 180, 185, 187-88, 191, 193
Navarre 91-92
Nebuchadnezzar 121
Neḥemiah Allony 55
Nestorians 166-67
New Testament 146
new year 16
Nicholas Donin 162
north pole 174

— O —

Old Testament 146, 148, 164, 168-69
ordering (*naẓm*) 47
Origen 159

— P —

Pablo Christiani 162
Pact of 'Umar 127
paganism 198
Pamplona 88
panegyric 1-2, 11, 22, 27-28, 31-34, 36, 43-44, 48
Paradise 163
Paris 162
Passover 161
pathetic fallacy 36
Paul Albar of Cordoba 141, 147
Pedro I 103, 157
Pelayo 94
Peter the Venerable 169
Petrus Alphonsi 156-77
Philip II of Spain 145
Philistine 89
piyyuṭ 69, 73-74
plagiarism 33
Plato 174-75
Pliny 173
Poema de Mio Cid ("Poem of the Cid") 117, 176
Primera Crónica General 143
Profiat Duran 68
Prophet of the Psalms 148
Protrepticu 156
Psalms, Book of 147-49, 151-53, 155
Ptolemy 173

— Q —

Qarmaṭī al-Ḥasan al-A'ṣam 39
qaṣīdah 1-48, 150, 178, 188, 191
qiyās 72
Qur'ān 50, 52, 54, 56, 58, 62, 69-71, 117, 124-25, 130-31, 134, 136, 164-67, 187, 194, 196
Quraysh 18, 23-24, 37, 44

— R —

Rabat 101
Rabbi Gamaliel I 161
rabbinic literature 160

rabbinic tradition 125
Ramaḍān 40, 45
Ramon Llull 207
Real Colegiata de San Isidoro 91
Recafred, Bishop of Seville 145
Reconquest, The (Reconquista) 42, 90-94, 96, 105
Refutation, The 123-27, 129-34
Reims Cathedral 103
Revelation, Book of 153
revelation 204
Richard the Lionhearted 205
Richelieu 27
Risālah (al-Kindī) 164-67
ritual reenactment 25
Rodrigo Ximenes 143-45
Romanesque art 78, 95, 102
Rome 162
root-play 38, 44, 47
ro'sh ha-golah 122

— S —

Saadia Gaon 55-56, 63, 70-72, 171
Saadia ibn Danān 117
sacred marriage 31
Sa'īd the Bishop 143
Saint-Jean in Liège 91
salvation 204-5
Samau'al al-Maghribī 120
Samuel the Nagid (see also Ibn Naghrīlah, Ismā'īl) 115, 117-20, 123, 127, 131, 133
San Juan de la Peña 92
Sancho García, Count of Castille 42
Sancho of Navarre 92
Sanhedrin, tractate 62
Saracen 169
Saragossa 83, 88, 131
sariqah 33
Sasanian 89
Sayf al-Dawlah 47
Sefer ṣaḥot 59
Septuagint 146
Sergius 166
Seville 101, 131, 178
Sharq 178
shrine of St. James 93
shu'ūbiyyah 52, 54-55
Silencing the Jews (see *Ifḥām al-yahūd*) 120
Solomon ibn Gabirol 62, 66
Son of Zebedee 154
Song of Roland 163, 169
Spanish Gothic 80
St. Augustine 156, 162
St. Bonaventure 205
St. Gregory I 147
St. Isidore of Seville 142, 147
St. James 93-94
St. Jerome 87, 146
St. Nicholas 94
St. Paul 94
St. Thomas Aquinas 205, 209
Sufi 178-79, 188, 191, 193
Sulaymān 11, 42-46
Sword of the Realm 91
synagogue 198
Syriac 62, 148

— Ṣ —

ṣaḥut ha-lashon 71
Ṣā'id al-Andalusī 109, 111-12, 118, 134
ṣaqāliba 107

— T —

Tábara 82
taḍmīn 32
tafsīr 124
tajnīs technique 74
Talmud 62-63, 69, 159-60, 162, 175-76
Tarjumān al-Ashwāq 178-96
tashbīb 31
Temple 161
Teruel 81, 96, 98-99, 101-3
Tervagant 163
Tiberian usage 74
time of ignorance 168
Toledo 83, 93, 128, 131, 143
Toledot Yeshu 159
Torah 49, 54-55, 60-65, 69, 125, 150, 194, 196
Tower of San Martín 99
Translation of Desires, The 178
Trinity, The 158, 171-72
trinity 163
Tunis 178

— U —

Umayyads 2, 17-24, 37-40, 42, 44-45, 47, 83, 87-88, 90, 93, 123, 127, 129
'Uthmān ibn 'Affān 24, 37-38

— V —

Valencia 93, 96, 105, 185
Velázquez 153
Vincentius 146, 148-49
Visigoth 78-79, 84, 89-90, 94-95, 106, 140
Vulgate 142

— W —

Walcher of Malvern 170
war poems 110
Whore of Babylon, The 83

— Y —

Yaḥyā b. 'Adī 172
Yaḥyá al-Qurṭubī 152
Yequtiel ibn Ḥasan 131
Yoma 161
Yuçaf de Huzmel 102
Yūsuf ibn Naghrīlah, see Ibn Naghrīlah, Yūsuf

— Z —

Zayd b. Ḥāritha 165
Zaynab bint Jaḥsh 165
Zechariah, Book of 148, 161
Zirid 110, 115-17, 127, 133
Zuhayr 133

— Ẓ —

ẓa'n theme 180, 185, 192, 196
Ẓāhirī 120

CONTRIBUTORS

SUZANNE PINCKNEY STETKEVYCH is Professor of Arabic Literature in the Department of Near Eastern Languages and Cultures at Indiana University.

ANGEL SÁENZ-BADILLOS is Catedratico de Lengua y Literatura Hebreas, Universidad Complutense, Madrid.

DEDE FAIRCHILD RUGGLES has taught the history of Islamic art and architecture at Ithaca College, SUNY Binghamton, Harvard, and Cornell. Dr. Fairchild Ruggles is currently Visiting Scholar in the Department of Near Eastern Studies, Cornell University.

ROSS BRANN is Chair and Professor in the Department of Near Eastern Studies, Cornell University.

HANNA KASSIS is Professor of Religious Studies at the University of British Columbia.

BARBARA GRANT was Visiting Scholar, Department of Near Eastern Studies, Cornell University, 1994–96.

MICHAEL A. SELLS is Professor in the Department of Religious Studies at Haverford College.

CIRIACO ARROYO is the Emerson Hinchcliff Professor of Hispanic Studies in the Departments of Romance Studies and Comparative Literature, Cornell University.